WITHDRAWN

FISH

ON A FIRST-NAME BASIS

FISH

ON A FIRST-NAME BASIS

HOW FISH IS CAUGHT, BOUGHT, CLEANED, COOKED, AND EATEN

Rob DeBorde

Thomas Dunne Books
St. Martin's Press ≋ New York

THOMAS DUNNE BOOKS.
An imprint of St. Martin's Press.

www.stmartins.com

Design by Rob DeBorde

Illustrations and interior photographs © 2006 Rob DeBorde, except: Photo on page 75 courtesy of the National Oceanic and Atmospheric Administration/Department of Commerce

LIBRARY OF CONGRESS CATALOGING-IN-PUBLICATION DATA

DeBorde, Rob.
    Fish on a first-name basis: how fish is caught, bought, cleaned, cooked, and eaten / Rob DeBorde.
        p.   cm.
    ISBN 0-312-34220-9
    EAN 978-0-312-34220-3
    1. Cookery (Seafood). 2. Seafood. I. Title
TX747 .D38 2006
641.6'92—dc22   2005051902

First Edition: April 2006

10   9   8   7   6   5   4   3   2   1

Contents

Here There Be Fishes

I like fish. No great mystery there (that is my name on the cover), but it's not just the taste that has me hooked. Fish are fascinating long before they reach the plate. From the time they're born to the moment of truth on my tongue the life of the average fish (or shellfish) is an excellent story, full of twists and turns, action and adventure, and even the occasional courtroom drama. It's a fun tale, and one that I am more than happy to tell. Ladies and gentlemen, allow me to introduce your dinner…

This book is the direct result of an encounter with a squid steak sandwich. It was hot, too hot to eat right off, which is how I found myself pondering my meal lest I singe my taste buds.

Let's see…a squid large enough to build a sandwich around probably didn't come from local waters. Mexico? Hawaii? The Pacific, parts unknown? I wonder how old it was. Did it swim a good life? Travel much? And what about that below sea level address? Did it dive to great depths or slip through the sunny surface waters? Was it days or weeks since it last shot beneath the waves squirting ink at would-be predators and sinking its beak into prey of its own? Months?

In a few minutes my lunch had a bio that included battling baby sperm whales and eluding schools of hungry tiger sharks. The wife, three bites into her chicken marinara, suggested I might want to seek professional help.

I wrote a book instead.

What's in a Name?

In addition to first names, I've also included the scientific names for all of the fish found in this book. The system for creating these names was developed in 1758 by Carl von Linné (more commonly known as Linnaeus) and breaks down into two parts, the genus and species. The fact that most names are derived from Latin or Greek roots has nothing to do with keeping the riffraff out of the sciences. (Or so the scientists would have us believe.)

Where's the Trout?

Unfortunately, there are too many fish in the sea, or at least too many to fit in a book like this one. The species found within were chosen (more or less) because they're the most popular and readily available fish and shellfish at most markets. No, you probably won't find every one at your favorite shop, but whatever's missing is only a few clicks away online and usually just as fresh.

About Those Numbers

It's hard to write about fish without mentioning numbers and there are a lot of them in this book (both fish and numbers). I've tried to be as accurate as possible when it comes to fish counts and catch totals, but each new season means new numbers, which may or may not look like last year's figures.

learn me about some fish

Enough with the calamari cliffhanger—what you really want to know is this: How do I cook it? I hear ya. Let's get that out of the way early, shall we?

> *Buy the freshest fish or shellfish you can find*
> *and cook it as little as possible.*

Yes, it's that simple. Granted, there are a few details that need to be addressed—how fresh is fresh and what exactly does that look like? What about fresh frozen or frozen at sea? In terms of time, how little is long enough? Is that in minutes or seconds? If I told you now, would you keep reading? Exactly.

The truth is every fish is unique. All may be best served fresh and fast, but each species has its own ideal set of guidelines for getting there. No, that doesn't mean memorizing a bunch of Latin names or over-written procedurals, but it does mean getting to know each fish on a first name basis. Will knowing that catfish have taste buds covering every inch of their bodies really make your dinner taste better?

Yes. Yes, it will.

(And if it doesn't, it'll at least make you more fun at parties.)

A round of applause

Thanks to all the fishermen and fishmongers who took the time to answer my questions, no matter how dumb. Thanks to Joe and Steve at Chesapeake Fish Company in San Diego for the tour. Thanks to Race Street Seafood & Poultry in San Jose for all the fish (and one turkey) over the years, and to Newman's Fish Market in Portland for what is hands down the freshest fish in town.

Thanks to Alton, Dana, and Tamie for the crash course on how to write about food. Thanks to Dave and Tako the Octopus for getting me into this mess in the first place.

Thanks to John Parsley at Thomas Dunne Books for actually getting a green light on a fish book. Big thanks to Michael Psaltis for setting the hook and stumbling around Fulton Street at four in the morning to look at fish.

Thanks to Dad for taking me fishing. Thanks to Mom for inspiration, information, and being my second in the kitchen. Finally, thanks to Sue for patience, for printing, and for putting up with all those fish. The book is done. Let's go get a steak.

No, not you, dear reader. For you, it's all about the fish!

FISH

ON A FIRST-NAME BASIS

WANTED

WHOLE OR FILLETED

PACIFIC "Wild Gill" SALMON

ALSO KNOWN to TRAVEL UNDER the NAMES:
"COHO" SALMON, "KING" SALMON, "CHINOOK" SALMON, "SILVER" SALMON,
"SOCKEYE" SALMON, "RED" SALMON, "KETA" SALMON, "CHUM" SALMON,
"PINK" SALMON, SILVERBRIGHT, STEELHEAD, and COPPER RIVER KING

REWARD

FOR CAPTURE and CONSUMPTION of fish includes:
SUPERIOR FLAVOR and HEART HEALTHY OMEGA-3s.

LAST SEEN SWIMMING in PACIFIC WATERS off the COASTS of
ALASKA, BRITISH COLUMBIA, WASHINGTON, OREGON, and CALIFORNIA.

Chapter 1

Wild Salmon

Gills Gone Wild

Salmon go by a lot of names. There are kings and cohos, sockeyes and silvers …actually silvers and cohos are the same thing. Chinook? That's a king. A pink is a pink, and a keta is a chum, as is a silverbright, but only sometimes, although some markets suggest other- wise. A steelhead is a salmon, but it used to be a trout, and if it says Yukon or Copper River it might be a king or a sockeye, but either way it's salmon and worth every penny. Sound complicated? It's not. Just remember this: For the tastiest, most nutritious salmon on the block, ask for a "wild" child.

When it comes to our favorite finfish, salmon is second only to tuna in the United States in terms of overall consumption. Discounting the canned varieties, salmon is tops at 150 million pounds annually. This is a very encouraging statistic, especially in light of the generally poor diet of most Americans (200 billion french fries annually).

In addition to being tasty, salmon is rich in omega-3 fatty acids, the unsaturated fats found primarily in fish. Study after study has pointed to the health benefits of these "good" fats, making omega-rich species such as salmon and tuna hot items with the healthfully inclined. Numerous seafood restaurants now actively promote the fat content of their fish, a concept that would have sent fat-phobic customers into a tizzy a few

VITAL STATS

FIRST NAME: Wild Pacific salmon (a.k.a. king/chinook, silver/coho, sockeye/red, chum, pink, and steelhead)

SCI. NAME: Genus *Oncorhynchus*

SIZE: Kings average 15-20 lbs; pinks 2-4 lbs

LIFESPAN: 2-7 years when caught

RANGE: Alaska to California

CATCH: About 500,000 metric tons annually (North American wild)

years ago. For proof of the omega-3's wondrous powers, look no further than the native peoples of the Great White North whose diet consists primarily of fish (and maybe a seal now and then), and who don't have a word for heart disease in their language (although they do have several for nosy nutritionists).

So, it's the fat that makes the salmon taste good, and all salmon are loaded with it thanks to their penchant for slouching about the ocean floor eating bonbons and watching their soaps. Actually…no.

In the Water
The long Journey Home

Salmon are anadromous fish, which means they spend parts of their life in both fresh- and saltwater. For most salmon, their story begins in freshwater, usually in some far-flung mountain creek or river. After hatching, the salmon fry (called "alevins") hide in the streambed until they're big enough to swim in the open water. Once they mature to the "smolt" stage, it's off to the ocean for some fun, sun, and as much krill as they can stomach.

Adult salmon will spend, on average, one to five years in the open ocean, depending on the species. Then it hits them: *I must spawn.* As biological imperatives go, it's a strong one. Salmon must reproduce in the streams where they were born, even though most find themselves hundreds, if not thousands of miles from home when the urge strikes. A road trip like that requires a lot of fuel, which is where a healthy fat reserve comes in handy. (This is not the case with farmed salmon, which build up their reserves by swimming in circles while eating carefully engineered feed formulas.)

*salmon eggs,
fry, and smolt*

Free-Range Salmon

Hatcheries in Alaska release millions of juvenile salmon into the wild each season in hopes that they will return years later. Just like true wild salmon they are driven to return to the streams and rivers where they were first cultivated.

Where's the map?

During the journey from sea to stream, salmon face numerous challenges, ranging from predation (bears, eagles, man) to rapids to various obstacles, both natural and man-made. Perhaps the most amazing feat is that the fish finds its way home at all. How does the salmon know where to go? Scientists aren't entirely sure, but speculation centers on the salmon's ability to discern subtle differences in the smell of the water from one creek to the next. As a young salmon makes its way out to sea, it gathers details about the journey that it will use years later to find its way home.

Pacific Salmon

king/chinook

The KING SALMON (*Oncorhynchus tschawytscha*) lives up to its reputation (and namesake) as the best-tasting salmon on the market. Its flesh is a pleasing reddish-orange color, which tastes so good thanks to the king's healthy fat reserves. A variation is the "white" or "ivory" king, which has a pale, almost white flesh and different (but equally tasty) flavor. WHERE AND WHEN: Kings range from Central California to Alaska and are available fresh from May to July. DISTINGUISHING FEATURES: Large size, black gums, and black spots along back and tail.

coho/silver

The COHO (*O. kisutch*) may be smaller, but it remains a tasty fish, and is interchangeable in recipes with king salmon. It is not as sought after as its big brother, partially because it's considered "threatened" in coastal runs south of the U.S.-Canadian border. WHERE AND WHEN: Cohos range from Oregon to Alaska and are available fresh from July to August. DISTINGUISHING FEATURES: White gums, flat tail end, and lightly spotted along back and top of tail.

For many, the SOCKEYE (*O. nerka*) is the salmon of choice because of its striking deep-red flesh. The color comes from eating more tiny crustaceans than other salmon species, which also gives the sockeye a more aggressive flavor bite. WHERE AND WHEN: Sockeyes range from California to Alaska and are available fresh from June to August. DISTINGUISHING FEATURES: Deep-red flesh, smaller size, and very few spots.

sockeye/red

chum

Because of a shorter spawning run, the fat stores of the CHUM (*O. keta*) are smaller than other wild salmon, thus its flavor is not quite as good. For the best results when buying whole chum, look for the shiniest, brightest skin and reddest meat. WHERE AND WHEN: Chum salmon range from California to Alaska and are available fresh from July to September. DISTINGUISHING FEATURES: V-shaped tail, and a few irregular black spots or splotches along back and tail.

The smallest of the Pacific breeds, the PINK SALMON (*O. gorbuscha*) has (not surprisingly) firm pink flesh. It's much leaner than other salmon and thus cooks more like a white-fleshed fish. For this reason, most of the catch ends up as canned salmon. WHERE AND WHEN: Pink salmon range from Oregon to Alaska and are available fresh from June to September. DISTINGUISHING FEATURES: Smallest size, pinkish flesh, and a hump on its back during spawning.

pink

![steelhead illustration]

steelhead

Steelhead

The STEELHEAD (O. mykiss) is primarily a sport fish, though a limited fishery does exist along the Columbia River. WHERE AND WHEN: Steelhead is found primarily along the Columbia River and its tributaries throughout the Pacific Northwest in the late summer months and early fall. DISTINGUISHING FEATURES: Smaller, pale flesh, silvery "salmonlike" appearance.

Atlantic salmon

Farmed ATLANTIC SALMON (Salmo salar) is of consistently good quality and size, almost always fresh, and available year-round at just about any store with a fish counter. It also contains artificial color and potentially higher biotoxin levels. Limit yourself to one serving a month, and avoid eating the skin, which is where most toxins reside. WHERE AND WHEN: Atlantic salmon is farmed in cold-water climates around the world and is available all year. There is no commercially available wild catch. DISTINGUISHING FEATURES: Large size, large black spots along head and back, much shorter anal fin.

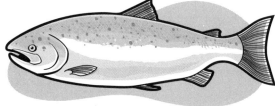

Atlantic

Cha-Cha-Changes

Wild salmon go through dramatic physical changes when they spawn. The skin darkens, sharp teeth appear; some develop humps, and others a hook in their upper jaw. One of the more dramatic changes is found in the sockeye (below), whose skin turns from silver to deep red.

before

after

Aiding their journey may be an "inner compass" that keeps the salmon attuned to the earth's magnetic fields, as well as an ability to track the seasons through fluctuations in water temperature and changes in the length of the day. Who needs a GPS when you've got one built in?

Ultimately, the salmon spawns and dies, leaving its body to decompose in the water, providing nutrients for its young in the process.

On the Boats
Wild West

The wild catch available at fish markets around the world comes primarily from Alaska. Each May through September roughly 80 million fish are plucked from the southeastern, central, and western coastlines and river deltas, using a variety of boats and fishing methods. The largely untouched Alaskan wilderness, coupled with a carefully regulated fishing industry, has kept wild salmon runs consistently healthy.

Seasonal salmon runs also provide West Coast fishermen with a springtime boon. King salmon are plentiful along the Northern California coast, and steelhead, a rainbow trout relative recently reclassified as a salmon, remains a popular sport fish and an up-and-coming commercial catch.

Unfortunately, many of the salmon runs that once dominated the waterways of the Pacific Northwest are not in good shape. Traditional runs in Washington, Oregon, and California have been decimated by dozens of hydroelectric projects built during the twentieth century. A single dam can destroy dozens of spawning runs, despite some reasonable efforts by the dam builders to protect the fish. It's estimated that over two hundred runs were wiped out along the Columbia River system alone.

Hydroelectric projects aren't the only problem affecting salmon stocks. Numerous forms of watershed erosion, pollution, predators, drought, and other natural and man-made problems have contributed to the decline of the non-Alaskan population. Efforts to restore native salmon runs, especially along the Columbia and its tributaries, have been modestly successful, but they're a long way from being commercially viable.

Out of the boat

Most of the wild Alaskan catch is transferred to a tender before it goes to a fish-processing facility. This helps both the fisherman, who can return to fishing quicker, and the processor, who can stagger deliveries to make processing more efficient. Because the majority of Alaskan salmon return in a brief window of time (3 to 4 months), keeping the industry from crushing itself under the weight of millions of salmon is a carefully planned and executed endeavor.

The highest-quality fish are often flown by helicopter directly from the tender to local airports and then around the world. Two days after being pulled from the sea, an Alaskan King can be the special at a restaurant in New York or London. The rest of the fish go to a processing facility where they are graded by species, size, and quality and then prepared for distribution either as fresh, frozen, or canned salmon. Fish to be frozen are individually quick-frozen (IQF), glazed with a thin layer

Golden Gill Rush

The Copper River Salmon is sought the world over for its wonderful flavor. With the help of a brilliant marketing campaign, it is the fish to have on the menu come May. For those in the know, however, Yukon River salmon is the real king of kings. In preparation for a two-thousand-mile spawning run, Yukons load up on tasty oils, two to three times that of Coppers. Unfortunately, the commercial fishery is very small, and only native Yup'ik and Athabascan peoples are legally allowed to fish it. Expect to pay as much as $25 a pound...if you can find it.

just a hop, skip, and a jump

QUICK QUESTION

Has the hydroelectric industry done anything to save native salmon runs?   Yes. Fish ladders (*left*), essentially artificial rapids, are in place at most dams to help spawning salmon get home. For young salmon heading out to sea, bypass channels and spillways get them past turbines and on their way. Believe it or not, some youngsters even get a ride downstream on barges that pump fresh water through their holds to familiarize the fish with the river.

of protective ice, and then placed in polyethylene bags. Properly stored, these fish will remain in excellent condition for up to six months.

The canned salmon industry, once the only significant market for Alaskan salmon, remains the largest arm of the industry due to its ability to handle an enormous volume of fish. Recent years have seen changes in canned salmon because consumers have demanded higher-quality products. While not up to the standards of fresh, canned nonetheless makes a great pantry staple for sandwiches, casseroles, and cakes (no, not the birthday kind).

Down on the farm

Farm-raised salmon is definitely not on anyone's endangered list. In 1980, commercial fishermen caught approximately 99 percent of the salmon consumed worldwide. By 2003, that number had dropped to about 40 percent. The dramatic rise of farm-raised fish has been bad for fishermen, but a boon for consumers, who can now find fresh salmon year round, even in markets thousands of miles from the nearest gill net. The majority of the farmed catch is Atlantic salmon, though some Pacific varieties are now also being farmed. The flavor of farmed fish, while not up to wild standards, is still reasonably good.

Salmon were first cultivated in the fjords and bays of Norway using large saltwater pens. Stocked with smolts spawned in freshwater hatcheries, farmers were able to grow market-sized salmon in just over a year. Unfortunately, a thousand (or more) salmon swimming in a circle for a year produces a lot of excrement, which has nowhere to go but into the local ecosystem. Farms have also been criticized for allowing salmon to escape their pens and threaten native stocks, though whether a force-fed salmon that only knows how to swim in a circle is truly a threat remains to be seen.

Farmers took another hit when it was revealed that unlike wild salmon, whose flesh is naturally orange because of a healthy diet of shrimp and krill, farmed salmon require an artificial dye to get that

Swatch This
Feed supplement manufacturers now provide salmon farmers with a color-coded system that, like a series of paint swatches, allows the farmer to pinpoint how orange his fish's flesh will be. Cool, huh?

healthy glow. Without a dose of canthaxanthin or astaxanthin in its diet, Farmer Brown's fish would be gray. About the same time "color added" labels began popping up at fish markets, an extensive study was released showing that biotoxin levels—specifically, PCBs, dioxins, and pesticides—were ten times higher in farm-raised salmon than in wild salmon. Why? Most farmed salmon chow down on pellets made from low-grade fish harvested in North Atlantic waters contaminated by industrial runoff. These fish can't catch a break.

While the U.S. Environmental Protection Agency and the Food and Drug Administration disagree on what constitutes a dangerous level of PCBs (the EPA says 50 parts per billion; the FDA 2,000 ppb), what matters is what the consumer thinks. That'd be you. Given the choice, would you rather eat salmon or color-corrected, farm-fattened, potentially PCBed salmon?

That's what I thought.

At the Market
Get It While It's Fresh

Thanks to improved distribution techniques, high-quality fresh salmon is no longer a rarity at most fish markets. When buying whole salmon, make sure the skin is silver, glistening, and free of any large splotches or dark marks. The eyes should be clear and a little bulgy, and if possible, check that the gills are bright red. As with any seafood, there should be no "fishy" odor, but perhaps only a salty-sea smell. If any part of the salmon seems overly dried out or the tail is curled up, throw it back.

When buying steaks or fillets, it's best to have the fishmonger cut them from a whole fish while you wait. You can also do this yourself and freeze what you don't use right away. If you buy precut fillets or steaks, make sure they're brightly colored, moist (but not wet), and free of any significant blemishes. If you're unsure of the quality, ask to take a sniff before they're wrapped up.

To Catch a Fish

Trollers, the smallest of the salmon boats, operate using numerous lines and baited hooks. In terms of catch volume, they're the least efficient, but they do bring in the most attractive and thus most valuable fish. Gillnetting uses a long, wide net to capture fish that attempt to swim through it, but instead wind up with their gills trapped in the netting. Purse seining uses the largest boats to set circular nets that can be drawn closed at the bottom, thus trapping the largest number of fish.

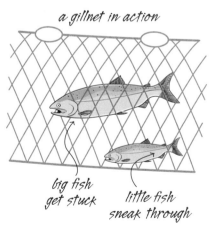

a gillnet in action

big fish get stuck   *little fish sneak through*

QUICK QUESTION

How do I tell a wild salmon from a farmed fish? If it says "Alaskan," or uses a specific Pacific salmon name, it's probably wild. If it says "Atlantic," "color added," or nothing at all, it's farm-raised. As of 2004 (in the United States), all fish must be labeled as either farmed or wild and indicate where in the world they came from.

Salmon Cuts

Salmon is available year-round in a variety of forms, including steaks, fillets, roasts, whole fish, smoked fish, and the ever-popular can-shaped salmon.

Fresh wild salmon is available from May to early October. (In some West Coast shops ocean-caught wild salmon begin appearing in March and April.) While finding fresh Atlantic salmon in January is not that unusual, anything labeled "wild" or "Alaskan" has undoubtedly been previously frozen. That doesn't mean it's bad, but it does mean the fish has been thawed out, something I prefer to do in my own kitchen. Ask your fishmonger for a frozen vacuum-packed whole fillet and thaw it at your leisure.

Old smoky

Many markets carry various smoked and cured salmon products, usually sold in pieces, fresh slices, or whole sides (presliced is best for easy eating), as well as in vacuum-sealed packages. A few of the more common forms include lox (traditionally brine-cured, although these days it's also lightly smoked), Nova style (similar to lox, but usually less briny due to a little added sugar), Northwest style (a Native American tradition often flavored by alder wood) and gravlax (a Scandinavian dish in which the salmon is cured using a salt, sugar, and herb rub).

Silverbrights

A "silverbright" is a chum that was caught prior to spawning, while it still had a beautiful silver sheen to it. It's fairly rare to find such a creature at the seafood counter, but that hasn't stopped resellers from usurping the name. Be wary of any grayish-green silverbrights.

QUICK QUESTION

Is it hot or cold? Smoked salmon comes in two forms: hot and cold. Cold-smoked fish is cured first and then smoked using "cold" smoke (usually around 90° F). It has fine texture, delicate flavor, and a moist, translucent appearance. Hot-smoked fish is more or less cooked (to an internal temperature of 145° F for 30 minutes) while being flavored by smoke. The result is a dryer, opaque fish, but often a more intense flavor.

HOW TO STORE: Salmon

FRESH: Fresh salmon steaks or fillets should be sealed in plastic wrap and set over a bowl of ice in the refrigerator. Whole salmon can be laid directly on ice, although if you intend to hold it overnight, plastic wrap will keep the aroma exchange to a minimum. *FROZEN:* Anything longer than a couple days, and your salmon should go in the freezer, where, sealed tightly in plastic wrap and aluminum foil, it will last for about two months. (Salmon frozen and vacuum-packed by the processor will last longer, usually 3 to 6 months.)

In the Kitchen
Simple Salmon

Chances are you're not going to have to clean or fillet your own salmon, but if you should find an intact fish in your kitchen, don't panic. With a little practice, you will find breaking down a salmon is almost as simple as cooking it.

Cleaning and scaling

Using kitchen shears or a small knife, cut the belly of the salmon from the small anal opening near the tail to the base of its head. Don't stick the blade in too deep or you'll slice open the guts and make a mess. Now reach in and pull out the guts. Go on, don't be a baby. You may need to trim the membrane holding the viscera in place. Next, use the kitchen shears to cut through the hard cartilage at the base of the head holding it in place. Remove the gills by cutting along the edge where they attach to the body. Now, thoroughly rinse out the inside of the salmon and you're done. See, that wasn't so bad, was it?

If you intend to cook the fish whole or serve it with the skin on, you'll need to scale it. Your fishmonger will probably be happy to do this for you, but it's really not that hard. Just be sure to do it outside or inside a large bag so the scales don't end up all over the kitchen. To make things as easy as possible, buy a fish scaler (the back of a knife will work in a pinch). Simply apply a little pressure as you run the scaler back and forth across the length of the fish. When you think you've got them all, run your fingers along the body to check for stragglers. Once again, rinse thoroughly.

Cut Up

Kitchen shears are great for cleaning, while a flexible boning knife works wonders on stubborn skin, but when it comes time to fillet, I switch to a long, slender fish knife similar to those used by sushi chefs. A good-sized cook's knife (a.k.a. a chef's knife) also does the job. Just make sure whatever you use is sharp and long enough to slice through the fish crosswise without the tip disappearing inside the fish. Did I mention it should be sharp?

Salmon Rounds

A popular way to cook salmon steaks is to turn them into rounds. (1) Begin by removing the pin bones and then cut around the backbone with a sharp knife, being careful not to trim away any of the flesh. Cut up to, but not through the skin at the top of the back. (2) Next, trim 2 inches of skin off of one of the flaps and wrap it around inside the steak. (3) Then fold the other flap around to complete the round. You may need to trim away a little extra skin to even it out. (4) Finally, use kitchen string to tie a double loop around the steak. It should be snug but not overly tight. You're done! Toss 'em on the grill.

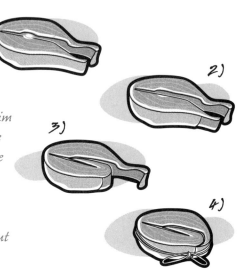

Filleting and skinning

Cutting a whole salmon into steaks is fairly easy. Simply remove the head, fins, and tail and then use a heavy cook's knife to cut the salmon crosswise into steaks as thick as you want them. You may need to use a little extra force to cut through the backbone, so keep a rubber mallet or rolling pin handy to punch it through (watch your fingers). Filleting a whole salmon takes a little more effort (*see illustration*), but is the best way to get the most out of your fish.

Skinning a salmon can be a tricky thing. Depending on the angle of the knife, the thickness of the flesh, and the whims of Neptune, you'll either zip through without a problem or end up with a jagged, mangled piece of salmon. For the best results, place the salmon skin side down on a cutting board and use a long, *sharp* knife to slice through the meat just above the skin. It may help to press down on the top of the fillet with your free hand to keep it from sliding around. Once you've made it all the way through, flip the fillet over to see if the gods were on your side. If any skin patches remain—there will be the first few times you try to do this—use the knife to carefully trim them away.

Even if you buy your steaks or fillets precut, you'll most likely have to remove the pin bones. To do so, run your fingers along the thickest part of the fillet to find them and then pull them out with a pair of needle-nose pliers or kitchen tongs. Try to pull them out straight, so as not to damage the flesh. If you're planning to remove the skin, do that first, as it will make pin bone removal easier.

removing the pin bones

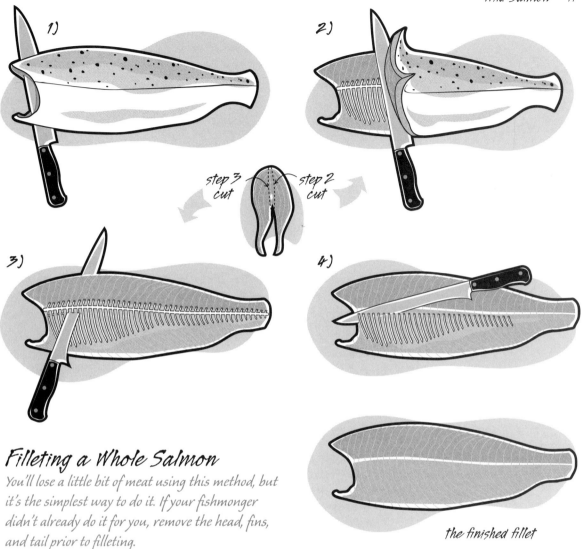

step 3
cut

step 2
cut

the finished fillet

Filleting a Whole Salmon

You'll lose a little bit of meat using this method, but it's the simplest way to do it. If your fishmonger didn't already do it for you, remove the head, fins, and tail prior to filleting.

(1) Slide the knife in crosswise, just above the backbone, and cut through the first few ribs. (2) Using the backbone as a guide, slice through the ribs toward the tail. This will leave you with two fillets, one with ribs, and one with ribs and the backbone. NOTE: Especially large salmon may require a few passes to get through all the flesh. Try to use long, even cuts, and not a sawing action, which will damage the flesh. (3) Cut through the first few ribs, and then, using the backbone as a guide, carefully slice through to the tail end to remove the spine. (4) Slip the knife behind the ribs and carefully slice down and back toward the bottom of the fillet, keeping the blade as flush as possible to the bones. Repeat on the rib only fillet.

No Time to Cook

Raw salmon is one of the more delicious things on earth, so if you've never tried it, run to a nearby sushi joint for a taste. For raw applications at home, be sure to buy salmon that was flash-frozen, preferably "frozen at sea" (FAS). Seven days in the deep freeze (below 0° F) will kill any parasites that happen to have hitched a ride. (For more information on preparing and buying raw fish, check out chapter 7, "Fast Food.")

QUICK QUESTION

What if my salmon doesn't have any pin bones? Closer to the tail, the pin bones disappear, but it's more likely the fillet had its bones removed during processing. It's a time-saver, but requires that the flesh rest a few days to allow the muscles to relax, which is why this treatment is usually applied only to farm-raised salmon.

Cooking: Just add heat

Cooking salmon is a treat, primarily because there's hardly a wrong way to do it. For proof of this, look no further than Bob Blumer, the Surreal Gourmet, who cooks his salmon in a dishwasher. One of the reasons salmon cooks up so nicely is because of its fat content. All that juicy fat lubricates the flesh, making it hard to overcook. This is good news for those afraid of the bad nasties that occasionally show up in fish. Go ahead and cook it through if you must; the salmon will make you look like a genius.

If you've picked up a whole salmon, try baking or poaching first, then try the grill when you're ready for a little more of a challenge. Steaks are perfect for the grill, especially after they've been made into rounds, but they're also nice pan-fried, poached, braised, or steamed. Fillets, perhaps the most versatile cut, cook up nicely sautéed, pan-fried, poached, grilled (skin-on), broiled, braised, steamed, and even microwaved. Salmon is also a great fish to use with hot- or cold-smoking techniques.

There is some discussion as to whether salmon should ever be deep-fried. I've had it turn out great and not so great. What's the solution? With so many other fish better suited for the fryer, why mask the salmon's delicious flavor with a bunch of batter (or worse, oil).

Salmon Recipes

Any wild or farmed salmon will work in the following recipes, although different flavors and fat content will affect the final outcome. For my dollar, nothing beats sockeye, which are always cheaper than kings, and equally delicious, if not more so. They're much leaner in terms of fat content (which is why so many folks crow about the kings—lots of tasty fat), but I like the sharper, "wilder" flavor. If you have the opportunity to try different varieties, by all means take it.

NUTRITIONAL INFO

Per 3.5 oz/100 grams (raw)

King/Chinook Salmon

Calories 180	
Calories from fat . . . 94	
Total fat . . . . 10.4 g	
Saturated fat . . . . 2.5 g	
Cholesterol . . . . 66 mg	
Sodium . . . . 47 mg	
Protein . . . . 20 g	
Omega-3 . . . . 1.9 g	
Mercury . . . . . 0.01 ppm	

Chum Salmon

Calories 120	
Calories from fat . . . 34	
Total fat . . . . 3.8 g	
Saturated fat . . . . 0.8 g	
Cholesterol . . . . . 74 mg	
Sodium . . . . 50 mg	
Protein . . . . 20 g	
Omega-3 . . . . 0.66 g	
Mercury . . . . . 0.01 ppm	

Coho Salmon

Calories 146	
Calories from fat . . . 53	
Total fat . . . . 6 g	
Saturated fat . . . . 1.3 g	
Cholesterol . . . . 45 mg	
Sodium . . . . 46 mg	
Protein . . . . 21.6 g	
Omega-3 . . . . 1 g	
Mercury . . . . . 0.01 ppm	

Pink Salmon

Calories 116	
Calories from fat . . . 32	
Total fat . . . . 3.5 g	
Saturated fat . . . . 0.6 g	
Cholesterol . . . . 52 mg	
Sodium . . . . 67 mg	
Protein . . . . 20 g	
Omega-3 . . . . 1.5 g	
Mercury . . . . . 0.01 ppm	

Sockeye Salmon

Calories 168	
Calories from fat . . . 77	
Total fat . . . . 8.6 g	
Saturated fat . . . . 1.5 g	
Cholesterol . . . . 62 mg	
Sodium . . . . 47 mg	
Protein . . . . 21.3 g	
Omega-3 . . . . 2.7 g	
Mercury . . . . . 0.01 ppm	

Atlantic Salmon

Calories 183	
Calories from fat . . . 97	
Total fat . . . . 11 g	
Saturated fat . . . . 2.2 g	
Cholesterol . . . . . 59 mg	
Sodium . . . . 59 mg	
Protein . . . . 20 g	
Omega-3 . . . . 1.4 g	
Mercury . . . . . 0.01 ppm	

Sautéed Salmon
(a.k.a. the Best Piece of Fish Ever)

Nothing in this world tastes better than a perfectly prepared wild salmon fillet. Nothing. Master this dish and you will be hailed as a culinary genius. For a little added color and a sweet twang, fresh blackberries are nice, but by no means necessary. NOTE: If you decide to cook fillets with the skin on, cook the skin side first and add an extra minute or two to crisp it up. To keep the skin from curling, make a few short, shallow cuts across it diagonally before cooking.

2 wild salmon fillets (6 to 8 ounces each)
Kosher salt and freshly ground black pepper
Olive oil
Blackberry Sauce (optional)

Season the salmon on both sides with salt and pepper. Place it in the fridge for a half hour or more. Before cooking, pat it dry to remove any moisture drawn out by the salt.

Place a nonstick pan over medium-high heat. Brush each fillet with just enough olive oil to coat both sides. Add the fillets to the pan, interior (pretty) side down. Give the pan a shake to help discourage any sticking. Cook for 3 to 4 minutes, flip the fillets, and cook for another 2 to 3 minutes. Thicker or thinner fillets may require more or less time. Slightly underdone in the center is ideal. *Yes, it is!*

Transfer the fillets to warm plates and top them with blackberry sauce, if desired.

Serves 2

NOTE: If you're cooking more pieces than you have room for in your pan, cook the thickest fillets first and hold them in a 200° F oven. Cut a little time off the sauté to keep them from overcooking while they wait in the oven. The last batch can be done normally.

Blackberry Sauce

If you manage to track down a blood orange, save a few slices and use them to garnish the prepared salmon along with the sauce.

1 tablespoon butter (+ ½ tablespoon if cooked in a separate pan)
Juice of one ruby grapefruit (or a blood orange if you can find it)
¼ cup dry sherry
8 ounces fresh blackberries

Set a pan over medium heat and add the butter, sherry, and juice. Allow the liquid to reduce for about 2 minutes. Add the blackberries and simmer over low heat until softened, 2 to 3 minutes. Spoon the sauce over the salmon (or vanilla ice cream).

Poached Whole Salmon

Poaching at home is a lot easier if you have a fish poacher, but any pan that's big enough to hold the fish and liquid will work (yes, you can remove the head and tail to make the fish fit). The following recipe uses a very straightforward court bouillon for the poaching liquid, but feel free to play with the ingredients to suit your own taste. NOTE: Serving a whole salmon requires your guests to hunt for the bones. Not everyone likes to do that.

3 quarts water
3 cups dry white wine
1 medium onion, chopped
1 large carrot, peeled and chopped
2 celery stalks, chopped
½ cup fresh flat-leaf parsley
1 bay leaf
1 teaspoon freshly ground black pepper
1 small whole wild salmon (5 to 6 pounds)
    or equivalent-sized salmon roast

To make the poaching liquid, combine everything (but the salmon) in a large pot and bring it to a boil. Simmer it for 25 minutes, allow it to cool, and strain it.

Set the fish in a large poacher and place it over two burners. Add enough of the poaching liquid to cover (if you don't have enough, add a little water). Bring the liquid to a simmer, but do not boil. Cook 10 minutes per inch of thickness at the thickest part of the fish. If you prefer to take the fish's temperature, shoot for 135° F (or a few degrees under).

Remove the salmon from the poacher, letting it drain briefly before transferring it to a serving platter. Carve the fish and serve it, or bone it and use the meat for another recipe.

Serves 6 to 8

NOTE: If you need help carving the salmon, see page 123 for instructions on how to dismantle a whole cooked fish. It's a different fish, but the same basic technique applies.

Grilled Salmon

Grilling salmon is a good idea. Yeah, I know, fish falls apart on the grill. Then why do so many restaurants serve grilled fish? Because it's a good idea... if you know what you're doing. Salmon works on the grill because it's a relatively firm fish, which keeps it from falling apart, and it's got enough fat to keep the grill lubricated so it doesn't stick. You can help the process along by adding a little oil to the fish and the grill, and by keeping your grill ridiculously clean. Steaks or fillets? Steaks are easier, thanks to the skin edge, but fillets tend to look a little prettier. If you leave the skin on, that'll help hold things together, but your fillets won't grill up as nicely (skin tends to stick).

4 salmon fillets (6 to 8 ounces each) or steaks (rounds preferred)
Kosher salt and freshly ground black pepper
1 tablespoon olive oil
Cucumber Salsa (optional)

Season the salmon on both sides with salt and pepper. Place it in the fridge for a half hour or more. Before grilling, pat it dry to remove any moisture drawn out by the salt.

Fire up the grill! (*If you don't know how to do this, refer to your grill owner's manual, or go out to dinner.*) The fish should cook about six inches from the heat. If you're using a gas grill, start it on high, and then turn it down a little before adding the steaks.

Brush both sides of the salmon with olive oil. Just prior to putting the fish on the grill, rub a little oil on the grill with a wad of paper towels. Place the steaks or fillets on the grill and cook for 3 to 4 minutes. Carefully flip the fillets (*see note*) using a spatula and a grilling fork and cook them for another 3 to 4 minutes or until done. Don't flip them more than once.

Carefully remove the fillets from the grill and place them on a serving platter. Spoon the Cucumber Salsa over them and serve.

Serves 4

NOTE: Don't just slide the spatula under the fillet when flipping it. First, test to see whether the fillet is ready to come up by sliding a grill fork under it and poking up on it (flat side to fish). If the fillet separates from the grill, slide the spatula under it and remove.

Cucumber Salsa

This cool salsa goes well with just about any salmon dish.

1 cup cucumber (preferably English), chopped
¼ cup tomato, diced
¼ cup red onion, diced
1 tablespoon fresh dill, chopped
Zest of 1 lemon
½ teaspoon crushed red pepper flakes (optional)
Kosher salt and freshly ground black pepper to taste

Combine all the ingredients, mix them thoroughly, and serve the salsa over the salmon. Generously.

Spicy Salmon Cakes

If you've skipped ahead, you will have discovered that I'm not a big fan of crab cakes. Sad, but true. I am, however, quite fond of these spicy little salmon treats, which to my taste sell the concept of a seafood cake much better. NOTE: If you don't like spicy, knock off a tablespoon (or two) of the horseradish.

1 large salmon fillet, about 12 ounces, skinned and boned
4 tablespoons unsalted butter
½ cup red onion, finely diced
½ cup celery, finely diced
1 large clove garlic, minced
½ cup mayonnaise
2 tablespoons creamy horseradish
Zest of 1 lemon
2 teaspoons fresh dill, chopped
½ teaspoon kosher salt
½ teaspoon freshly ground black pepper
½ teaspoon paprika
¼ teaspoon red pepper flakes
1 cup *panko* (Japanese bread crumbs)
Lemon wedges

Prepare the salmon, using whatever technique you like (see previous recipes). Don't worry about making it pretty since you're just going to crumble it up. *NOTE: You can also use cold salmon cooked the day before.*

Melt 2 tablespoons of butter in a sauté pan over medium heat. Add the onions and celery and sauté, stirring occasionally, for 3 minutes. Add the garlic, and cook for an additional 2 to 3 minutes, until the veggies are softened but not browned. Remove the veggies from the heat and allow them to cool.

Combine the mayonnaise, horseradish, lemon zest, dill, salt, pepper, paprika, and red pepper flakes in a large mixing bowl. Add the cooked onion, celery, and garlic and stir to combine them. Break up the salmon and fold it into the mix, trying not to break up the flakes any more than necessary.

Use your hands to form 10 to 12 balls, each about 1 inch in diameter, flatten them to ½-inch rounds, and refrigerate for 30 minutes or up to 4 hours.

Prior to cooking the cakes, roll them lightly in *panko*. Melt 2 tablespoons of butter in a large sauté pan over medium heat. When it starts to bubble, add the cakes (4 to 6 at a time) and cook them for 3 to 4 minutes, flip them, and cook for 3 to 4 additional minutes. The cakes should be golden brown and heated through. Serve immediately with lemon wedges.

Serves 4 to 6 (appetizer) or 3 (main course)

Dill Salmon Wraps

This is a recipe that really demands you make it your own. After the salmon, tortilla, cucumber, and dill, everything is open to reinterpretation. I like the sinus-clearing burn you get from a little wasabi or horseradish, but it's not for everyone. Have fun.

1 salmon fillet (8 ounces), skinned and boned
1 medium cucumber, seeded and cubed
1 tablespoon fresh dill
1 medium tomato, diced
1 radish, slivered
2 tablespoons cilantro, chopped
1 tablespoon lime juice
1 tablespoon capers
Baby spinach
Crumbled feta or blue cheese
Freshly ground black pepper to taste
1 tablespoon horseradish or wasabi aioli (optional)
2 large spinach tortillas

Prepare the salmon, using whatever technique you like (see previous recipes). Don't worry about making it pretty since you're just going to crumble it up. *NOTE: You can also use cold salmon cooked the day before.*

Combine the cucumber, dill, tomato, radish, cilantro, and lime juice in a bowl and set the mixture aside.

Place the tortillas between two damp paper towels and microwave for 20 seconds. Move them onto individual plates and spread a little of the horseradish over each (optional). Cover them with baby spinach leaves, one layer only. Break up the cooked salmon with a fork and add half of it to each tortilla, making sure to spread it across the entire surface, stopping just short along one side. Sprinkle the tortillas with the crumbled cheese, capers, and cucumber mix and top each with a little freshly ground pepper.

Carefully roll up the tortillas, trying to keep them in as tight a spiral as possible. The edge you left empty should lay flat against the tortilla, holding it together. Hopefully. *NOTE: If the tortilla falls apart, who cares? It'll still taste fantastic.*

Serves 2

Chapter 2
Dungeness Crab
The West is Best

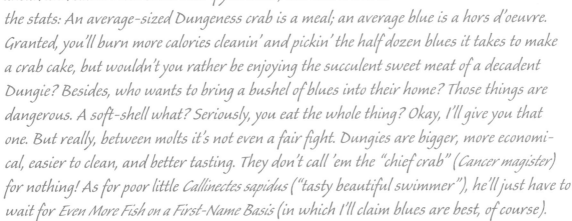

Dungeness crab is better than blue crab. Hey, no yelling in the kitchen. I'm sorry, but it's true. Go ahead and claim West Coast bias if you must, but take a look at the stats: An average-sized Dungeness crab is a meal; an average blue is a hors d'oeuvre. Granted, you'll burn more calories cleanin' and pickin' the half dozen blues it takes to make a crab cake, but wouldn't you rather be enjoying the succulent sweet meat of a decadent Dungie? Besides, who wants to bring a bushel of blues into their home? Those things are dangerous. A soft-shell what? Seriously, you eat the whole thing? Okay, I'll give you that one. But really, between molts it's not even a fair fight. Dungies are bigger, more economical, easier to clean, and better tasting. They don't call 'em the "chief crab" (Cancer magister) for nothing! As for poor little Callinectes sapidus ("tasty beautiful swimmer"), he'll just have to wait for Even More Fish on a First-Name Basis (in which I'll claim blues are best, of course).

VITAL STATS

FIRST NAME: Dungeness crab

SCI. NAME: *Cancer magister*

AVERAGE SIZE: 1.5-3 lbs, 6-8 in wide across the carapace

LIFESPAN: 4-5 years (when caught)

RANGE: Alaska to California

CATCH: Cyclical, but averages about 40 million lbs annually

Now that I've alienated half of the folks reading this book, let's see if I can't win them back by introducing the left coast's answer to lobster, the Dungeness crab. Come mid-November, San Francisco is awash with boats loaded with these fat and (not so) happy crustaceans. I doubt Thanksgiving crab will catch on nationally, but the locals have embraced the Dungeness as a surrogate sea turkey, and have done so for decades.

The first commercial West Coast crab fishery opened in San Francisco in the mid-1800s, operated primarily by Italian immigrants and a few miner-forty-niners searching for a way to make up for losses in the mountains. Back then, the local crustacean was simply called crab or, for those in need of a little reassuring, "edible" crab. The modern moniker didn't become widely used until well into the next century, although it wasn't some deep, dark corner of Alcatraz that gave us the name Dungeness, but rather a homesick English explorer. It seems that during his passage through the Strait of Juan de Fuca, Captain George Vancouver came upon a thin stretch of land that reminded him of a similar locale near the cliffs of Dover. Not being a terribly original fellow, he named the spit for its English counterpart and in so doing inadvertently tagged the crab that populated local waters.

In the Water
M & M (Molting and Mating)

Today, Dungeness crabs are plentiful in coastal waters from Alaska to California. They prefer cooler water, which is why you'll rarely find a Dungie sunning himself south of Santa Barbara. Unlike lobsters, which seek out rocks and crevices, the ideal landscape for a Dungeness is the sandy bottom of a bay or inlet where it can burrow in search of food or lie in wait for something to swim by. The sand also provides a necessary hiding place from predators eager to put that "west is best" theory to the test.

Why does a critter wearing body armor need to bury its head in the sand? Like most crustaceans, Dungies periodically shed their shells to increase their size. If you've found a dead crab on the beach, there's a good chance it was simply the shell of a crab that had recently molted. During the first few years of its life, a Dungeness crab will molt a dozen or more times before settling into the once-a-year pattern of adulthood. To molt, a crab absorbs extra water into its body tissue, expands, and then literally bursts at the seams. After backing out of its old shell, the now vulnerable soft-shelled crab spends most of the following four to six weeks buried in the sand while its shell hardens.

British Columbia

Dungeness Spit

Seattle

Oregon

San Francisco

Dungeness crab

Soft-shell Dungies?

Unlike blues, there's no market for soft-shell Dungies. Why? Take a look inside. Who wants to eat that much gunk?

QUICK QUESTION

Why do crabs walk sideways? Because their legs lack ball-and-socket joints, most crabs are limited to side-to-side locomotion along a single plane of movement. Since they have slightly more evolved appendages, Dungies (and a few other species) are capable of moving in any direction they like and can do so rather quickly when underwater.

The Dungeness Experience

For the truly crab crazy, some charter companies now offer crabbing trips that allow the general public to take part in the process. The cost is generally around $50 per person and includes a day at sea, an education in crabbing, and an ice chest full of feisty Dungeness crabs.

crab boats

How to make little crabs

In addition to providing a way to regenerate a lost limb, molting also plays an important part in the mating cycle of Dungeness crabs. By the age of three, most Dungies molt only once or twice a year, allowing them more time to focus on the singles scene. For the bachelor, that means mixing it up with as many partners as possible. Monogamy is not popular with male crabs.

For the female Dungie, mating is only the beginning. Once the male has shoved off to find another filly, the female goes into a holding pattern, waiting for just the right time to release her eggs. She can wait for months. When she does release her eggs (and only then does she fertilize them) there may be a million or more in a single clutch. A few weeks later, the water will be filled with tiny, shrimplike crustaceans called "zoea," which after another four months of growth will finally start to look like little crabs.

On the Boats
Crab Catchers

One of the reasons why it's easy for males to find multiple partners is because there are simply more females. This is your fault. No, really, if you've eaten a Dungeness crab, it was male. In order to ensure a healthy supply from year to year, fishermen only harvest male Dungies, tossing any girls back into the bay. Seems like a raw deal for the boys, but then most have been sexually active for a year or two before they reach the minimum legal size (6.25 inches across the carapace; 6.5 inches or 39 centimeters, in Canada), so it's not all bad.

Like the crab itself, the Dungeness fishery ranges from California to Alaska, and is considered one of the most sustainable large-scale commercial crab fisheries in the world. Although overlapping seasons keep Dungies on the menu year-round, the bulk of the catch is landed in December and January. This is the time to find the best deals on Dungies, although not always the best crabs. Some of the initial catch is made up of crabs still filling out their shells after a late summer molt. Come February, most Dungies are as plump as they're going to get, so dig in.

Pot-o-crabs

The Dungeness fishery remains primarily a mom-and-pop business, with most boats being owned and operated as small family-run enterprises. Crews of two to four fishermen spend their days hauling crab pots, 3- to 4-foot-wide circular traps made of durable wire mesh. A single boat will work 250 to 300 pots at one time, although some larger boats haul upward of 1,000. The pots are set on the ocean floor, usually at depths between 30 and 180 feet, and allowed to "soak" overnight. Later in the season, as the crabs thin out, fishermen will keep their pots down longer to increase their chances of hauling up more than just water.

Much like lobster traps, crab pots are designed to catch and hold primarily market-sized Dungies. Small holes in the mesh allow undersized crabs to escape. A larger trap can hold 30 or more crabs, although 10 to 15 is considered a reasonable catch. On the menu inside most pots: herring, squid, or razor clams (I can think of worse last meals).

stacked crab pots

At the Market
Dungies on Deck

If you live near the coast (the left one), the best place to get a Dungeness crab—short of trapping your own—is to buy it live, right off a boat. Not only are you getting the freshest crab at the lowest price, but you're also supporting the fishermen who, in most cases, are living on a very tight budget. Not all fishermen sell direct to the public, so check with your local harbormaster (or favorite fishmonger) to find out when and where crabs will be available. Be sure to bring a cooler packed with ice for the return trip. Some docks have large boiling pots of water on hand for cooking crabs on the spot. (Not a bad way to start a picnic.)

For those who don't live next door to the ocean, start with a fishmonger or market you trust. If they're reasonably near the coast, they might have a few Dungies live in a tank, otherwise precooked is your only option (fortunately, not a bad thing for crab).

If you decide to buy live, pick a feisty fellow. Live Dungeness crabs can last up to two weeks in an aerated tank, but they do tend to wither after a while. Never buy a deceased uncooked crab unless the fishmonger killed and cleaned it on the spot. Once they've kicked the bucket, a crab's own digestive juices will go to work on the meat, turning it rather bitter. If the crab is cooked alive, this isn't a problem.

Crab Economics

Dungies are about 25 percent edible by weight. That means, if the picked meat costs less than four times the per-pound price of a whole crab, it's cheaper. Whole crabs are usually fresher, however.

blue

Crab Conversion

Can't find a Dungie? Don't despair; there are other domestic crabs in the sea, and chances are at least one of them is available in your area.

The dominant species on the east coast is, of course, the BLUE CRAB (*Callinectes sapidus*), which can be had live, whole cooked, in pieces, or as picked meat. In general, the prep and cooking procedures are similar to those for Dungies, except that, because they're smaller, more blues will be needed to satisfy the average eater. Live, they do tend to be fairly aggressive, so don't turn your back on 'em. In terms of flavor, it's probably a toss-up. I prefer Dungeness, but that's what I grew up on. It's not your fault if you were forced to eat an inferior crab. (Please direct all hate mail to my publisher.)

Two East Coast crustaceans, JONAH (*Cancer borealis*) and ROCK CRABS (*Cancer irroratus*), look very much like small Dungeness crabs, save for the front claws, which are fatter. If you find whole or live specimens, they can be treated the same as a Dungie, although don't expect the end result to be quite as flavorful. A "peekytoe" crab is simply a rock crab with a clever marketing name.

jonah

In Florida, they eat only the claw, at least when it comes to STONE CRABS (*Menippi mercenaria*). Fishermen catch 'em, snap off the big claw, and toss the angry stony back in the water, where it will grow a new appendage in a year or two. Claws are available cooked, both frozen and fresh. My experience with the frozen variety has not been good, but fresh they're a real treat.

stone

On the other hand, the best crabmeat I ever tasted came from the frozen leg of an ALASKAN KING CRAB (*Paralithodes camtschaticus*). Huge, spiny, and full of meat, the legs of a king crab are simply sublime. Due to the critter's size (up to 6 feet across from toe to toe), it's extremely rare to see a live king crab. This is not a problem. Frozen legs are excellent thawed and served cold, or steamed back to life. Once you've tried king crab, lobster will never taste the same again.

king

snow

SNOW CRAB (*Chionoecetes opilio, C. bairdi*, and *C. tanneri*) tends to be less life-changing, but still tasty. Frozen cooked leg clusters are the most common product, and can be found in many grocery stores. Both king and snow crab tend to be richer and a little saltier in flavor than Dungeness.

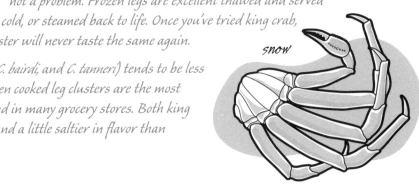

QUICK QUESTION

Can I use other crabmeat? Yes, you can substitute blue for Dungeness in any recipe that calls for crabmeat. Most of the picked crabmeat available at stores (except on the West Coast) is blue crab, so you probably won't have a choice.

There are three basic grades of processed blue crabmeat: jumbo or jumbo lump, which includes the best of the body meat; lump or backfin, the smaller flakes of body meat (sometimes called "special" or "flake"); and the least desirable (but still tasty) brownish claw meat. Some picked crabmeat is pasteurized to extend its shelf life, but fresh has a better flavor.

What the...Krab?

It looks like crab (sorta), it tastes like crab (kinda), it's spelled like crab (more or less), but what is it? "Krab," also known as surimi, is fish paste that has been processed to approximate the look and feel of crabmeat. It's not great, but if you're low on funds it'll do in a pinch (or a crabcake).

Both live and cooked Dungies should seem heavy for their size when lifted. A lightweight means less meat. The shell should be hard and without visible cracks or breaks. For cooked crabs, the legs should be pulled up to the body, indicating the crab was alive when cooked. A missing leg isn't necessarily a bad thing, as crabs will sometimes release one as a defensive maneuver. (Doesn't help much in a pot of boiling water, but no one ever said crabs were smart.) Do, however, avoid any that show signs of black discoloration where the legs join the body. This is an indication of an undercooked crab.

If you decide to buy picked crabmeat, look for flesh that is opaque white with a fresh, slightly briny aroma. For frozen crabmeat, check for freezer burn and discoloration before buying.

In the Kitchen
Dungeness Dinner

To truly enjoy a Dungeness crab you're going to have to accept that there's some work involved. Sure, you can buy fresh-picked crabmeat at the market and start dipping into it on the way home, but that's not really an honest culinary experience, is it? At the very least, you should have to do a little cracking and digging. Trust me, the effort will make the meat taste that much sweeter. And while cooking a live crustacean is not for everyone, it's usually not the disaster found in urban legends and sitcom kitchens.

Let's say you took the initiative and brought home a couple of live Dungeness crabs. Way to go! What next? Boil them. Or steam them. Or zap them. Seriously, each method can result in tasty crabs cooked to perfection. Which is best? Let's take a look:

Pincher Protection

Dungies aren't as mobile or "pinchy" as certain other crabs, but they can turn nasty if provoked. To avoid getting pinched, hold the crab from behind and keep any fingers (and other body parts) out of reach of the claws. Taunting a live crab is not recommended.

Shocking

Dunking a freshly cooked crab into an ice bath stops the cooking process and causes the flesh to contract, making it easier to pull from the shells intact. Some chefs claim this damages the crabmeat's flavor, making it tough and stringy, but I haven't found this to be the case.

HOW TO STORE: Dungeness crab

LIVE: Live crab can be stored safely in the fridge, preferably in a damp paper bag, but should be cooked on the day of purchase. Don't slip these puppies into the tub overnight (extended exposure to freshwater will kill 'em). *FRESH:* Whole cooked crab can be kept in the fridge, on ice. A plastic bag will keep any odors from mingling. Cooked crabmeat will last 2 to 3 days in the fridge, or up to four months frozen. *FROZEN:* Chill recently cooked crabs in an ice bath, dismantle, and then store the leg clusters in individual freezer bags. To use, thaw overnight in the fridge.

Boiling

On the plus side, it's not complicated: Bring a large pot of heavily salted water to a boil and add crabs—that's more or less it. The salted water approximates the crab's home, helping it maintain its natural salinity. Boiling is also a good way to cook several crabs at once, and it's a speedy and relatively humane way for them to meet their maker.

While it doesn't take a long time to cook the crabs once they go into the pot, it can take a while to bring a gallon or two of water to a boil. And after the crustaceans are cooked, there's still the issue of what to do with that big old pot of hot, crabby water.

Steaming

Of the basic methods, steaming is the best way to introduce accent flavors to the crab by way of the liquid. Add a little beer or wine, or maybe some fresh herbs and you've got yourself a party. Some chefs prefer steaming because they believe boiling waterlogs the crab. I prefer steaming because it doesn't require bringing several gallons of water to a boil.

The crabs will take a little longer to cook, however, especially if you're cooking more than two, and they may not expire quickly (or quietly). It's also necessary to keep an eye on the liquid to make sure it doesn't completely boil off.

Zapping

Seriously, cooking a crab in the microwave is a legitimate method of preparation. Many well-known chefs have taken to nuking lobster, so why not crab? In terms of time, this is the fastest way to go. Even the largest of Dungies will be done in 10 minutes in the microwave. In terms of flavor, this is the purest form of cooking since the crab is steaming in its shell, thus the only flavors available to it are its own juices. There's very little prep time, no big pot needed, and cleanup is a snap.

QUICK QUESTION

Do Dungies have to be cooked alive? No, but crab should be cooked (or at least dismantled) very soon after killing to prevent its digestive juices from affecting the flavor of the meat. *What's the most humane way to kill a crab?* A quick cut through the central nervous system will do it instantly, but will leave you with a cleaved crab. Chilling the crab first then dropping it in a pot of boiling water is effective, though there is some debate as to whether the crab feels any significant pain. Bottom line: relax. It's not that cute.

The downside? It's best to only cook one crab at a time, a big drawback if there are many mouths to feed. And, yes, there might be a little kicking inside the box as the crab expires. It's the same thing that happens in the pot, but there's no convenient viewing window in that case.

The bottom line is that each method works. Choose whichever feels most comfortable in your kitchen.

Precooked crab

For many consumers, cooked crabmeat is their only option. No problem. Most precooked crab is prepared soon after hitting dry land, meaning it's cooked fresh, which, in some cases, is better than live. Think about it: Is it better to buy cooked crab that was prepared at its peak of freshness or a live crab that's been hanging out in the lobster tank for the past week? That's not to say you shouldn't seek out a live Dungie if they're available, but don't skip crab simply because they're not.

Do you need to reheat Dungeness crab? No, it tastes great cold. If you want a little heat, dip it in some warm clarified butter. If you absolutely must eat your meat hot, try not to overdo it. Cooked crab needs only to be heated, not cooked again. Reheating in the shell offers some protection from the elements and imparts of bit of flavor in the process. For the best results, simply steam legs for 5 minutes, or 7 to 10 minutes for a whole crab. Steaming with beer or wine is perfectly acceptable. If the microwave is your thing, wrap the legs in several damp paper towels and a layer of plastic wrap and cook on high for 3 to 4 minutes for a half dozen legs. (Times will vary, so you may need to adjust.)

Pickin' and grinnin'

There's no great mystery to retrieving the meat from a crab shell. You just have to get to it and be patient. Some advocate heating the crab briefly under a broiler to color the meat, making it easier to distinguish from the cartilage, but I find this unnecessary. Once you've cleaned out the crab, give your bounty the once-over for stray pieces of shell.

Live-backing

Methods such as charcoal grilling and stir-frying often call for crabs that have been "live-backed," that is, dismantled while still alive. Basically, this means chopping the Dungie in half with a cleaver, and then cooking only the good parts. If this seems a little gruesome, ask your fishmonger to do the honors, or simply boil the crab for a minute and then plunge it into ice water to stop the cooking.

Crab Butter

Ah, crab butter, a.k.a. "crab mustard." Lovely stuff. What is it? Mostly it's an organ called the hepatopancreas, which acts as a liver for the crab. And some folks like to eat it, usually by stirring it into a sauce where it imparts a nice crabby flavor. But should you eat it? (See the Health Question for the answer.)

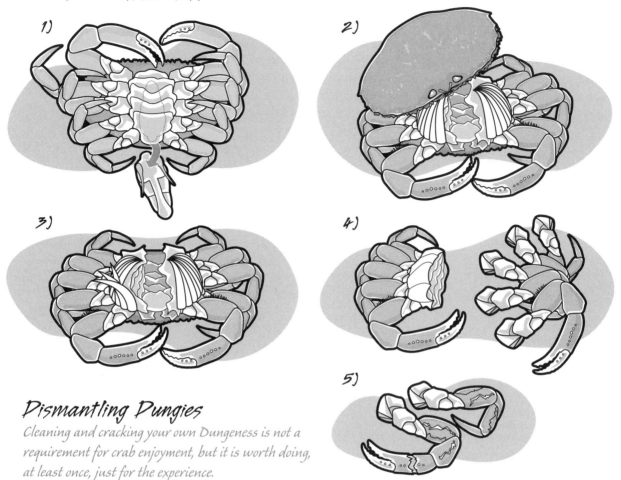

Dismantling Dungies

Cleaning and cracking your own Dungeness is not a requirement for crab enjoyment, but it is worth doing, at least once, just for the experience.

(1) Pull off the triangular shaped apron from the underside of the crab, including the two spines. (2) Turn the crab right side up. Pull off the top shell (the carapace). Give it a twist if necessary. Not a pretty picture, eh? (3) Remove the gills (the white feathery fingers; clear, when raw), the intestines, and the beaklike mouthparts. Some folks like to use the yellowish (when cooked; gray when raw) fat known as "crab butter", but I don't trust it (see "Health Question"). Scoop it out and give the insides a good rinse, clearing out any residual gunk. (4) If you're delivering whole legs to guests, break the crab in half and slice each half into 5 sections by cutting through the body between each leg. That'll give you 8 legs and 2 claws, each with a bit of body meat attached. If you're just after the meat, break the legs off the body and clean out the body halves separately. For first-timers, it might be difficult to tell the body meat from the shell (both are white). What you've got is essentially a honeycomb structure with very thin walls and lots of meat. A small fork will help with the digging, but it's not a necessity. (5) Crack each leg section with a mallet (or other blunt instrument), but be careful not to overdo it. A single fault line along the shell is enough to get at the goods. For raw crab, this will help any additional flavor sneak into the meat. For the cooked variety, it will make getting at the flesh a lot easier.

Dungeness Crab Recipes

Before jumping straight to the crab fritters it's worth taking the time to cook a live crab, at least once. Nothing tastes quite like a fresh-cooked Dungie. Yeah, it's messy, and it takes some time, and there's wiggling involved, but in the end the flavor is more than worth the trouble. And let's be honest: if you don't like "plain old crab," what are you doing making crab fritters, anyway?

NUTRITIONAL INFO

Per 3.5 oz/100 grams (raw)

Dungeness Crab

Calories:	86
Calories from fat:	8.1
Total fat:	1.0 g
Saturated fat:	0.1 g
Cholesterol:	59 mg
Sodium:	295 mg
Protein:	17.4 g
Omega-3:	0.3 g
Mercury:	0.06 ppm

HEALTH QUESTION

Are there health risks associated with eating Dungeness crabs? Domoic acid, a natural biotoxin, has been found in the hepatopancreas (crab butter) of some Dungeness. In fishing areas where the level is high, it's required that the butter be removed prior to bringing the crab to market. Basically, as long as you don't eat the crab butter, you'll be fine.

Boiled Dungeness Crab

For boiling 2 large Dungies, a 12-quart pot is fine, but for 3 or more I prefer a 16-quart pot. If you need to cook a bunch of Dungies and don't have a large enough pot, use two or more pots or boil the crabs in batches.

½ cup kosher salt
2 gallons water
2 live Dungeness crabs, about 2 pounds each
Melted butter
Lemon wedges

Add the salt and water to a large stockpot and stir to dissolve. Cover the pot and bring the water to a rolling boil over high heat. This could take a while, so be patient. *NOTE: The water should not be any closer than 4 inches from the top of your pot prior to adding the crabs.*

When the water starts to bubble (still a long way from boiling), move your crabbies from the fridge to the freezer to calm them down prior to cooking. Ten to fifteen minutes should do it. Any longer and they might start to freeze (not good).

When the water is rolling, remove the Dungies from cold storage, rinse them off, and carefully drop them headfirst into the water. Cover the pot and return it to a boil. Once the pot is boiling again, lower the heat, just enough to maintain a modest boil, and cook for 12 to 15 minutes (a little longer for larger crabs), until the shells are bright red. It's okay to leave the lid slightly askew to allow the steam to escape.

Carefully remove the crabs with a pair of tongs. If you are serving them hot, rinse them under cold water briefly before dismantling them (easier on the digits). If serving them chilled, plunge the crabs into ice water and drain thoroughly, dismantle, and refrigerate them on ice until dinner.

Serve the crabs with melted butter, lemon wedges, and a bunch of napkins.

Serves 2

QUICK QUESTION

What kind of wine goes best with crab? The short answer is white—something a little fruity and not too oaky, like a sauvignon blanc. The long answer is that your choice of wine will be determined as much by the added flavors as by the crab itself. A crab kicked up with garlic and hot spices needs something a little sweet to tame the heat, like a dry Riesling. Sparkling wines are also a good pairing (maybe it's the bubbles the crabs like), especially with a spicy dish. In general, I'd avoid most chardonnays because of their strong oak-flavored tendencies, but if you like it, knock yourself out.

Drunken Dungies
(Steamed Crab)

Beer makes everything better. Really. This is a fun way to add a little something extra to the flavor of steamed crab. If you don't have a big enough steamer, place a collapsible steamer basket or small metal colander at the bottom of a large (12-quart) pot. (The crabs won't know the difference.)

3 or more bottles of microbrew (something flavorful but not too heavy; quality counts!)
2 live Dungeness crabs, 2 pounds each
Old Bay seasoning
Melted butter
Lemon wedges

Place your crabs in the freezer for 10 to 15 minutes to calm them down prior to cooking.

Fill a large pot with about 3 to 4 inches of beer. Add the steamer basket, cover the pot, and bring it to a boil over high heat. *NOTE: Beer has a tendency to bubble excessively, so if you end up using a smallish pot, keep an eye out for overflowing bubbles.*

When the beer is at a full boil, remove the crabs from cold storage, rinse them off, and carefully add them to the basket. Dust them liberally with Old Bay. Cover the pot and steam them for 20 to 25 minutes, until the shells are bright red. Leave the lid slightly askew to watch the steam. If the beer level gets low, add a cup of very hot (or boiling) water.

Carefully remove the crabs with a pair of tongs. If you are serving them hot, rinse them under cold water briefly before dismantling them. If serving them chilled, plunge the crabs in ice water, drain thoroughly, dismantle, and refrigerate on ice until dinner.

Serve the crabs hot or cold with melted butter, lemon wedges, and a bunch of napkins.

Serves 2

NOTE: You could use this recipe to reheat precooked crab, but only steam it for 7 to 8 minutes. If you're using precooked crab portions instead of a whole crab, steam for about 5 minutes.

Zapped Dungeness Crab

If you have a teenage son, now is the time to introduce him to cooking. Trust me, putting a crab in the microwave will thrill him no end. Hey, at least you're cooking together, right?

1 live Dungeness crab, 1½ to 2 pounds
Lemon wedges
Melted butter

Place the crab in the freezer 10 to 15 minutes prior to cooking.

Remove the crab from the chill and immediately slide it into a heavy-duty microwave-safe plastic bag, along with a couple tablespoons of water and a few lemon wedges. Seal the bag and place it in the microwave.

Microwave on high for 6 minutes for the first pound, plus 1 minute for each additional ¼ pound. (For example, a 1½-pound crab will cook for 8 minutes.) *NOTE: If you're a little squeamish about cooking a live critter in the microwave, you may want to step out of the kitchen for the first couple of minutes. There may be some flinching.*

When the beeper goes off, let the crab rest in its bag for a few minutes. When you do retrieve it, watch your fingers, as it will be hot. If you are serving it warm, rinse the crab under cold water briefly before dismantling it. If you are serving it chilled, plunge the crab into ice water, drain thoroughly, dismantle, and refrigerate on ice until dinner.

Serve with melted butter, fresh lemon wedges, and a bunch of napkins.

Serves 1

Dungeness Roll

Decadent and delicious. In New England, they make these rolls with lobster, but for an equally tasty (and less expensive) treat, try it with crab. Be sure to double-check picked crabmeat for shell pieces. Nobody wants a crunchy crab sandwich.

8 ounces cooked crabmeat
¼ cup mayonnaise
1 tablespoon creamy horseradish
¼ cup celery, finely chopped
¼ cup red bell pepper, finely chopped
1 tablespoon fresh flat-leaf parsley or tarragon, chopped
1 tablespoon lemon juice

Kosher salt and freshly ground black pepper
2 sweet French rolls (or other soft-crust rolls)
Olive oil

In a medium-sized bowl, combine the crabmeat, mayonnaise, horseradish, celery, red pepper, parsley, and lemon juice. Add salt and freshly ground pepper to taste. Chill the mixture briefly.

Cut a triangular section out of each roll from the bottom. The idea is to create a V shape for the crab to sit in. Lightly brush the inside of the rolls with olive oil and toast them under the broiler for a minute. Don't overdo it; we're just looking for a light toast to keep the bread from getting soggy.

Stuff the toasted roll with crab filling and enjoy. For a warm crab roll, place it under the broiler for 2 to 3 minutes. Very tasty either way!

Serves 2 (or 4 as half-sized appetizers)

Crab Quesadilla

Traditionalists will balk at broiling a quesadilla, but it's a great way to brown the quesadilla to perfection if you don't have a professional quesadilla press. (Plus it's fun to watch.) You can top with any salsa, but the mango complements the crab beautifully.

8 small (taco-sized) flour tortillas
3 tablespoons melted butter
Freshly ground black pepper
1 cup cheddar cheese, shredded
1 cup Monterey Jack, shredded
8 ounces (about 1½ cups) cooked crabmeat
1 small jalapeño pepper, seeded and diced
Mango salsa (*see recipe on page 61*)

Turn the broiler on high and set the rack about 4 to 5 inches from the heat source.

Lightly brush one side of each tortilla with butter. Set four tortillas (butter side down) on a foil-lined sheet or broiler pan. Evenly distribute half the cheese among the tortillas. Top them with crab and jalapeño. Add pepper to taste and top with the remaining cheese. Cover each with a tortilla, butter side up.

Slide the quesadillas under the broiler and cook them until the tops begin to brown (watch closely). Remove them from the heat, carefully flip them using a wide spatula, and return them to the broiler. When the opposite sides are toasty, remove the quesadillas from the heat, cut them in quarters, and serve them immediately with Mango Salsa.

Serves 3 or 4

Buttermilk Crab Fritters

I know, I know. . . where are the crab cakes? Here's the deal: I think most crab cakes are too much about the cake and not enough about the crab. Yes, there are good crab cake recipes out there, but I'd rather eat a fritter loaded with crabmeat any day.

1½ quarts (6 cups) peanut (or other vegetable) oil
¼ cup all-purpose flour
1½ teaspoons baking powder
¼ cup yellow cornmeal
¼ teaspoon freshly ground black pepper
¼ cup buttermilk
1 egg, lightly beaten
1 tablespoon lemon juice
8 ounces (about 1½ cups) cooked crabmeat
¼ cup fresh corn kernels
Lemon wedges
Spicy Aioli (*see recipe on page 47*)

Heat the oil in a heavy 4-quart or larger pot to 370° F. Preheat the oven to 200° F.

Sift the flour and baking powder into a medium-sized bowl and whisk them together thoroughly. Add the cornmeal and pepper and stir to combine. Add the buttermilk, egg, and lemon juice and stir until a thick batter forms. Fold in the crabmeat and corn until just combined.

Carefully drop heaping tablespoon-sized dollops of batter into the oil. Fry the fritters (no more than 6 at a time) for 3 to 4 minutes, until golden brown. Flip the fritters occasionally to ensure even cooking. Transfer the finished fritters to a wire rack set over a baking sheet in the oven. Repeat until all fritters are fried (making sure the oil is at least 360 °F before adding the next batch).

Serve the fritters with lemon wedges and Spicy Aioli.

Serves 3 or 4

For more details about deep-frying, see "Deep Fried Cod Laws" on page 58.

BONUS CRAB!
Soft-shell Second Opinion

Hey, nobody's perfect.

Dungies don't do deep-fried, so if you want a soft-shell sandwich, it's going to have to be a blue crab. I can live with that. Next to a mouthful of squid tentacles, there's no seafood experience quite as tactile as eating a soft-shell blue crab. Crunchy doesn't begin to describe it. Crunchy, crabby, and a wee bit creepy? Now, you're talking.

Soft-shell signs

There's no point to trying to catch a soft-shell crab; not only are they difficult to find, but unless they're pulled from the water immediately after molting, their shells will already have begun to stiffen up. The trick is to harvest blues while they're hard and check for signs of an impending molt. What begins as a faint white line along the second segment of the back swim fin will turn pink a week before molting. When it turns red, start the 48-hour countdown.

Most soft-shell crabs are harvested during the summer (spawning season), as fishermen capture blues that are about to molt and hold them in tanks or floating cages, sometimes referred to as "peeler pounds." Immediately after molting, crabs are pulled from the water, which halts the hardening process, and then are shipped to markets live, or processed to be sold fresh or frozen. In some cases, crabs may perish on their way to market, which is okay, as long as the crab still smells fresh.

Soft-shells are often sold by size, with the largest being "whales" at 5½ inches across the carapace. Next come "jumbos," followed by "primes," "hotels," and, finally, "mediums." As with other seafood sized for sale, there is no such thing as a small soft-shell crab. In terms of softness, crabs should feel papery and thin, but not mushy.

Soft-shells at home

Fresh soft-shell crabs should be stored in the fridge, preferably in a moist environment, such as between a few wet paper towels. If you've brought home a few live softies, sticking them in the fridge will kill them (it's too cold), but won't necessarily ruin them. Whether live or fresh, soft-shell crabs are best eaten on the day of purchase, unless you happen to know they came out of the water only recently.

Cleaning a Soft-shell Crab

This method works for both fresh and live softies. Live specimens may complain a bit more, but without a hard pair of pinchers, they can't do much damage. If you're uneasy about chopping up a live critter, toss them in the freezer for 10 to 15 minutes to calm them down.

(1) Rinse under cold running water and pat dry. Cut off the face (the front ¼ inch of the body). Pull or squeeze out the small sac that remains.   (2) Lift up one side of the carapace and remove the gills. Repeat on the other side.   (3) Flip the crab and remove the apron. Cook at once!

Frozen soft-shells should be defrosted in the fridge, ideally in a colander or a makeshift draining rig that allows the water to drain away from the crab. In most cases, frozen softies have already been cleaned by the processor.

Softy sauté

Whether you decide to deep-fry or sauté a soft-shell crab will most likely depend on how comfortable you are with eating one. Deep-fried softies are safer (to eat, not to cook), and depending on how much batter or spices are used, can be as mild-mannered or wild-flavored as you like. A soft-shell crab dusted lightly with seasoned flour and sautéed in butter or oil leaves very little to the imagination. Guess which one I prefer?

There's no real trick to either method. Be sure to get a complete coating over the entire crab, including between the legs. In terms of time, count on 3 to 4 minutes per side to sauté, about the same to fry in oil heated to 375° F. For softy sandwiches, be sure to choose a roll that's not so big that the legs don't hang out on the sides. Who says food isn't a visual medium?

NUTRITIONAL INFO	
Per 3.5 oz/100 grams (raw)	
Blue Crab (Soft-shell)	
Calories:	87
Calories from fat:	10
Total fat:	1.1 g
Saturated fat:	0.2 g
Cholesterol:	78 mg
Sodium:	293 mg
Protein:	18.1 g
Omega-3:	0.3 g
Mercury:	0.06 ppm

Chapter 3
Halibut
Flatfish Flip-flop

"I painted a profile nose into a frontal view of a face. I just had to depict in sideways so that I could give it a name, so that I could call it 'nose.'"
—Pablo Picasso

Picasso was referring to a painting when he said that, but he could just as easily have been talking about a fish. I'm not sure what name he would have given it, but there's no more cubist leviathan than the sideways-seeing halibut. Sure, it may look odd, but that illustration is no abstraction. Halibut really do have eyes on only one side of their head. They aren't born with a blind side, but it isn't long before the left eye is taking a road trip to the right. Why? All the better to see you with…assuming you happen to be lunch…and on the right.

VITAL STATS

FIRST NAME: Pacific halibut (a.k.a. Alaskan, northern)

SCI. NAME: *Hippoglossus stenolepis*

SIZE: Commercial average: 20–40 lbs; max: 8 ft, 500+ lbs

LIFESPAN: Average when caught: 12–14 years; max: 50+

RANGE: California to Alaska, Russia to Japan

CATCH: About 75 million lbs annually (U.S. and Canada)

Flatfish are, for lack of a better word, flat. Their bodies are compressed laterally, meaning the average flatfish looks more like aquatic roadkill than a highly evolved underwater predator. All that's missing are the tire tracks. Were it possible to take the SUV on a deep-sea drive, you might soon find numerous flatfish beneath your wheels—sole, turbot, flounder, and the largest of the pancake clan, halibut.

Both Pacific halibut and its Atlantic counterpart are capable of reaching 8 feet in length and topping the scales at more than five hundred pounds, making halibut one of the largest bony fishes in the world. It also happens to be one of historical importance, which explains the name. Broken down Middle English style, halibut or "halybutte" means flatfish that was eaten on holy days. Hallelujah.

What makes halibut worthy of such high praise? For most folks, it's the flavor. There's something about firm, moist, and sweet that puts the average eater in the mood for fish (be it a holy day or a Tuesday). But this bottom-dwelling flip-flopper is more than a menu favorite; it's an evolutionary curiosity.

In the Water
The View from the Bottom

Halibut turn sideways not to impress art critics or confound ichthyologists (folks who study fishes), but rather to orient themselves to life on the bottom of the sea. If part of your daily routine involved burrowing in the sand to stake out lunch (or avoid becoming it), you'd keep two eyes above ground, as well. A little camouflage also helps, which is why halibut skin tends to be a splotchy dark green, brown, or black—very similar to the ocean floor.

For the young halibut, the ability to get out of sight is a prerequisite to becoming an old halibut. It takes eight years for males to hit sexual maturity, females closer to twelve, though the girls do grow faster and much larger. Nearly all Pacific halibut more than one hundred pounds are female.

Once they're all grown up, Pacific halibut prefer to hang out along the continental shelf from California to the Bering Sea. While you might find a few Russian- or Japanese-speaking halibut, the majority of the population swims in Alaskan waters. Despite being able to travel great distances, most adults remain fairly local, with only seasonal migrations to shallower waters in summer to feed and then to deeper waters in winter to mate. A large female halibut (250 pounds or more) can produce as many as four million eggs in one go, which the male will fertilize only after they've hit the water (bummer). Two weeks later, the eggs hatch, releasing tiny larvae that drift in the current toward shallower waters. By the time they're strong enough to break free of the Alaskan stream, some halibut will have drifted hundreds, even thousands of miles.

Age Old Fish

Like many fish, the age of a halibut can be discerned by examining the otolith, less scientifically known as the earbone. Summer and winter rings are added each year, similar to the rings of a tree trunk. Beats a fake ID every time. Incidentally, the oldest halibut on record was a fifty-five-year-old male. No word on how he tasted.

Eye Slide

Late in the postlarval stage of halibut development, the left eye begins to migrate to the right, following a path just above the snout (1). As the fish leans more and more to the left, the mouth twists slightly sideways (2), while its new underside loses pigmentation. By the age of six months, the inch-and-a-half-long halibut is ready to live life on the down low (3).

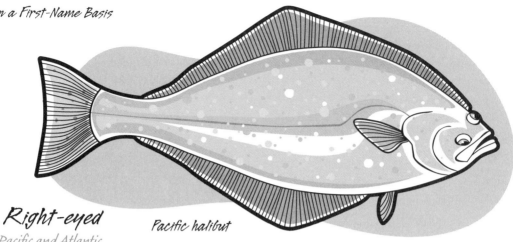

Pacific halibut

Right-eyed

Both Pacific and Atlantic halibut are "dextral" flatfish, meaning their eyes are on the right side of their bodies. "Sinistral," or left-eyed, halibut are very rare, with only about 1 in 20,000 swimming that way. The exception is the much smaller California halibut, which is naturally left leaning... crazy Hollywood halibut.

First Fishery

Long before the first commercial boat hit the water, Native Americans fished for Pacific halibut using hooks made of crooked cedar branches and line made of tightly twisted cedar bark.

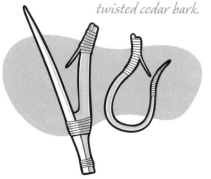

On the Boats
How to Hook a Halibut

Oddly enough, the first Pacific halibut caught commercially took a several thousand-mile journey *after* they were plucked from the sea. A trio of boats fishing off the Olympic Peninsula of Washington State in 1888 shipped their haul back to Boston via the new transcontinental railroad. Improved refrigeration techniques (not to mention the heartiness of the halibut) made the journey possible, and thus the Pacific halibut fishery was born.

The first commercial halibut boats were actually launching pads for much smaller, two-man dories, which would spend the day fishing, then return to the main vessel at night. Landing several hundred pounds of unhappy halibut in a small boat was no easy feat and was often made more difficult by rough weather. Despite the dangers, it would be 30 years before larger vessels began hauling in halibut without the dories.

Modern halibut boats use longline techniques and crews of five or six fishermen to catch and dress as much as 50,000 pounds of fish in a day. While most boats rarely stay out more than a week, it wasn't long ago that the entire Alaskan fishing season lasted only 24 to 48 hours. During the mid-1980s, increases in halibut price and population (as well as declining crab stocks) convinced many more fishermen to try their hand at the popular flatfish. The result was a "derby" style fishery that opened and closed in the blink of an eye to protect the fish population. Unfortunately, this meant dangerous, rushed working conditions for fishermen whose annual incomes were dependent on only a few days' fishing. It also meant that fresh halibut was a no-show at fish markets eleven months out of the year.

QUICK QUESTION

How does the IPHC set catch limits? No, they don't pick a number out of a hat. It's simple: start by determining the total number of fish available for fishermen to catch...let's call that the "exploitable biomass" (655 million pounds in 2002). Next, multiply the exploitable biomass by an appropriate harvest rate (based on current stock conditions) to find the total number of fish that can be taken that year. Subtracting allotments for sport fishing, tribal fishing, and bycatch will produce the commercial catch limit (76.5 million pounds in 2004), which is then divided among the fishermen based on individual quotas. Easy!

Enter science

By the mid-1990s, the International Pacific Halibut Commission (IPHC) had seen enough. The IPHC regulates both the commercial and sport halibut fisheries and has done so for more than seventy-five years. They rule by research and biomass assessment (total number of fishies) rather than fishy politics. The result has been one of the more consistently stable fisheries on the planet. To dismantle the Alaskan derbies, the IPHC adopted an Individual Fishing Quota (IFQ) system that allotted each fisherman a specific amount of halibut they were legally allowed to catch. This meant fishermen could fish whenever they wanted from March to November, theoretically when the prices (and the weather) were at their best. What's in it for you? Fresh halibut, practically year-round. The middlemen who buy from the fishermen aren't as fond of the system, nor are the fishermen who weren't able to obtain quotas during the original allocation, but overall the system has been very successful.

California, Oregon, and Washington continue to use a derby-style fishery, but with fewer fishermen and significantly lower catches than that of the Alaskan fishery, the system works better and is less dangerous. Still, it's best not to get in the way of a halibut boat on derby days.

Halibut on Skates

Longline halibut boats use a gear set known as a "skate," which consists of short branch lines, called "gangions," attached at regular intervals along a groundline. Hooks baited with herring, octopus, salmon, and other bycatch are left to "soak" a few hours, and then hauled back, hopefully heavy with halibut.

The Norwegian Way

Many of the original halibut fishermen were Norwegians who had immigrated to the Pacific Northwest intent on catching the same fish they had in Norway.

QUICK QUESTION

What about Atlantic halibut? Haven't said much about Atlantic halibut (*Hippoglossus hippoglossus*), have I? Here's why: The U.S. fishery is currently closed while the stock rebuilds. Atlantic halibut from Canada and Europe are available, as is farmed fish from Scotland and Norway, but the Pacific breed dominates most domestic menus and markets.

At the Market
Where's the Fish?

Now, for the big disappointment: You're not going to find whole halibut at the market. I know, I know…I built up the "eyes on one side of the head" thing and now you want to see it with your own. Sorry about that. The truth is, pretty much every halibut loses its head at the processor and is then cut into steaks and fillets. The few fish that do sneak through the system intact are most likely missing at least one anatomical feature: their cheeks.

halibut market forms

Cheeky and chalky

Traditionally, halibut cheeks were a favorite of fishermen, who would remove them before handing the fish off to the processor. Why? They taste like a cross between a scallop and Dungeness crab. Need I say more? What's shocking is that it took so long for the guys in marketing to figure this out. If you see halibut cheeks at the local fish stand, grab 'em.

The more likely market finds are steaks, fillets, and occasionally whole sides (called "fletches") or tail sections. All are good, but if given a choice I'll always go with the fillet (or fletch if the family's in town). Don't be afraid if you notice a slightly metallic smell during an up close and personal examination of the flesh. Unless it's particularly off-putting, that'll disappear during the cooking process. (If it smells *bad*, don't buy it.) In terms of appearance, fresh halibut has a translucent ivory cast to it; frozen tends to be more pure white. Frozen halibut is also more susceptible to dehydration than some fish, which is why much of the ice-box product is "glazed" during processing. A glazed fish has been frozen and then dipped in water several times to add a protective layer of ice.

Occasionally, higher acidity levels will cause halibut flesh to appear chalky. While this isn't dangerous to your health, it can result in a dryer, more fibrous fish when cooked, potentially dangerous to your reputation as a master chef.

In the Kitchen
Flatfish Society

A question I'm often asked (okay, once) is whether halibut is a good fish for beginners or better left to advanced students. My answer: How deep are your pockets? Halibut isn't the highest priced fish on ice, but sometimes it's close. This is not a practice fish like tilapia, which is cheap

Other Halibuts

CALIFORNIA HALIBUT (Paralichthys californicus) is a much smaller variety caught off the coast of California. It has a milder flavor than Pacific halibut and is considerably leaner. Overall, not a bad option, but with less fat, moist cooking methods are a must. You won't find GREENLAND HALIBUT (Reinhardtius hippoglossoides) at the market, but you will find "Greenland turbot," which is the same thing. U.S. regulations require that the fish be labeled as such to keep it from competing with more expensive (and better-tasting) Pacific halibut.

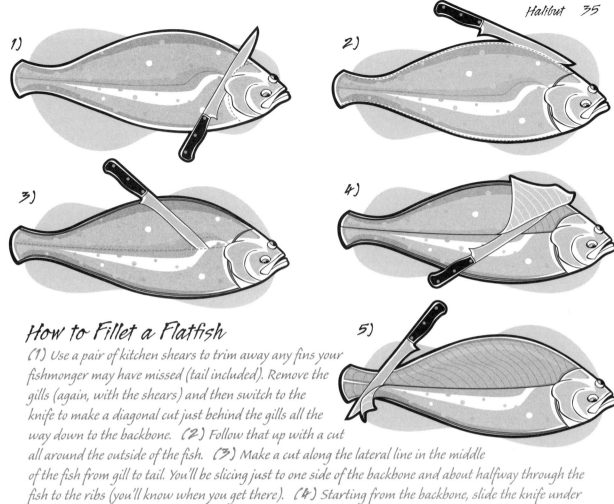

How to Fillet a Flatfish

(1) Use a pair of kitchen shears to trim away any fins your fishmonger may have missed (tail included). Remove the gills (again, with the shears) and then switch to the knife to make a diagonal cut just behind the gills all the way down to the backbone. (2) Follow that up with a cut all around the outside of the fish. (3) Make a cut along the lateral line in the middle of the fish from gill to tail. You'll be slicing just to one side of the backbone and about halfway through the fish to the ribs (you'll know when you get there). (4) Starting from the backbone, slide the knife under the flesh, keeping the blade as flat against the ribs as possible. Using short strokes, slice toward the outer edge of the fish. Keep slicing until you've completely removed one fillet. (5) Next, remove the fillet on the other side of the backbone, and then flip the fish over and repeat the process two more times.

and fairly foolproof when it comes to preparation and cooking. Leaner flesh makes halibut more susceptible to drying out, although that can be prevented with proper preparation.

Let's just say halibut is for advanced beginners.

Skin and boning

In the unlikely event that a whole halibut (or similar flatfish) appears in your kitchen, don't panic. Simply locate a good-sized cutting board and a very sharp filleting knife (flexible, if possible), and follow the instructions shown in the illustration. It takes a little practice, but with four fillets to be done, by the end you'll be a pro. Don't bother gutting the fish unless little Johnny needs an impromptu biology lesson.

No Bones About It

One of the reasons for halibut's popularity with fish-phobics is the fact that even the boniest halibut steak has very few bones. An especially big steak can even be turned into four boneless quarter steaks by simply cutting out the backbone and the thin strip of ribs that run through the center of the fillet.

Chickens and Whales

A "chicken" is what commercial fishermen call a halibut that weighs less than 20 pounds; at 20 to 40 pounds they're called "mediums;" more than that, you've got yourself a "whale."

HOW TO STORE: Halibut

FRESH: Unless you're going to be cooking your catch right away, it's best to discard the market's bag and butcher paper and rewrap the fish before storing it in the fridge. Give it a quick rinse, a pat dry, and then wrap in plastic or foil (or both) to keep the fish from absorbing (or adding to) any local aromas. Place it in the coldest part of the fridge or on ice if you've got room to spare.

FROZEN: Commercially frozen halibut can last up to six months, but if done at home (not recommended for previously frozen fish...duh), I'd eat it inside of a month. If you do intend to freeze your fish, look for skin-on fillets. Halibut like to swim where it's really, really cold, so that skin is going to protect the flesh better than even the most stupendous freezer-bag technology.

If your halibut happens to be a big boy (or girl), say 25 pounds or more, be sure to harvest the cheeks, which reside in a well just behind the mouth on either side of the fish. To remove, insert the knife at an angle and cut in a circle.

While you may never have to carve up a whole halibut, removing a side of skin is a definite possibility, which is trickier than it sounds. Sliding a knife along the bottom of the fillet doesn't work. I've tried. What does work is sliding the bottom of the fillet along the knife. See? Tricky.

Place the fillet on a cutting board, skin side down. Using a sharp knife, separate the skin and flesh at one end of the fillet. This is going to be a bit of pain, but stay with it until you've got about an inch of skin free. Now, you've got something to hold on to with your fingers, tongs, pliers—whatever works. Get a good grip on the skin, slide the knife back into position, and then pull the skin back against the knife, moving it from side to side as you go (the skin, not the knife). This does put pressure on the knife, so be sure to point the blade away from any body parts or miscellaneous children.

Wetter is better

What's the secret to happy halibut? Moisture. On a fishing boat that might mean cooking with a dollop of mayonnaise on board, but for us landlubbers olive oil, white wine, and butter work just as well. It's the fat in the fish—or lack of it—that's a problem. Halibut is not devoid of fat, but compared to such fin favorites as salmon and tuna, it's the skinless chicken of the sea. The best methods for cooking leaner fish are those that involve a bit of moisture, such as steaming, braising, poaching, and—my personal favorite for halibut—pouch cooking.

Papier-mâché Fish

The French call pouch cooking en papillote, which means "in paper." Yes, it's that simple. Start with a sheet of parchment (or foil) roughly 12 inches wide by 24 inches long. (No need to cut any fancy heart shapes…unless you really want to.) Fold the sheet in half, and then place your fish and fixings just slightly off center on one side of the fold. Don't build it too high, or you won't be able to close the pouch. Fold the top over the fish and start crimping from one corner. Neatness isn't a big deal here, but make sure you've got a tight seal. Overlapping the crimps usually does the trick. A little oil or melted butter brushed on the outside of the pouch will brown nicely, but is not necessary.

It's in the bag

Cooking in a pouch made of folded parchment paper is an excellent way to prepare numerous fish, but it's especially good for halibut, which appreciates the moist environment, the delicate cooking method, and the subtle (or not so subtle) addition of other flavors. The cool thing is that the fish is, more or less, cooking itself. Moisture inside the fish heats it from the inside out, essentially steaming it in its own juices (along with whatever else you added to the bag). Best of all, that steam stays in the pouch, infusing the fish with even more flavor, as well as protecting it from overcooking. Pouch cooking is more forgiving than other methods, which is especially nice for a finicky fish like halibut.

Pouch cooking is also an excellent low-fat cooking method, if that's what you're after. As long as there's enough moisture in the pouch—from the fish, veggies, wine, or even water—no additional fats are needed. This is also a surefire way to impress dinner guests. Let 'em tear open their own bag and watch their faces light up as the aroma fills the air; less work for you, more fun for them. Speaking of less work, cleaning up after cooking in a piece of parchment paper is a snap.

If you're thinking about tossing a piece of halibut on the grill, think steaks or thicker fillets. If sauté is the way, go with a thinner fillet. Halibut has a bit of firmness to it, meaning it'll hold together better than your average flaky white fish, but it does cook quickly, especially if it spent some time in the deep freeze. Don't be afraid to stop cooking a fillet that's just shy of opaque in the center to save it from drying out.

In recent years, deep-fried halibut has become a popular replacement for cod in many fish-and-chips establishments, especially on the West Coast. Halibut doesn't have the generous moist qualities of the best cod, but it does offer a flavorful, slightly firmer alternative.

Big Catch

For those who don't think recreational fishermen account for much in the way of poundage, consider: In 2003, sportsmen landed nearly 8.5 million pounds of halibut.

NUTRITIONAL INFO

Per 3.5 oz/100 grams (raw)

Pacific Halibut

Calories	105
Calories from Fat	20
Total fat	2.2 g
Saturated fat	0.4 g
Cholesterol	32 mg
Sodium	63 mg
Protein	20 g
Omega-3	0.5 g
Mercury	0.26 ppm

Halibut Recipes

On the West Coast, Pacific halibut is almost as popular as salmon in terms of availability and devoted fan base. In the early spring it's definitely the "it" fish, outselling everything else at the market. If your market happens to be a bit farther to the east, with no halibut in sight, there are alternatives to burning the place down. (1) Ask the fishmonger to get some halibut. He has connections. He can make it happen. (2) Comment loudly that a competitor's market down the street just received a lovely shipment of fresh halibut fillets and while you hate to shop elsewhere. . . (3) Shop elsewhere. (4) Shop online. Seriously, there are lots of good, reliable online resellers who will ship fresh fish direct to your doorstep. My advice: stick with those outfits located on the West Coast, specifically those based in the Pacific Northwest or Alaska.

Halibut en Papillote

The hardest part about cooking in parchment paper is mastering the fold. The rest is cake. What's up with the vermouth? Just a little flavor boost. A dry white wine will do the trick, too. Feel free to try with orange, grapefruit, Meyer lemon, etc.

1 large lemon, plus zest
1 large lime, plus zest
2 halibut fillets (6 to 8 ounces each)
Kosher salt and freshly ground black pepper
Olive oil
1 tablespoon dry vermouth (optional)

Preheat the oven to 425° F. Remove the zest from both lemon and lime and then cut each into 6 to 8 slices.

Fold two sheets of 12-by-24-inch parchment paper in half like a book. On each piece, place 3 to 4 of the largest citrus slices slightly to one side of the fold in a triangular or square layout. Season the halibut with salt and pepper and place each fillet on its own citrus platform. Drizzle with olive oil (no more than a tablespoon) and sprinkle with zest. Top with the remaining citrus slices and sprinkle with dry vermouth if desired. Secure the parchment pouch as directed in the illustration on page 37.

Place both pouches on a baking sheet and bake for 12 minutes (15 minutes for fillets more than 1 inch thick). Serve each pouch unopened to preserve the full aroma or slice them open and place the contents on a plate for a cleaner presentation.

Serves 2

Halibut en Papillote
with Wild Mushrooms

If you don't like mushrooms this is probably not the recipe for you. Then again, if you don't like mushrooms, you might want to seek professional help. I'm just sayin'. . .

½ pound wild mushrooms (oysters and chanterelles are excellent)
2 tablespoons unsalted butter
1 shallot, finely chopped
¼ cup dry white wine
Kosher salt and freshly ground black pepper
2 halibut fillets (6 to 8 ounces each)
Olive oil

Rinse and dry the mushrooms and chop any oversize specimens into manageable pieces (no bigger than 2 inches).

Melt the butter in a large pan over medium-high heat. Add the mushrooms and sauté, stirring regularly, for 5 minutes. If the butter starts to burn, turn the heat down slightly. Add the shallots and sauté until softened, about 2 minutes. Pour in the wine, stir to combine, and continue to stir until the liquid has reduced by 75 percent (or thereabouts). Season with salt and pepper and set aside.

Preheat the oven to 425° F. Fold two sheets of 12-by-24-inch parchment paper in half like a book. Season the halibut with salt and pepper and place each fillet on its own sheet of parchment paper slightly to one side of the fold. Drizzle with olive oil (no more than a tablespoon) and then top each fillet with the mushrooms including the remaining liquid. Secure the parchment pouch as directed in the illustration on page 37.

Place both pouches on a baking sheet and bake for 12 minutes (15 minutes for fillets more than 1 inch thick). Serve each pouch unopened to preserve the full aroma or slice them open and place the contents on a plate for a cleaner presentation.

Serves 2

Sautéed Halibut Cheeks

Because of their size, halibut cheeks tend to cook quickly, smaller pieces more so than larger ones. If your catch has multiple sizes, cook them in two batches or slide the thinner cheeks to the outside of the pan as they firm up. Very large cheeks (more than 4 ounces) will require more time to heat through and should be cooked separately or cut into smaller pieces.

1 tablespoon olive oil
½ tablespoon unsalted butter
2 tablespoons capers
1 pound halibut cheeks
Kosher salt and freshly ground black pepper
Juice of 1 lemon

Heat the olive oil and butter in a large nonstick pan over medium-high heat. Add the capers and swirl to coat.

Season the halibut cheeks lightly with salt and pepper. Add the cheeks to the pan, giving each its own space (overcrowding equals uneven cooking). Sauté until the cheeks tighten up and the edges turn opaque (1 to 3 minutes, depending on size). Turn them with a spatula and cook until just opaque in the center (1 to 2 minutes). NOTE: *Halibut cheeks become stringy as they overcook, so don't be afraid to remove fatter cheeks before they're completely cooked through. They'll finish up on the plate.*

Sprinkle lemon juice over the finished cheeks and transfer them to serving plates. Drizzle with cooked capers and oil.

Serves 4 to 6 (appetizer) 2 or 3 (main course)

Broiled/Grilled Halibut

The longer the halibut marinates in this recipes, the stronger the flavor will be. Plan accordingly. This is also great on the grill, but you'll find the flipping easier using steaks rather than fillets.

4 halibut fillets (6 to 8 ounces each)
Kosher salt and freshly ground black pepper
2 teaspoons (total) fresh rosemary or thyme leaves
1 tablespoon lemon juice
Extra virgin olive oil

Season both sides of the halibut with salt and pepper (light on the salt; as heavy as you want with the pepper). Place in a single layer in a shallow dish (a large zip-top bag also works) and spread the herbs over the top. Sprinkle the fillets with lemon juice and olive oil, cover (or seal), and marinate them in the fridge for at least 20 minutes or up to 3 hours.

Preheat the broiler, placing the rack 5 to 6 inches from the heat. NOTE: *The top of the fish should be about 4 inches from the heat; if your broiler pan adds an inch, take that into account.*

Remove the fish from the chill 10 minutes prior to blastoff. Place the fillets on a broiler pan (or baking sheet) and slip them under the heat for 4 to 5 minutes, by which time the top should be starting to show some color. Turn them and cook an additional 4 minutes, or until the outer edges start to flake. Thicker fillets may take a little longer to cook through; dropping the fish down one rack to finish will keep the surface from getting overly crispy (which isn't necessarily a bad thing).

Serve the fillets on warm plates with a few whole herb sprigs to dress things up.

Serves 4

Deep-Fried Halibut

Halibut steaks are ideally suited for deep-frying. The uniform size and shape actually makes them just right for small strip-sized pieces, best for quick frying between french fry batches. (I mean "chips," of course.)

1½ quarts (6 cups) peanut (or other vegetable) oil
4 to 5 whole halibut steaks, about 1½ pounds
½ cup all-purpose flour
1 teaspoon baking powder
1 teaspoon dried dill
¾ cup very cold water
Kosher salt
1 lemon, cut into wedges
Tartar sauce (*see recipe on page 60*)
Chips (*see recipe on page 60*)

Heat the oil in a heavy 4-quart or larger pot to 370° F. Preheat the oven to 200° F.

Quarter and skin the steaks as illustrated on page 36. You should be left with 4 strips of roughly equal size from each steak.

Sift the flour and baking powder into a medium-sized bowl, add the dill, and stir thoroughly to combine. Stir in ½ cup water until a paste forms, and then add the remaining water. (You need to use the batter within 20 minutes.)

Dredge half of the strips through the batter and lower carefully into the oil using a fry basket or spider tool. Fry them for 1 to 1½ minutes, then roll over and fry them for an additional minute or until golden. Transfer the finished pieces to a wire rack set over a baking sheet in the oven. Repeat the process with the second batch (making sure the oil is at least 360° F before adding the fish).

When both batches are done, sprinkle the strips with kosher salt and serve them with lemon wedges, tartar sauce, and chips.

Serves 3 or 4

NOTE: *For more details on deep-frying see "Deep Fried Cod Laws" on page 58.*

Chapter 4
Squid
Call Me Calamari

I want you to eat bait. Not just any bait, but squiggly, slimy, many-legged bait with big eyes and a suction-cup grip. Seriously. I want you to grab it by the tentacles and chow down. Yum. Hey, where are you going? Come on, my grandmother eats squid. I've seen her do it, one ring at a time, cringing after each and every chew. This from a woman who thinks peanut butter and jelly is spicy. If it's creamed it's cuisine, and if it's not, well...pass the cream. Perhaps she was afraid her recently relocated grandson would turn tail and run back to California if she didn't try his precious calamari fritti. Score one for octogenarian anxieties. But that's it, isn't it? You want me to call it calamari. I can dig it. Calamari is cultured cuisine. Calamari is fast food for the cool kids. Calamari is deep-fried, nonthreatening, and downright delicious. Squid is a fish with no bones, too many legs, and a beak. Who says names don't make a difference?

VITAL STATS

FIRST NAME: Squid, a.k.a. calamari

SCI. NAME: *Loligo opalescens* (market), *L. pealii* (longfin), *Illex illecebrosus* (shortfin), *I. argentinius* (Argentine), *Todarodes pacificus* (flying)

SIZE: A few ounces up to 5 lbs; 6 in to 2 ft total length

LIFESPAN: 6-18 months

RANGE: Wherever it's salty and wet

CATCH: 2 million-plus metric tons annually, worldwide

How did this happen? How did a fish that has been used primarily to catch other fish suddenly become a restaurant standard? Was it simply a name change that made squid—sorry—calamari, palatable?

Not exactly.

While it's true that until recently calamari has been used mainly as bait in the United States, nearly every other costal country in the world has been eating *and enjoying it* for centuries. Calamari is practically a staple in Italy, as is *ika* in Japan, *lula* in Portugal, and *smokkur* in Iceland. No matter what name it's given, squid is on the menu to the tune of 2 million metric tons annually. That's a lot of bait.

Thus, it must have been an effort by restaurateurs to broaden the cultural horizons of all Americans that finally introduced squ—calamari to the nation.

Nice idea, but no.

Here's the deal: Squid is cheap. Restaurants can deep-fry a dollar's worth, call it calamari, and charge eight bucks an appetizer. Not a bad profit margin, eh? What's remarkable is that when delivered to the table, a pile of tender tubes and tentacles doesn't look or taste like a rip-off. Properly prepared, calamari has a mild flavor, not really fishy, yet reminiscent of the sea, that appeals to Joe Meateater, at least when it's safely battered and fried. Not everyone is on board with eating the spidery legs, but more and more restaurants are serving them, which is a step in the right direction.

Logically, the next step would be to bring this easy-to-cook cephalopod home. Too soon? Relax. Before we can eat a squid, we're going to have to catch it.

In the Water
Escape Artist

Calamari is the second most widely consumed shellfish in the world (behind shrimp), which begs to question: Where the heck is the shell? Take the time to dismantle a dozen, and you'll find what appears to be a piece of clear plastic stuffed into the mantle. That would be the gladius, also called the quill or pen. While it doesn't provide much in the way of protection, it does help stabilize the squid's movements, which thanks to a clever bit of bioengineering, can be either forward or backward. A small tube on the mantle (the "funnel") ejects water, propelling the squid in whatever direction the tube happens to be pointing. It's a fairly effective method of swimming, assuming your primary locomotive needs include short bursts of speed and sharp turns. If that sounds like running away, remember that squid have long been used as bait for a reason: Fish like to eat them. Chicken of the sea? In more ways than one.

In addition to being fast on their fins, squid are capable of squirting a cloud of ink at hungry fish to mask their escape. They can also modify their appearance instantaneously thanks to quick-change

Big Squid
You've heard of giant squid, right? Meet the colossal squid, an even larger deep-sea demon that comes equipped with large, swiveling hooks on the end of its tentacles. How big is bigger? It has an eye the size of a dinner plate (see above). Which, of course, begs the question: does it taste good? Alas, probably not. The one fellow who admitted to cooking a giant squid claimed it tasted of ammonia.

market squid on the move

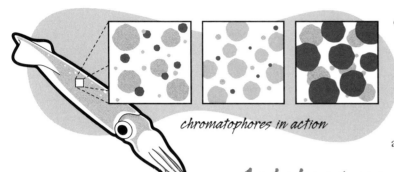

chromatophores in action

color cells in their skin. These cells, called chromatophores, expand and contract on command, changing the color, pattern, even the perceived luminosity of the skin. Defensively, this means squid can blend in with their surroundings, or at the very least, startle enemies with a sudden costume change.

Cephalopod sex

Squid do have occasion to use their defense skills for offensive purposes, specifically when trying to impress potential mates. Males will run though a series of color combinations hoping to attract females. The girls respond in kind, although whether they're reciprocating or merely telling would-be suitors to get lost is anyone's guess.

The life of a squid is short and sweet. Most barely make it past their first birthdays before the biological imperative kicks in, inspiring them to spawn and then die. The fertilized egg sacks lie on the ocean floor or possibly become attached to seaweed. After a few weeks, they hatch, each releasing hundreds of tiny squid that disappear into the open ocean. Remarkably, those that survive will return to the place of their birth within a year to fulfill their reproductive duties…and die. Such is the life of the terminal spawner.

In the case of the California market squid, mating is actually a group event. During the spawning season, enormous schools arrive in costal waters after dark to engage in what can only be described as nocturnal squid orgies. Tens of thousands of tentacles grasping at one another, hungry for love, or whatever it is that arouses squid. Unfortunately, massing in the shallows is the underwater equivalent of ringing the dinner bell. Any critter with a craving for calamari needs only to dive headfirst into the buffet. What's a poor squid to do? Swim into the light, of course.

Barbed Tentacles

In addition to eight regular arms, squid have two longer tentacles that they use to grab or stun prey. In many species, these clubs come equipped with barbs built into the suckers, making it easier for the squid to hold on tight.

Heart Healthy

Squid have three hearts—a primary engine, plus two minor motors to help pump blood through the squid's gills.

On the Boats

Like Moths to a Flame…

Mating squid are naturally drawn to the surface by the light of the full moon. Why? Nobody seems to know, but nineteenth-century Chinese immigrants fishing in Monterey Bay learned to exploit this fact. A single lantern was enough to attract the evening's catch, most of which was dried the next day for easy transport to markets in San Francisco and beyond. Modern boats lure squid to the surface using mercury vapor lamps

QUICK QUESTION

Do squid really have blue blood? A squid's blood is blue thanks to hemocyanin, the fluid responsible for transporting oxygen throughout its body. Unlike hemoglobin (the red stuff inside us), hemocyanin contains copper, which gives squid blood the blues.

Seal Bombs

Some fishermen use small explosive devices to scare off seals that might make off with the catch or get tangled in the squid nets. Do they work? Sure, right up to the point where the seals figure out that the BOOM means dinner is served. Sneaky seals.

totalling 30,000-watts and then employ purse seines to haul in the bounty. On a good night, a single boat can land twenty tons of squid. Is it fair to take advantage of a love-struck cephalopod? The heart says no, but the taste buds say, "You bet!" (Hey, they're going to croak, anyway.)

Gettin' jiggy

Another popular method for catching squid is jigging, which uses hundreds of lures set along multiple lines dropped directly into the water on either side of the boat. A machine automatically jigs the lines up and down, luring squid to attack and (hopefully) snagging them in the process. The lines are then reeled in over rollers that dislodge the squid from the barbless hooks, depositing them in a holding tank.

Prior to the 1990s, the Japanese employed a huge fleet of drift-net boats to fish the North Pacific for several species of squid, including the much larger Japanese or neon flying squid. Unfortunately, the nets, some of which stretched more than forty miles, were notorious for ensnaring marine mammals, birds, and untargeted fish species in addition to the squid. International pressure forced the Japanese (as well as other Asian and European nations) to abandon drift nets and switch to boats outfitted with large jigging rigs.

The Wild West hangs up its spurs

Until recently, conservation was not a word often associated with squid fishing. Huge increases in the California catch, however, finally got a few of the fisherman thinking about the future. In a remarkable move, state officials implemented boat restrictions and fishing quotas *before* the first signs of trouble. What was once a wide-open, anything-goes fishery is now a carefully regulated system of calamari catch and release…sans the release part.

Protecting squid is smart, not only from a bottom-line perspective, but also because they're a valuable part of the aquatic food chain. A collapse of the squid population could damage many of the species that depend on squid for their survival, including other fish, seals, dolphins, whales, and dockside restaurateurs.

fishing with light

Lab Squid

Squid have long been a favorite for research scientists due to an oversized set of nerve cells.

Squid Ink

Like octopuses, squid are capable of squirting a cloud of ink to help make their getaway. Naturally, someone decided to eat the stuff and now we have squid ink pasta, squid ink risotto, squid ink soup...you get the idea. Squid ink imparts a mild seafood flavor and turns just about anything it gets into black. For Goth fans, it's a pantry must-have.

At the Market
Well-Traveled Squid

Because of squid's global presence, there are rarely shortages at the market, at least in the freezer section. Fresh supplies are occasionally hard to find, depending on weather or seasonal changes in water temperature. In 1998, landings of market squid practically fell off the map due to everyone's favorite oceanic anomaly El Niño. Thanks to the squid reproduction cycle, the catch bounced back the very next year.

The California market squid fishery accounts for about 100,000 metric tons annually, about 90 percent of which is shipped to overseas processors. Traditionally, this made sense, since Asian and European markets were the primary buyers of squid. The recent increase in domestic demand has changed the market, but not the squid's travel plans. The United States continues to export most of its catch, but now also imports nearly 50,000 metric tons of squid, primarily from China, Taiwan, and India. Even more striking is the fact that many of the imports are simply California squid processed and packaged overseas. A calamari conspiracy? Nope. It's just cheaper to do the dirty (okay, slimy) work overseas.

Frozen is the new fresh

In general, fresh domestic squid are better than imports, but the best option may actually be found in the freezer section. Unlike practically everything else on the cutting board, calamari can be frozen and thawed multiple times with little or no loss of quality (assuming they were fresh at the start). This is how squid can be shipped halfway around the world and back again and still taste terrific. Which squid-cicle is the best? Block-frozen whole squid have had the least amount of processing, but whole tubes and tentacles are usually a worthwhile time-saver.

If you're in the market for fresh, your choices are probably going to be between "whole" and "cleaned tubes and tentacles." If there are multiple varieties, give a cheer and go for a tenderer *Loligo* species such as Californian market squid or "longfin" squid (one of two common Atlantic varieties, the other being the less popular "shortfin"). Squid are cheap, so this is definitely one of those times when paying a premium is worth the extra buck or two. Is it okay to buy squid (mostly) precleaned? If you're feeling squeamish and don't need the ink, go for it.

squid products

FROSTY SQUID
BLOCK FROZEN SQUID

HOW TO STORE: Squid

FRESH: Fresh squid is best used soon, preferably the day it was purchased. Kept refrigerated on a bed of ice, fresh squid will remain so for a day, although it's wise to clean whole specimens right after purchase. *FROZEN:* A block of properly frozen squid will last up to a year in the freezer. To thaw it, simply place it under cold running water (if in a hurry) or in the fridge overnight.

tasty squid products from Japan

When buying, make sure the flesh is as white as white can be. If the squid is still wearing its mottled outer skin, that's okay, but once the flesh starts to turn yellow (or the skin overly pink), it's time to fish elsewhere for dinner. Once again, the eyes are your guides to freshness, as is your nose; clear eyes and a clean scent means you're good to go.

In the Kitchen
Fastest Food

Cook calamari less than two minutes or more than twenty. Congratulations, you are now a squid expert. Okay, there's a little more to it than that, but remember that simple equation and your chances for success with suckers will greatly increase. Forget to do the math and be prepared to face numerous rubber band jokes at the dinner table.

Squid cooks fast because (*a*) there's not a lot to cook, and (*b*) it contains high levels of protein in its flesh. This makes it nutritious, but also notorious for toughening up in a hurry. Sautéed over high heat, most squid will cook through in about a minute, with only larger specimens needing a full two count. Deep-fried, squid goes from tender to tire in the blink of an eye, before coming back to tenderness after another 20 minutes. Of course, it will also be burnt to a crisp, which is why a longer cooking time requires a low heat method to gently break down the muscle fibers. There's always room for a few tubes and tentacles in cioppino.

Big squid (bodies 5 inches or longer) are delicious stuffed or grilled, preferably skewered to keep them from curling up (lightly scoring the mantle also helps). In most cases, this means cooking the calamari naked, save for a little olive oil and seasonings. Naked calamari looks like…well, squid, which is a problem for some eaters. You can try to disguise it with some clever cutting or a sauce, but ultimately a tentacle is a tentacle.

Thus, we've come full circle. To eat calamari you must eat squid, and anyone who isn't prepared to do that is going to miss out. If you can't convince your grandmother to at least give it a try, threaten to move. That always seems to work.

Calamari Equation

if X < 2 or > 20 then :)
where X = cooking time in
minutes and :) = yum!

Milk It

Some restaurant chefs marinate squid for up to 48 hours in milk or buttermilk, using the lactic acid as a tenderizer.

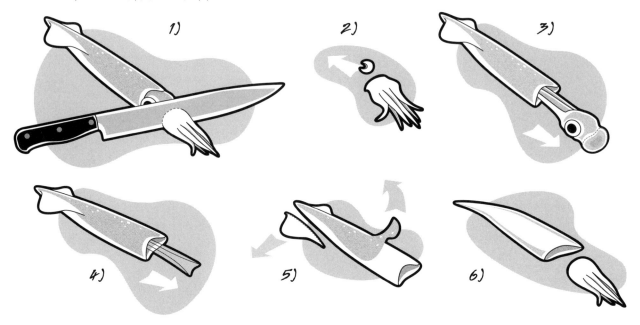

How to Dismantle a Squid

Slimy? A little. Educational? Sure, get the kids. Economical? Now, you've got it.

(1) Cut off the tentacles just below the eyes. Don't cut too low, or they'll fall apart. (2) Find the beak in the center of the tentacles and pop it out. (3) Pull the head away from the mantle. Most of the inner workings (the guts) will slide right out.* (4) Pull out the transparent quill and then slide a finger inside the mantle to clear away any remaining viscera. (5) The skin is edible and colorful and adds a bit of flavor, so I leave it on. If you prefer the clean white look, scrape at the body with the back of a knife to get things started, then pull the skin away with your fingers. (6) Thoroughly wash the tubes and tentacles (inside and out) and pat dry. Trim the tubes as desired (rings, strips, etc.).

*Ink Sack: You can harvest your own gourmet squid ink by carefully removing the silvery ink sack from the viscera.

QUICK QUESTION

I know what a squid is, but what is a SQUID? A SQUID, or Superconducting Quantum Interference Device is used to measure extremely low-level magnetic fields, such as those associated with neural activity inside the brain. How low is low? Try 1/1,000,000,000 of a Tesla (a refrigerator magnet is about 1/10 of a Tesla).

Squid Recipes

I realize this whole "cook the squid as little as possible" thing has a few of you tweaked. Here's what you do: Sauté a few small tubes and tentacles in olive oil over medium-high heat until you think they're done. (What did you give them, 3 minutes?) Okay, try them. Not great, but not horrible, right? Toss a few more squid in the pan, but this time stop cooking after 2 minutes. How'd they turn out? A little bit more tender, perhaps? Good. Now cook them again, this time for only 1 minute. Seriously. What do you think? Best yet? Care to go for 30 seconds?

QUICK QUESTION

What if I want a steak? Calamari steaks are cut from the mantle of either Japanese flying squid or Argentine squid, both much larger species that account for roughly half of the worldwide squid landings each year. Because they tend to be a little tougher, most steaks are tenderized using a cube steak machine or a natural enzyme, such as those found in papayas or pineapples. Look for squid steaks in the freezer section.

NUTRITIONAL INFO

Per 3.5 oz/100 grams (raw)

Squid

Calories	92
Calories from fat	13
Total fat	1.4 g
Saturated fat	0.4 g
Cholesterol	233 mg
Sodium	44 mg
Protein	16 g
Omega-3	0.5 g
Mercury	0.07 ppm

Calamari Fritti

Master this recipe and you'll never order calamari at a restaurant again. Okay, maybe you will, but you won't be as impressed once you see how easy it is to make. WARNING: *Hot oil splatters if not treated with respect. For more tips on deep-frying, see "Deep Fried Cod Laws" on page 58.*

1 quart (4 cups) peanut oil (or other vegetable oil)
1 pound cleaned tubes and tentacles (about 2 pounds whole)
1 cup flour
Kosher salt
2 small lemons, cut into wedges
Spicy Aioli

Clean the squid (if necessary) and cut the mantles into ½-inch-thick rings.

Heat the oil in a large, heavy-bottomed pot or deep fryer to 370° F. Dredge a third of the squid in flour, shake off the excess, and carefully lower the pieces into the oil with a spider or in a fry basket. Cook for 30 seconds to 1 minute—just until the squid are a light golden brown. Drain briefly and transfer the squid to a paper towel-lined cooling rack. Once the oil kicks back up to 370° F, repeat, using the second and third batches.

Sprinkle the calamari with salt and serve it immediately with lemon wedges and Spicy Aioli.

Serves 3 to 6 (depending on how hungry folks are)

Spicy Aioli

If you want to go traditional, omit the red pepper flakes.

3 to 4 large garlic cloves, peeled
2 egg yolks
½ teaspoon kosher salt
Freshly ground pepper, to taste
¼ teaspoon red pepper flakes
1 tablespoon lemon juice
¾ cup extra virgin olive oil

Crush the garlic into a smooth paste (using a mortar and pestle or a garlic press). Transfer the paste to a mixing bowl, add the yolks, salt, pepper, red pepper flakes, and lemon juice, and whisk to combine them.

Add a small amount of the olive oil and whisk until it is absorbed. Continue to gradually work in oil until the sauce forms a smooth emulsion. If the aioli seems overly thick, add a little more lemon juice. Adjust the seasonings as desired.

Makes about 1 cup

Grilled Squid Skewers

This is calamari for grown-ups, without the deep-fried safety net. Be sure to get the grill good and hot so the squid have a chance to crisp up a little. Larger squid are more impressive on the stick, but the little guys are just as tasty (maybe more so).

2 pounds whole squid (about 1 pound cleaned)
Extra virgin olive oil
Kosher salt and freshly ground black pepper
Flat-leaf parsley, chopped

Clean the squid, but don't cut the mantles into rings. (Skin on or off is up to you, but the color looks especially nice when grilled.) Thread the body and its tentacle cluster onto a skewer (metal or water-soaked wood). Larger squid each get their own stick; the little guys can share. Drizzle the skewers with olive oil and sprinkle with salt and a few twists of pepper.

Get the grill going (the hotter the better). Once it's good and hot, lay the skewers across the grill. *NOTE: Larger squid may sit fine parallel to the bars, but as they cook they're going to shrink, which may result in their falling through into the fire. You will be very sad if this happens.* Cook the squid for 1 minute, or less if the squid start to shrink up before the minute is up. Turn and cook for another 30 seconds to a minute.

Serve the squid immediately (on skewers or plated with a sprinkle of flat-leaf parsley) with lemon and aioli (or other dipping sauce).

Serves 3 or 4 (appetizer) or 2 (main course)

Squid Bruschetta

This could easily top a salad or sit by itself on a plate as the main attraction. NOTE: Any kind of tomato will work, but high-quality heirlooms, especially those found at summertime farmer's markets, are vastly superior to most supermarket options.

2 large heirloom tomatoes (or 4 to 6 Romas), chopped
Kosher salt and freshly ground black pepper
6 to 8 large basil leaves, chiffonade (see note)
3 tablespoons extra virgin olive oil
1 sourdough baguette (or other small diameter loaf)
4 large garlic cloves
½ pound cleaned tubes and tentacles (smaller squid are better)

Place the tomatoes in a bowl and season with salt and pepper. Toss with basil and 1 tablespoon olive oil. Set aside.

Slice the baguette into 8 (or more) ¼-inch-thick slices and toast both sides until golden brown. Cut 2 garlic cloves in half and rub over one side of each toasted slice. Arrange on a serving platter. Finely chop the remaining garlic and set it aside.

Cut the squid tubes into ¼-inch rings and chop the tentacle clusters in half. For larger squid, tentacle clusters should be quartered and rings cut in half. Season with salt and pepper.

Heat the remaining olive oil in a large sauté pan over medium heat. Add the chopped garlic and cook, stirring frequently, until the garlic begins to sizzle (but not brown). Turn the heat to high and add the squid. Cook, stirring continuously, until the squid has shrunk up noticeably, about 1 minute. Add the tomatoes, stir to combine, and cook for 1 minute more.

Remove the squid from the heat and spoon them evenly over toasted slices. Serve immediately.

Serves 3 or 4 as an appetizer

NOTE: The best way to cut basil is by using a method called "chiffonade." Simply stack the leaves, roll them up, and cut them into fine strips.

"A vast pulpy mass, furlongs in length and breadth, of a glancing cream-color, lay floating on the water, innumerable long arms radiating from its centre, and curling and twisting like a nest of anacondas, as if blindly to clutch at any hapless object within reach. No perceptible face or front did it have; no conceivable token of either sensation or instinct; but undulated there on the billows, an unearthly, formless, chance-like apparition of life."
—*Moby-Dick, Herman Melville, 1851*

Slow-Cooked Calamari
with Squid Ink (and) Pasta

Some stores now carry black "squid ink pasta," which is certainly the easy way to go. For those feeling a little more adventuresome, buy whole squid and harvest your own ink. If you can't find whole squid, don't worry. This dish is equally delicious without the ink.

2 pounds whole squid (about 1 pound cleaned)
2 tablespoons olive oil
1 red onion, chopped
3 large garlic gloves, minced
1 large can (about 28 ounces) whole peeled tomatoes plus juice
½ cup red wine
1 tablespoon capers
6 Kalamata olives, pitted and chopped
½ pound linguini or spaghetti
Kosher salt and freshly ground black pepper

Clean the squid, but save the entrails. Look for the silvery little pouch filled with black liquid and remove it, discarding the rest of the guts. Strain the ink sacs through a fine mesh strainer to release the liquid. Discard the sacs. Cut the remaining mantles into ½-inch-wide strips or rings. For larger squid, cut the tentacle clusters in half.

Heat the olive oil in a large saucepan over medium-low heat. Add the onions and garlic and cook until tender. Do not allow them to brown. Break up the tomatoes with a fork and add them along with the tomato juice, red wine, capers, and olives to the pan. Bring the mixture to a boil and then add the squid and ink, reduce heat to a bare simmer, and cook for 30 to 35 minutes until the squid are tender (the second time around). Season with salt and pepper to taste.

While the squid are simmering, bring a large pot of salted water to a boil. Once the squid nears the finish line, cook the pasta. NOTE: *It's okay if the squid simmers a few extra minutes—better to get the pasta right.* Once the pasta is done, drain thoroughly, and toss it with the squid (in the saucepan is fine). Serve immediately.

Serves 3 to 4

Calamari Steak Sandwich

Calamari steaks are usually sold frozen, pretenderized. If yours don't have a bunch of tiny holes in them (left by a tenderizing machine), grab a fork and liberally puncture each side. If you aren't fond of Old Bay seasoning, salt and pepper are fine by themselves.

2 sandwich-sized French baguettes
Olive oil
1 large egg
½ cup *panko* bread crumbs
¼ teaspoon Old Bay seasoning
Freshly ground black pepper (to taste)
2 squid steaks (4 to 6 ounces each)
2 tablespoons vegetable oil (preferably peanut oil)
4 slices of provolone or Swiss cheese
¼ cup marinara sauce (store-bought is fine)
1 whole dill pickle, sliced lengthwise (optional)

Preheat broiler. Place the egg, Old Bay, and a few twists of ground pepper in a shallow bowl and beat with a fork until combined. Add the bread crumbs to a second shallow bowl.

Slice the baguettes in half and brush the interior faces with olive oil. Toast both the top and bottom halves until just golden. Set aside (but leave the broiler on).

Heat the oil in a large saucepan over medium-high heat. Dredge the steaks in the egg, then in the bread crumbs, shake off the excess, and carefully lay them in the pan. Cook them until golden brown, 2 to 2½ minutes, flip them, and cook another 1½ to 2 minutes.

Place the cooked steaks on a foil-lined broiler pan and top each with two slices of cheese. Spread the marinara sauce over the toasted baguette bottoms and set next to the steaks. Broil until the cheese is thoroughly melted and the sauce is warm (about a minute).

Place the cheesed steaks on the bottom half of the baguette, top with pickle slices (if you dare), and complete the sandwich with the baguette top. Slice the sandwich in half and serve it with Japanese shrimp-flavored chips. Or potato chips. Whatever.

Serves 2

Chapter 5
Cod
Joe Fish

What can I say about cod? I think this ad, which first appeared in Ultra Modern Homemaker Magazine in 1955, pretty much says it all. (No, really, it did. Honest.)

Ladies and Gentlemen, allow me to introduce the fish stick that changed the course of history: cod. Nations were built on it, populations sustained by it, wars fought over it, and children delighted by it (when accompanied by copious amounts of tartar sauce). This is the fish found in most definitions of the word: white, flaky, and preferably deep-fried and bone-free. This is the fish in fish-and-chips, the cod in scrod, and the fillet that modified the menu at McDonalds. Look up "fish" in any history book and there's a good chance it'll point you to a picture of a cod.

That may seem like a lot of baggage for one fish to carry, but for most of its multimillion-year existence, cod has been up to the task. It was only in the last half century that cod finally hit the back of a net it couldn't escape. Still, even after decades of overfishing, cod is second only to a cod clone (pollock) in terms of annual worldwide catch. Despite our best efforts to catch and eat every last one, cod survives (albeit barely in some places).

Atlantic cod

Forrest Gump of the sea

How did cod become so important? Why not salmon or tuna or swordfish? While it may seem like a case of right place, right time, there's a reason cod continually pops up in the historical record, in fact, there are three of them. First, this was a fish that preindustrial fishermen could catch using the simplest of methods. Cod are not deep thinkers; dangle a hook in front of 'em (bait optional) and chances are they'll take it. Tales of fishermen dunking baskets into the water only to retrieve them full of cod are exaggerations—but not by much. Ultimately, the steam engine made it possible to land thousands of cod in a single net, but the cod kept coming.

Of course, to be the fish on every man's plate, cod had to be available to every man. Thanks to curing techniques pioneered by Norse and Basque fishermen, long-lasting, protein-laden cod was widely distributed to the masses. It may have required a little moisture to make it palatable, but for a populace in search of cheap, winterized nutrition, cod was a godsend. (Conveniently, cod was exempt from Church-sanctioned fast days because it was considered a "cold" food.)

Finally, to make a difference on a global scale, there would have to be a lot of cod—and there was. Until the invention of the factory trawler, it was doubted fishermen could ever catch all the cod in the sea. This feat of prodigious proliferation was accomplished thanks to a bit of practical codfish philosophy: Eat everything in sight, don't get sick, and make lots of little fish.

In the Water
The Tao of Cod

If we learn anything from cod it should be this: Swim around with your mouth wide open and you'll never go hungry. Sure, you might occasionally swallow a sea cucumber or an old shoe, but it's hard to complain with a mouth continually full of something. A few folks (fish included) might not be able to stomach the menu of an omnivorous bottom-feeder, but

A Fish with No Name

Sure, its name may be synonymous with fish, but where did "cod" come from? Honestly, no one's really sure. The earliest form is found in the thirteenth century Middle English word "cotfish," which doesn't seem to have been based on anything. Another obsolete Middle English word, "codd," or bag, would appear to be a contender, but no definitive link has ever been made.

VITAL STATS

FIRST NAME: Cod (a.k.a. Atlantic cod, Pacific cod, Icelandic cod, true cod, scrod, fish)

SCI. NAME: *Gadus morhua* (Atlantic), *G. macrocephalus* (Pacific)

SIZE: Commercial average: 5-25 lbs; max: 200 lbs, 6 ft in length

LIFESPAN: Average when caught: 4-8 years; max: 25 years (Atlantic), 12 years (Pacific)

RANGE: Continental shelf of northern Atlantic and Pacific

CATCH: 1.5-2 million metric tons annually, worldwide

Alaskan pollock

The Other White Fish

Historically, "fish" meant cod, but these days it might mean haddock, whiting, hake, or pollock. All are very similar to cod, but ALASKAN POLLOCK (Theragra chalcogramma), also known as walleye pollock, represents the largest fishery in the world. Between 3 and 4 million metric tons are caught each year in the North Pacific from Alaska to Japan. In terms of flavor, pollock is fairly bland, which is exactly what most processors love about it. It's going to taste like whatever it's next to when it cooks. Right about now you're probably thinking: "But I've never seen pollock at the fish market—what gives?" Because its flesh is fairly fragile, most pollock is processed into fish paste (surimi) and used to make "value added" products such as artificial crab. Curiously square products like fish sticks are cut from large blocks of pressed, frozen pollock fillets.

for the cod it's ideal. Whether this lack of dietary discrimination has anything to do with cod being a supremely disease-resistant fish is purely speculative, but it probably doesn't hurt.

Besides eating and staying healthy, cod like to multiply, a feat they accomplish through overwhelming numbers. The average 4-foot-long female can produce more than 9 million eggs during its annual spawning period. Do the math, and by all accounts we ought to be up to our armpits in cod. Fortunately, nature, or more specifically harsh currents and other fish, thin out the numbers. At best, only a handful of cod eggs from each spawning event will ever develop into full-grown adults, but that's more than enough to keep the population stable.

Most cod prefer to spawn close to shore, although how close varies from one region to another. Young cod emerge from their eggs after 2 to 3 weeks, and then spend the next month or so chomping on plankton and krill, before realizing they'd be a heck of a lot safer swimming along the ocean floor. The first year of a cod's life is the most dangerous; after that, they have very few natural predators, no doubt another reason for their success. Unfortunately, life on the bottom does have its drawbacks, the most obvious being that fishermen know exactly where they are.

On the Boats
Fishing Boat to Factory

If you've ever been to Newfoundland in the winter and wondered why anyone would want to live there, the answer is cod. Centuries before it was "discovered" by John Cabot, Basque fishermen used Newfoundland as a staging area for drying their catch. Practically every nation that has fished the great cod stocks of the Grand Banks has sought to use it for similar purposes, resulting in its colonization by English, French, and Spanish fishermen. For years, cod was so important to the local economy, it earned the nickname "Newfoundland currency." These days the locals just call the fish gone.

For much of the fishery's existence, the primary method for catching cod was through the use of handlines. Small two-man dories launched from a larger ship would spend the day at sea, hauling cod using only a long line, a hook, and two pairs of very strong shoulders.

A Cod in Time

Need a little convincing of the cod's greatness? Check out its impressive historical highlight reel.

3000 B.C. Native Americans begin fishing for cod in the Gulf of Maine.

982-1002 A.D. En route to Greenland and North American, Vikings just happen to sail through all the major North Atlantic cod stocks. Guess what they eat along the way?

1450-1500 Age of Exploration kicks into high gear thanks to newly printed charts, readily available shipbuilding plans, and barrels full of dried cod. When the barrels run dry, a quick stop in Newfoundland fills the tank.

1500s Salted or dried cod becomes the energy bar of its day, providing inexpensive, shelf-stable nutrition for the masses of Europe. Let them eat fish!

1602 Cap Pallavisino is renamed Cape Cod by Bartholomew Gosnold, in honor of the fish that continually hinders his efforts to get to Asia.

1620 At the first (and only) Thanksgiving feast held by the Plymouth Pilgrims, cod is served prominently alongside turkey. Later, cod (along with lobster) is used to fertilize crops, hold off starvation, and make New Englanders rich.

late 1600s Cod becomes a part of the infamous triangle trade, providing the means to purchase slaves in Africa, as well as food for slaves in the West Indies.

1776-1782 Issues surrounding tea, molasses, and cod are primary reasons for patriot ire aimed at England. Once the war is over, the final sticking point to the Treaty of Paris is cod rights on the Grand Banks (which the United States gets).

1784 The "Sacred Cod," a five-foot wooden cod, is hung in the Massachusetts House of Representatives. It remains there today, facing north when the Democrats hold a majority, south when the Republicans...oh, like that's ever going to happen.

1800s In England, codfish and chips are the edible fuel that runs the Industrial Revolution. It's entirely possible the British Empire would collapse without cheap, deep-fried fish. (Think I'm kidding? Ask a Brit.)

1865 During the Civil War, the Union army is kept afloat thanks to various cod products, a tactic the British navy had been using to combat the French for ages.

1933 Members of the Harvard Lampoon use a pair of wire cutters and a long flower box to steal the Sacred Cod. Upon its return, the fish is hung a bit higher to prevent future cod-nappings.

1950s Fish sticks are a hit. Children everywhere squeal in delight, wonder why their pet goldfish isn't square.

1958-75 Three times over 17 years, Iceland and England kick up the Cod Wars. Though no lives are lost, numerous nets are cut, nerves frayed, and international borders redefined. Inspired by Iceland's seaward expansion, coastal nations around the world soon claim the sea within two hundred miles of their own shores. Today, only 10 percent of the world's fishing stocks swim in international waters.

1963 McDonalds introduces the Fillet-O-Fish sandwich, the first-ever addition to its original menu.

1997 Mark Kurlansky publishes tell-all biography of cod (*Cod, A Biography of the Fish that Changed the World*, Penguin), making it impossible for anyone to write about the fish without referencing his book.

COD WARS
EPISODE III
ICELAND STRIKES BACK

Counting in Tongues

Handliners were commonly paid for each cod they caught. To keep track of an individual's catch, the throat piece, called the cod tongue, was removed and kept for counting purposes. This is why dead cod tell no tales.

Handliners gave way to long-liners, which could catch cod more quickly and efficiently. Around the dawn of the twentieth century, the proliferation of steam engines helped introduce another weapon into the fisherman's arsenal: the trawl net. Rather than wait for the cod to come to them, fishermen could now chase them down with nets designed to fish just above the ocean floor. Bigger engines begat bigger boats, which meant bigger nets and bigger catches. Throw in improved freezing techniques and the stage was set for the cod killer: the factory ship.

Another day at the factory

Centuries of fishing failed to put a dent in cod stocks, but all that changed with the introduction of the factory trawler in the 1950s. These mammoth ships could catch, clean, and process cod on the spot, converting several thousand tons of cod into a consumer-ready product while still at sea. Soon, factory ships from around the world were pouring into the North Atlantic, armed with monster trawls that not only swallowed up cod, but also did considerable damage to the seafloor. Cod landings more than doubled during the 1960s to nearly 2 million tons, but the bonanza didn't last. By the time the first disco ball started spinning (that'd be the mid-seventies, kiddies), cod landings had fallen back to half of what they were before the factory ships arrived.

Tired of seeing its inshore cod stocks ransacked by offshore fishing, Iceland finally stopped kidding around and announced the waters within two hundred miles of its shores were off limits to foreign fleets (especially the Brits). By 1977, both the United States and Canada had followed suit, establishing their own "exclusive economic zones," and taking control of many of the most valuable cod stocks in the process.

For those who like happy endings, best to stop reading right about now.

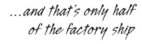

...and that's only half of the factory ship

Meet the new boss, same as the old boss

In short order, North American fishermen were flocking to the newly wide-open fishing grounds in big numbers and even bigger boats. Despite some efforts to protect the population, cod landing declined throughout the 1980s. By the early 1990s, Canada was limiting and later closing areas to cod fishing off the coasts of Newfoundland and Labrador in an effort to rebuild the population. In 2003, the Canadian government declared several of their native cod stocks "endangered" or "threatened." Today, only two of the nine primary Canadian stocks are considered to be in a fishable state.

QUICK QUESTION

Trawler? Troller? Which is it? A trawler is a boat that fishes by pulling (or dragging) a wide-mouthed net along the seafloor, scooping up just about everything in its path. Trolling refers to fishing using multiple baited hooks set on lines in the water. Trolling has a reputation as a high-quality, low-bycatch method; trawling…not so much.

Cracker Jack of the Sea

Catch a cod, win a prize: Ducks, octopuses, shoes, jewelry, cans, and rocks have all been found in the stomachs of cod.

The situation for the U.S. cod fishery is not much better. Both major stocks (Gulf of Maine and Georges Bank) are considered "overfished," with "overfishing occurring" according to the National Marine Fishing Service. How bad is it? Even with significant restrictions placed on fishermen in 2002, it's likely to take decades before cod stocks are rebuilt to sustainable levels.

Hard to believe a fishery that produces over a million tons annually is in trouble, but without increased and continued conservation efforts, Atlantic cod may one day be rendered commercially unviable.

Pacific praise

Okay, now for a little good news: despite a whole lot of fishing going on, Pacific cod stocks are healthy and by all accounts should remain so for the foreseeable future. Another Alaskan success story? You bet. Good management goes a long way in the Great White North. Or maybe it's the cold…who wants to fish for long in that weather?

At the Market
Great White

Once upon a time, cod was the "it" fish at markets. Finfish came and went, but the one fillet you could count on week in and week out was the ubiquitous cod. These days overfishing and more media-savvy competition have pushed cod to the corners of most display cases. Despite its former star status, cod is an excellent choice for those seeking a mild-mannered dinner; for fish-and-chips purists it's the *only* choice.

Atlantic cod remains the most popular variety, although it's sometimes sold as Icelandic cod or scrod. Due to domestic closures, most of the Atlantic catch now comes from Iceland, Canada, and Norway. On the west coast, Pacific cod dominates, with U.S. vessels fishing in Alaska being the primary domestic provider. It has been given the rather

Whiskers

That funny little goatee hanging down beneath a cod's chin is called a "barbel" and is thought to help the fish feel its way along the seafloor.

Cod-liver Oiled

Cod-liver oil was used to prevent rickets prior to the fortification of milk with vitamin D in the 1930s. More recently it's been touted as a remedy for arthritis and as a way to prevent cardiovascular disease, though neither claim has been proven conclusively. Most experts agree that it's probably healthier to just eat the fish. Most kids agree cod-liver oil tastes spectacularly bad. Bottom line: yuck.

QUICK QUESTION

Should I eat an overfished fish?   Tough question. Are you contributing to the demise of the species by eating it? Or will it send a message to the industry if you stop buying the bad fish? Or is it bad fishermen? Or bad politicians? What about a boycott? It worked for the dolphins, right? True, but cod aren't as cute as dolphins. What's a cod-loving, environmentally responsible person to do?

The easy answer is to buy Pacific cod. It comes from a well-managed fishery and the stocks are plentiful. Haddock, hake, and whiting also make suitable substitutes, but if you're only option is Atlantic cod, you've got to ask yourself: Am I an activist or am I hungry? More often than not, I opt for lunch, but then I usually root for the bad guy in most movies, too. It's your call.

unnecessary name of "true cod" by fishmongers apparently trying to make up for past transgressions. You might also find it labeled as "Alaskan cod" or "p-cod."

If you happen to spot something labeled *Bacalao*, congratulations, you've stumbled onto a bit of history. Bacalao is the Spanish word for salt cod, a must-have if you happen to be on a seventeenth-century high-seas reality show. It's actually pretty common in some ethnic stores and fish markets that sell plenty of smoked fish.

The White Way

Whole cod are rare these days, but even if you do happen to spot one (check for the barbels), I'd still head for the snowy white fillets. I don't have much reason to cook a whole cod, and in this case I'd like to see inside the fish before buying (see "Fishing with Candles" sidebar…if you dare).

Cod has long been prized for being the whitest whitefish on the block, a trait it acquired thanks to a dedication to laziness. Seriously, cod are built for short bursts of speed, not long-distance swimming, which means they're loaded with white fast-twitch muscles. When buying, whiter is usually better (duh), but a slight pinkish cast shouldn't be a deal killer. Pacific cod sometimes has a gray cast to it, and is occasionally marketed as "gray cod" because of it. Beyond color, look for fillets that are moist (but not wet) and not falling apart. A quick sniff should result in a reassuring sea breeze or less.

Don't be afraid to buy frozen fillets. Cod freezes well, and may be better than fresh, depending on when it was caught. Frozen cod fillets should be very white and free of any noticeable ice crystals.

Lingcod

LINGCOD (Ophiodon elongatus) is not a cod or a ling, but it does share characteristics of both. Its long, slender body resembles the European ling, while the white flesh is similar to that of a cod.

QUICK QUESTION

What the...scrod? For years I thought this was a name used by fishmongers who didn't know what they were selling. "What kind of fish is it? Err...well, um...it's a scrod!" Turns out, a scrod is a small cod, usually between one and two pounds. Of course, it might also be a small haddock, which is why the FDA requires that it be sold with a species name attached ("scrod cod," "scrod haddock," etc.).

The name scrod most likely evolved from an ancient Dutch term, "schrood," which loosely translated means "to fillet."

Fishing with Candles

Fresh cod fillets are generally observed over a light table in a process called "candling." The light makes it possible to spot any nematodes (worms) the cod might be carrying. Didn't want to know that, did ya?

Fish sticks and friends

Cod opened the door to the frozen fish market with the introduction of frozen fillets in the 1930s. Unfortunately, the venture was not a success. Housewives in the heartland just weren't ready for fish in their kitchen. But their kids would be. A few decades later, frozen fish took off like a shot and never looked back. Today's frozen entrées and the like are a few notches above the good old fish stick, but they're not exactly gourmet eats, either. Not that this matters to your kids.

If you do find yourself in the market for a fish stick, check the ingredient list—the fewer, the better. And unless it says cod, assume that it's not. In fact, assume that it's Alaskan pollock and you'll rarely be wrong.

In the Kitchen
Just Add Chips

After all that talk about worldly importance and endangered stocks, the true value of cod still boils down to one thing: fish-and-chips (or is that two things?). Sure, cod can be baked, sautéed, stir-fried, pan-fried, braised, poached, and steamed—but let's be honest: This is a fish best served fresh from the fryer. Cod's mild flavor, firm texture, and perfect flake are ideally suited for a light coating of starch and few minutes of hot oil treatment. And that's okay.

What's not okay is screwing up a sweet piece of cod by overcooking it, using too much oil, not using enough oil, or drowning it in batter. Frying is not the hardest thing you'll ever do in your kitchen, but it can be daunting to anyone with a fear of splattering oil. Thus, I present the Deep Fried Cod Laws. Break them at your own peril.

resistance is futile

Deep-Fried Cod Laws

The pot   Choose a heavy pot that's big enough to hold at least double the amount of oil being used. Is a deep fryer worth the investment? Sure, if you fry a lot. I don't have the counter space.

The oil   How much is enough? As little as possible. Sorry, that's mean. You'll need enough oil to maintain a relatively constant temperature once the fish is added, but not more than half the depth of your pot. You can get away with less by cooking fewer fish pieces at one time, but that means more total fry time.

    What kind of oil? Canola, corn, safflower, and other vegetable oils are all popular choices. They're cheap, readily available, and have a high enough smoke point not to complain at most temperatures. I prefer peanut oil. It's a little more expensive, but the flavor is better than most other vegetable oils.

The temperature   350-370° F, and keep it there. Invest in a thermometer; it'll help. The oil temperature is going to drop slightly when the fish goes in, so if you're using less oil than you should, pump up the temperature a few degrees to compensate. If the temperature drops much below 350°, the fish will overcook before the outside has a chance to form a nice crisp shell.

The fish   Cod, preferably cut into thin strips. Small chunks are fine; large wedges are not advised. Whatever you choose, try to keep them relatively similar in shape and size. Pat the fish dry before dipping them in the batter.

The batter   For the best batter we're going to need some air: beer, baking soda, club soda—it's got to be something bubbly to give the fish a light crunch. Flour and water will work, but it's not the same without the bubbles. Prepare the batter last so the air doesn't escape before hitting the oil.

The drop   Use a fry basket or Asian "spider" tool (a wire-mesh spoon thing—one of the world's few perfect utensils) to lower the fish in *slowly*. No dropping. Oil splatters. If the fish sinks or doesn't immediately start to bubble, the oil isn't hot enough. And remember, too many fish swimming around will ruin the batch. Ideally, two-thirds of the oil's surface area should be clear of fish.

The fry   Depending on fish size, fry time will range from 1 to 3 minutes per side, although very small pieces or strips may take less than a minute total. We're after a light golden color and a crisp crust; deep brown and impenetrable is not what we're after.

The finish   Unless you're eating as you go, the first batch of cod needs a place to rest while the second batch cooks. Best option: on a wire rack set over a sheet pan in a 200° F oven. Any excess moisture will drip away, keeping your cod crisp.

The cleanup   Once the oil has cooled, strain it through a few pieces of cheesecloth or a fine-mesh strainer and save for future fries. You might be able to get four or five uses out of it, but once it darkens noticeably or starts to smell burnt, it's time to change the oil.

    In the end, pure white goodness wrapped in a golden fried shell—that's what cod is all about. And malt vinegar. Some people just love that stuff. Some people are weird.

Cod Recipes

If you're new to deep-frying, the first thing to do is take a deep breath. A pot full of extremely hot oil is nothing to mess around with, but it needn't be feared. Treat it with respect and it will deliver nothing but tasty fish. The most common mistake is not using enough oil, which will result in wild temperature fluctuations as you try to stay in the zone. Don't skimp. It's better to stretch more expensive peanut oil with vegetable oil than to not use enough. Just be sure not to use more oil than your vessel of choice can handle. A half-full pot is full enough.

NUTRITIONAL INFO

Per 3.5 oz/100 grams (raw)

Atlantic Cod		Pacific Cod	
Calories	82	**Calories**	82
Calories from fat	6	Calories from fat	6
Total fat	0.67 g	**Total fat**	0.63 g
Saturated fat	0.1 g	Saturated fat	0.1 g
Cholesterol	43 mg	**Cholesterol**	37 mg
Sodium	54 mg	**Sodium**	71 mg
Protein	17.8 g	**Protein**	17.9 g
Omega-3	0.18 g	**Omega-3**	0.21 g
Mercury	0.11 ppm	**Mercury**	N/A

HOW TO STORE: Cod

FRESH: If you're not going to use cod on the day of purchase, remove any excess moisture and rewrap the fish in fresh plastic wrap. Fresh cod will keep for a few days in the fridge, preferably in the coldest part or on ice. Direct contact with ice won't hurt most white fish fillets, but they might pick up (or share) an aroma or two if not protected. Any fillets that develop a strong smell should be discarded. *FROZEN:* Properly frozen cod fillets will last upward of twelve months. Of course, if you're not going to eat something within a year, why did you buy it? (Yeah, I do that, too.)

Classic Fish-and-Chips

Light, crispy, and tasty. What else is there to say?

1½ quarts (6 cups) peanut (or other vegetable) oil
2 pounds cod fillets
½ cup all-purpose flour
½ teaspoon garlic powder (optional)
½ teaspoon onion powder (optional)
1 teaspoon baking powder
¾ cup very cold water
Kosher salt
1 lemon, cut into wedges
Malt vinegar (optional)
Tartar sauce (optional)
Chips (a.k.a. french fries—not optional)

Heat the oil in a heavy 4-quart or larger pot to 370° F. Preheat the oven to 200° F.

Cut the cod fillets into uniform strips about 1 to 1½ inches wide, 3 to 4 inches long, and no more than an inch thick. *NOTE: Any size will do, as long as all are relatively the same. Larger pieces will take longer to cook, however, and should be fried at a lower temperature (closer to 350° F).*

Sift the flour and baking powder into a medium-sized bowl, add the garlic powder and onion powder, and stir to combine them. Add ½ cup water, stir until a paste forms, and then add the remaining water. Use within 20 minutes.

Dredge half of the cod strips through the batter and lower them carefully into the oil using a fry basket or spider tool. Fry them for 1½ to 2 minutes, then turn and fry them for an additional 1½ minutes until golden. Transfer the finished pieces to a wire rack set over a baking sheet in the oven. Repeat the process with the second batch (making sure the oil is at least 360° F before adding the fish).

When both batches are done, sprinkle the strips with kosher salt and serve them with lemon wedges, malt vinegar, tartar sauce, and chips.

Serves 4

Chips

The trick to perfect chips is to cook 'em twice. That's what gives 'em their crispiness. This process also makes cooking fish and chips together manageable at home since the second fry is short and batches of chips can be alternated with fish batches.

1 pound russet or Kennebec potatoes (4 inches long is ideal)
1½ quarts (6 cups) vegetable oil
Kosher salt and freshly ground black pepper

Wash each potato, dry it, and cut it into wedges of roughly equal size. (I like the rough edges, but feel free to peel 'em if you want.) Soak the chips-to-be for at least five minutes in cold water to remove some of the surface starch.

Heat the oil in a heavy 4-quart or larger pot to 325° F.

Drain and dry the potatoes thoroughly. DO NOT PUT WET CHIPS IN THE FRYER; THEY WILL SPLATTER. Add just enough wedges to allow for free movement at the top of the oil. Fry for 4 to 5 minutes, stirring occasionally, until the wedges are softened, but not browned. Drain and remove the chips to a cooling rack set over several layers of paper towels. Repeat the process until all the wedges are fried. Allow all batches to cool for at least 10 minutes.

For the second fry, the oil temperature should be raised to 370° F (convenient, no?). Fry the wedges in small batches until golden brown (1 to 2 minutes). Remove to a paper towel-lined basket, sprinkle with salt and pepper, and serve hot with fish.

Tartar Sauce

Yeah, you can use the store-bought stuff, but tartar sauce is really easy to make, so. . . why wouldn't you? If you don't like a little heat, tone down the horseradish or omit it altogether.

1 cup mayonnaise
1 tablespoon dill pickle, finely chopped
1 small shallot, finely chopped
1 tablespoon fresh Italian parsley, finely chopped
1 tablespoon lemon juice
2 teaspoons horseradish
Kosher salt and freshly ground black pepper

Combine the mayonnaise, pickle, shallot, parsley, lemon juice, and horseradish in a small bowl. Mix thoroughly. Season the sauce with salt and pepper to taste.

Manly Drunken Fish-and-Chips

Light, crispy, tasty, and beery. What kind of beer? Lighter is better, which means no stouts or porters. An overly hop-happy beer is also not a good idea. Too bitter. NOTE: In this case, "manly," means bigger, but feel free to use the smaller pieces of the previous recipe if you like (adjust frying times as necessary).

1½ quarts (6 cups) peanut (or other vegetable) oil
4 thick cod fillets (4 to 6 ounces each)
½ cup all-purpose flour
1 very cold beer
Kosher salt
1 lemon, cut into wedges
Chips (see previous recipe)

Heat the oil in a heavy 4-quart or larger pot to 350° F. Preheat the oven to 200° F.

Place flour in a medium-sized bowl and pour in ½ cup of the beer. Stir until a paste forms, but don't overdo it. Excessive stirring will scare away the bubbles. Add additional beer, until the batter is the consistency of pancake batter. *NOTE: Prepare the batter just prior to use or the beer will go flat.*

Dredge two of the cod fillets in the batter and lower them carefully into the oil using a fry basket or spider tool. Fry them for 3 minutes, then turn and fry them for an additional 2 to 3 minutes until golden. Transfer the finished pieces to a wire rack set over a baking sheet in the oven. Repeat the process with the second batch (making sure the oil is back up to 350 °F before adding the fish).

When both batches are done, sprinkle the pieces with kosher salt and serve them with lemon wedges, chips, and more beer.

Serves 4 regular folk or 2 "men"

Tempura Cod

For a lighter, more airy dish, dip your cod in Japanese-style tempura batter. The trick is to leave the batter lumpy, which gives the shell a unique bumpy quality that looks accidental but tastes great. NOTE: I've gone with a traditional Japanese hot-oil treatment of 3 parts vegetable oil to 1 part refined sesame oil, which has a higher smoke point and milder flavor than other sesame oils. Do not use "pure" or "toasted" sesame oil in place of refined. If you can't locate refined sesame oil, use 6 cups of vegetable oil plus 1 tablespoon of either pure or toasted sesame oil for flavor.

4½ cups vegetable oil
1½ cups refined sesame oil
1½ pounds cod fillets
3 cups all-purpose flour
1 large egg, lightly beaten
1½ cups ice-cold water, plus a few ice cubes
Soy sauce (for dipping)

Heat the oil in a heavy 4-quart or larger pot to 370° F. Preheat the oven to 200° F.

Cut the cod fillets into uniform strips about 1 to 1½ inches wide, 3 to 4 inches long, and no more than an inch thick.

Sift 2 cups of flour into a medium-sized bowl. Combine the egg and ice water separately, and then add it to the flour. Stir roughly with a chopstick (for tradition) until the batter is combined but still lumpy. Add a few ice cubes to keep it cold. Place the remaining flour in a separate bowl.

Dust half of the cod strips with flour, shaking off the excess. Dip them in the batter and lower them carefully into the oil using a fry basket or spider tool. Fry the strips for 1½ to 2 minutes, then turn and fry them for an additional 1½ minutes until golden. Transfer the finished pieces to a wire rack set over a baking sheet in the oven. Repeat the process with the second batch (making sure the oil is at least 360° F before adding the fish).

Serve the cod with room-temperature soy sauce or other dipping favorite.

Serves 3 or 4

Roast Cod
with Mango Salsa

Okay, you don't have to deep-fry cod. Of course, the crispy crust created by roasting a fillet topped with bread crumbs is kind of like frying without the fryer. Sneaky, no?

1 cup fresh bread crumbs, toasted
2 tablespoons extra virgin olive oil
Juice of one lemon
4 cod fillets (6 to 8 ounces each), skinned
Kosher salt and freshly ground black pepper
Mango Salsa (see below)

Preheat the oven to 400° F. Combine the toasted bread crumbs, olive oil, and lemon juice in a small bowl, and mix until the oil is evenly distributed.

Season both sides of the cod with salt and pepper and place the pieces on a lightly oiled baking sheet. Spread the bread crumb mixture evenly on top of each fillet. Bake until the crust is golden and the fish is cooked through (8 to 10 minutes). For a toastier flavor, switch to the broiler after 6 to 8 minutes and cook the fillets until browned (2 to 3 minutes).

Transfer the fillets to warm plates, top them with Mango Salsa, and serve immediately.

Serves 4

Mango Salsa

Watch out for overripe mangos. Soft is good; squishy is not.

1 whole mango, peeled, pitted, and chopped (about ¾ cup)
½ cup cucumber, seeded and finely chopped
¼ cup red onion, finely chopped
2 tablespoons cilantro, chopped
¼ teaspoon red pepper flakes
1 tablespoon lime juice plus zest of one lime
Kosher salt and freshly ground black pepper

Combine the mango, cucumber, onion, cilantro, red pepper flakes, lime juice, and zest in a small bowl. Season with salt and pepper to taste. Store in the fridge for up to 3 days.

Chapter 6
Scallops
Marshmallow of the Sea

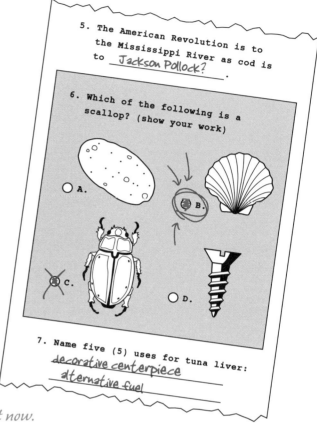

5. The American Revolution is to the Mississippi River as cod is to _Jackson Pollock?_ .

6. Which of the following is a scallop? (show your work)

A.
B.
C.
D.

7. Name five (5) uses for tuna liver:
decorative centerpiece
alternative fuel

POP QUIZ! What does a scallop look like? A fishy marshmallow? No, that's only a part of the scallop, merely a single muscle, in fact. I'm talking about the whole critter. What does that look like? No, it's not a fish. Not a potato, either. Here's a hint: there might be part of one holding a bar of soap in your bathroom right now.

That's right, it's a bivalve. Scallops have a shell, a pretty one, in fact. The last time you were at the beach, you probably picked up a few scallop shells and didn't even know it. Ready for another one? Why does your fish-hating cousin love scallops? Because she thinks they're potatoes. Next question: How do I persuade you to cook scallops at home? (Hey, nobody said these questions were going to be easy.)

shucked sea scallops

The French call the scallop *coquille Saint-Jacques*, or shell of Saint James. Seems back in the day, Jimmy saved a knight from drowning, forever linking him with the bivalves that clung to the wet soldier as he emerged from the brine. During the Crusades, knights loyal to the Order of Saint James wore scallop shells as a symbol of their patron saint. Today, a scallop shell is used as the symbol of one of the world's largest oil companies. So…would that be progress or blasphemy?

Religious icons and corporate logos notwithstanding, I'm more interested in what's inside the shell—namely the sweet, tender goodness that is the scallop. I'm not alone in this. Scallops recently cracked the top

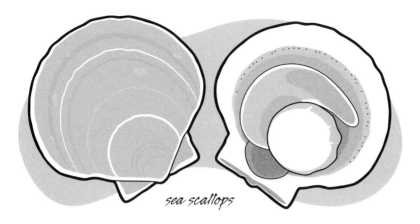

sea scallops

VITAL STATS

FIRST NAME: Sea scallop, bay scallop (also calico, weathervane, pink, spiny)

SCI. NAME: *Placopecten magellanicus* (sea), *Argopecten irradians* (bay)

SIZE: *Sea:* 10-40 per lb, *bay:* 60-100 per lb (both are meat only)

LIFESPAN: *Sea:* 3-5 years when caught, 10+ max; *bay:* 1-2 years when harvested

RANGE: *Sea:* North Atlantic, from Newfoundland to N. Carolina; *bay:* Atlantic coastal and gulf waters of the United States, cultured in China

CATCH: *Sea:* about 50 million lbs annually; *bay:* about 22,000 lbs

ten of America's favorite seafoods, just edging out halibut and its flatfish buddies. Not bad for a product that remains a mystery to many who eat it. Perhaps you've heard the rumor that most scallops are simply chunks of shark or skate flesh cut out with a cookie cutter. Trust me, if that were true, scallops would not be so popular.

Despite their status as a restaurant superstar, scallops are often left off the shopping lists of many fanatics. Why? Even though they lack bones, scales, skin, and anything else that would make them a challenge to cook, scallops are a challenge to cook. Actually, the challenge is more in the buying than in the cooking. Bring home the right scallop and yours can be every bit as super as the restaurant's.

In the Water
Putting the Bi in Bivalve

If a battle of the sexes were held between bivalves, choosing sides would prove problematic for the scallops. While most shellfish have separate sexes, many scallops are sequential hermaphrodites, meaning each individual is both a male and a female, though not at the same time…usually. Bay scallops are simultaneous hermaphrodites, which means they can produce both sperm and eggs at the same time. (If this seems confusing, imagine what it must be like for the scallop.)

Sea scallops spawn in late summer or early fall, releasing millions of eggs (or sperm) into the current at one time. Once an egg is fertilized, it only takes a few hours for the embryo to develop small cilia and begin swimming. In about a month's time, the young scallop will head for the seafloor in search of a secure bit of ground or eelgrass to call home. Much like a mussel, it secretes a byssal thread to cement itself in place, but unlike its steadfast cousin, the scallop doesn't stay put.

Along for the Ride

Spiny scallops often allow sponges to attach to their shells, which helps ward off sea star attacks and barnacle infestation, while offering the sponge a bit more mobility.

Takeout

Locomotion allows the scallop to be pickier about what it eats. As a filter feeder, scallops dine on phytoplankton and other nutrients filtered from the water. If a scallop doesn't like what the local current has to offer, it can always move.

A Scallop's Age

Sea scallops grow more slowly than most bivalves, taking as long as four to five years to reach full sexual maturity. If the water is warmer, the scallop will grow faster.

QUICK QUESTION

Where do scallop shells come from? Scallops aren't born with a shell, nor do they hang around bivalve retirement homes waiting for an elderly scallop to give up the ghost (and his shell). Rather, a thin inner membrane called the mantel secretes a matrix that, when combined with calcium carbonate, hardens to form a shell. The mantel will continue to add on to the outer defenses until the scallop is fully grown.

Mollusk in motion

Oysters, mussels, and clams are all fine examples of undersea engineering, but can any of them swim? Scallops can. Thanks to an overdeveloped adductor muscle, a scallop can generate enough thrust to launch itself across the seafloor simply by opening and closing its shell. This is an especially good tactic for escaping slow-moving predators such as sea stars (starfish). It also means that the muscle grows up big and tasty, though that doesn't really help the scallop.

A herd of hermaphroditic bivalves galloping along the sea floor may sound bizarre, but for an even more amazing sight, take a peek inside a live scallop. Situated on the mantle, along with a row of short sensory tentacles, are thirty to forty tiny blue eyes. Although weak, each peeper has a lens, cornea, and optic nerve, enabling it to see just enough light and movement to recognize approaching danger.

On the Boats
Raking Them In

Sea scallops are fished year-round, but due to day-at-sea restrictions, local area closures, and bad weather, most of the fresh catch is available in spring and summer. Most wild scallops are harvested using trawl nets and metal-framed dredges that rake the seafloor, collecting scallops and anything else that happens to get in the way.

Not surprisingly, dredging is not a popular form of fishing with environmentalists. In scraping the ocean floor, dredging disrupts and occasionally destroys the natural habitats of many nontargeted species. There's also substantial bycatch, particularly of groundfish species such as skate and monkfish. Improvements have been made to reduce both bottom damage and bycatch, but those in search of the most eco-friendly scallops look for farm-grown or diver scallops.

Scallop Varieties

There are hundreds of scallop varieties, but as far as most American markets are concerned there are only two: sea and bay. The SEA SCALLOP is the larger of the two, with a shell size regularly exceeding 8 inches across, and an edible muscle that looks like a moist, ivory marshmallow. BAY SCALLOPS are much smaller (think mini marshmallows), with an average shell size of about 3 inches. Many scallop enthusiasts prefer bays, whose flavor tends to be a little sweeter.

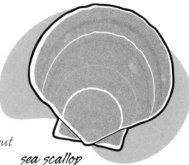

sea scallop

Though harder to find, a few other species occasionally appear at the market. Tiny CALICO SCALLOPS (*Argopecten gibbus*) are harvested off the coast of the southern United States and are often sold as bay scallops. Fishermen in Alaska capture a larger breed called WEATHERVANE SCALLOPS (*Patinopecten caurinus*), most of which are shipped to market frozen. In Washington State, divers harvest PINK and SPINY SCALLOPS (*Chlamys rubida* and *C. hastata*), both of which go by the nickname "singing scallops." (I'm told pinks prefer pop, but spiny scallops lean toward late-seventies punk rock.)

bay scallops

shucked bay scallops

Aw, shucks

Most scallop boats stay at sea for one to two weeks at a time, the result of which is a lot of shucking. Scallops don't do well out of the water—they can't close their shells tight—so nearly all of the harvest is cleaned at sea. Crews of six or more stand on deck shucking and icing scallops as long as the catch comes in. When the fishermen return to port, wholesalers will often pay them a premium for what's known as "top of the catch," presumably the freshest scallops on the boat.

Chinese culture

The domestic bay scallop fishery took a huge hit in the 1980s when a brown algae blight decimated the eelgrass where so many bays liked to hide. Left without a place to mature in safety, bay scallop stocks plummeted. In less than a decade, the fishery was practically wiped out…and yet, walk into any fish market today and there are bay scallops for sale. What gives?

In 1982, a handful of live bay scallops made the trip from New England to China, where, with a little coaxing, they were persuaded to spawn, thus launching the Chinese scallop industry. Today, nearly all of the bay scallops sold in the United States come from farms in northeast-

Quick Fix

Sea scallops were declared overfished in 1997, but recovered quickly with the help of fishing restrictions and area closures. In many cases, closures intended to help rebuild groundfish stocks actually benefited the shellfish by reducing scallop bycatch.

a scallop dredge in action

ern China. The scallops, most of which are the East Coast native, *Argopecten irradians,* are grown on suspension nets for about a year before being harvested, frozen, and shipped to foreign markets.

What remains of the traditional bay scallop fishery in the United States provides the only fresh bay product in the market, usually from November to March. Two southern subspecies also contribute to the harvest, though neither is as commercially important as the true bay scallop.

At the Market
Don't Get Soaked

Canada Dry

One shortcut to getting dry scallops is to buy Canadian. Most scallops imported from the Great White North arrive in this country untreated. Hockey, Rush, and dry scallops—what a country!

There should be very little mystery to buying scallops. There's no shell (usually), no scales, no skin, no bones—these puppies are all muscle. What you see is what you get. If it looks good and smells good, you're good to go, right? Wrong.

The scallop industry has a dirty little secret, and it's called "soaking." Once upon a time, someone discovered that frozen scallops (and other seafood) retained their moisture better if treated with sodium tripolyphosphate (STP) prior to freezing. Don't panic; it's perfectly safe. Unfortunately, someone else discovered that *fresh* scallops soaked in a STP solution not only retained their moisture, they gained some, enough to add as much as 25 percent to their weight. In other words, you're paying for water. To combat the problem, the FDA now requires all scallops with a moisture content of 82 percent and higher to be labeled "water-added" products, and any above 86 percent cannot be marketed at all.

The good news is that because of the abuse, more retailers are offering untreated, or "dry," scallops. They cost more, but the quality (assuming the scallops are fresh) is universally better. If the label doesn't say "dry," the product probably isn't, but how do you tell? Fresh, treated scallops are usually much whiter than dry, and can often be found sitting in a pool of milky liquid. Are the scallops sticky? If so, they're probably dry; soakers slip and slide all over one another.

What the nose knows

Dry or otherwise, scallops are going to smell—hopefully in a good way. A bouquet that can be described as "sweet and briny with a hint of seaweed" is ideal. "Fishy with a overpowering stench of sour iodine" is less than ideal. In terms of color, some scallops may have a slight orange or pink tint to them, but most should fall into the "translucent ivory" band of the rainbow. When handled, the freshest scallops will seem elastic and springy...kind of like slightly moist Jell-O.

Frosty the scallop

Despite being a year-round fishery, much of what now reaches the market is frozen. Fortunately, scallops freeze well, and if it's a choice between one that was frozen right after being caught or one that's been sitting around "fresh" for a week or more, I'll take the Popsicle.

Frozen scallops will be white—very white. That's normal, whether they've been soaked a little, a lot, or not at all. Look for IQF (individually quick frozen) scallops and beware of previously frozen product. Scallops may take to the cold just fine, but once they've thawed, there's no going back.

Buying live

If you magically happen upon a pile of live in-the-shell scallops, don't scream—you'll only alert others to the treasure. After confirming the scallops' liveliness (an open shell will close up when tapped), scoop up as many as your little arms will carry and run. Yes, run. Live scallops won't be that way for long, so head straight home and cook 'em.

Calico No-no

Tiny calico scallops are often marketed as bay scallops, even though they lack the flavor punch of their northern cousins. To spot a pseudo bay, check the outer edges of the scallop; if they're opaque white (a sign that the shell was steamed open), it's a calico.

Raw

Eating raw or undercooked scallops is perfectly safe since most of us only eat the adductor muscle, a part of the scallop that rarely comes in contact with any toxins that might have been filtered through its body.

HOW TO STORE: Scallops

FRESH: If you're not going to be cooking them right away, remove any excess moisture from the scallops and store them in the fridge, preferably in a container that is surrounded by ice. Fresh scallops will remain in reasonably good condition for two or three days, although I recommend using them on day 1. **FROZEN:** If you choose to freeze your scallops, make sure they weren't previously frozen. Freezing cooked scallops is okay. Three months is a safe cutoff point for most frozen scallops. When it's time to thaw, a night in the fridge is the best method.

In the Kitchen
Hot, Fast, and in Control

There was a time when I couldn't cook scallops. My seared scallops never soared, my scallop kabobs ka-crashed, my poached scallop meatloaf…well, that never made it out of the testing phase. Any scallop that entered my kitchen was, at best, destined for mediocrity, and at worst… Let's just say Superman had kryptonite, I had scallops. That's when I started reading comic books starring the Flash.

If you haven't figured it out by now, I like things that cook fast. "From pan to plate in minutes," that's my motto. Because they're all muscle, scallops cook especially fast—sea scallops in a few minutes, smaller bays in mere seconds. As soon as the outside turns opaque, the inside is cooked to perfection. Larger scallops might be only medium rare, but like a good steak, scallops benefit from a little tenderness at the center. Yes, undercooked scallops are perfectly safe (see "Raw" sidebar). The trick, of course, is not to overcook 'em.

Cleaning

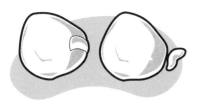

removing the extra muscle

Scallops require very little preparation prior to cooking, so it's best to wait until the last minute to do it. Start by removing the small, crescent-shaped muscle attached to the side of each scallop. It should peel right off. Some scallops will have already lost their's, so don't go crazy if you can't find every one. Left intact, the small muscle will be unpleasantly tough, but won't ruin dinner.

Rinse the scallops under cold water and pat dry. Now, pat them dry again. Yes, it's that important. Wet scallops don't sear as quickly, but they cook through just as fast. If you want the best of both worlds, make sure they're dry before hitting the pan.

Scallop Shucking

For those few lucky enough to snag a bag of live (or very recently passed on) scallops, it's time to get shucking.

1-2)

(1) Carefully pry open the shells by inserting a knife (an oyster shucker works well) at the hinge and giving a twist. (2) Before opening up wide, slide the knife under the top shell to detach the scallop. Keep it flush with the shell so as not to damage the goods. (3) Repeat on the bottom shell to fully detach the scallop. At this point you can toss the shell or keep it for presentation purposes. (4) Find the pearly white adductor muscle and remove it. You can also keep the orange coral if desired. Everything else goes in the trash. (5) Finally, remove the crescent-shaped muscle on the side of the scallop and give everything a rinse.

3-4)

Hot, hot, hot

High heat is the key to success when it comes to searing scallops. Dry sea scallops on a hot nonstick pan will brown up nicely by the time they're ready for the plate. Unfortunately, this is when most folks discover they bought "wet" scallops. When a soaker meets the heat, all that added moisture is going to jump ship, drowning out any chance you had for golden, brown, and delicious.

What do you do if your scallops look suspiciously moist? Make a sauce! (Hey, if you can't beat 'em, join 'em.) Cook wet scallops over medium low heat, allowing them to release their moisture into the pan. Pull them just before they're done, and get to work on that sauce, combining the scallop juice with white wine and butter. After the sauce has reduced by half (or to desired thickness), toss in a few fresh herbs, reintroduce the scallops, cook briefly, and serve.

Cold cooking

Skewered scallops cook up nicely on the grill or under the broiler. Lightly steamed bay scallops make a flavorful addition to salads, while deep-fried they put popcorn shrimp to shame. One of the more creative uses for scallops is in ceviche, a traditional Mexican dish that uses lime or lemon juice to "cook" fish and shellfish without heat. The acid in the juice causes proteins in the scallop flesh to coagulate, though it doesn't actually cook the shellfish. The end product is opaque enough to slip past most folks' raw fish radar. (Not that we're trying to sneak anything by our friends. Heavens no.)

Eurocentric

Order a few scallops in Europe and you're in for a surprise. What the heck is that big orange thing on the plate? It's the roe (some say "coral"), which is quite popular outside the United States. (Go ahead; eat it. It's pretty tasty.)

I ♥ Scallops

In Sandro Botticelli's painting Birth of Venus, *the Roman goddess of love is seen rising from the ocean's depths in a giant scallop shell.*

Scallop Recipes

Okay, time to put that whole counterfeit scallop story to bed: Nobody is going to try to sell you cookie-cutter skate, shark, or halibut nuggets masquerading as sea scallops. It just isn't done. Or, at least, it isn't done by any fishmonger with an ounce of common sense. Skate meat doesn't look anything like a scallop: It has a series of lines running across the flesh. Shark meat is closer, but not close enough to convince anyone who's ever eaten a scallop. And halibut? While it's true halibut cheeks look and even taste similar to scallops, they're usually more expensive if sold as cheeks.

Relax. Your scallops are scallops.

Sautéed Scallops

When cooking scallops, be sure not to overcrowd the pan. Each scallop deserves a little elbow room (at least ½ inch). If you don't have a large enough pan, use two, or cook the scallops in batches. NOTE: While it's tempting to use a nonstick pan for this recipe, I don't recommend it due to the high heat necessary for searing scallops.

12 large (or 8 very large) sea scallops
Kosher salt and freshly ground black pepper
1 tablespoon unsalted butter
1 tablespoon olive oil

Remove the small crescent-shaped muscle from the side of each scallop, dry them thoroughly, and season (both sides) with salt and pepper.

Heat the butter and olive oil in a large sauté pan over high heat until the butter just starts to show some color. Add the scallops and cook them for 1½ to 2 minutes, by which time they should be nicely browned. Flip them, and cook for an additional minute (2 tops) until the scallops are firm to the touch.

Transfer the scallops to warm plates and serve immediately.

Serves 4

NOTE: if you're dealing with folks who aren't accustomed to undercooked anything, slice each of the scallops into two (roughly) ½-inch-thick discs. You'll have twice as many scallops and they'll cook faster (1 minute per side) and all the way through without burning.

Sautéed (Wet) Scallops
with White Wine Sauce

Got watery scallops? No worries. This recipe will make the wetness work for you. NOTE: Yes, you can use dry scallops, but add 2 tablespoons of water along with the wine (or double the wine).

2 tablespoons unsalted butter
1 tablespoon olive oil
1 shallot, finely diced
1 large garlic clove, minced
12 large sea scallops
Kosher salt and freshly ground black pepper
2 tablespoons dry white wine
1 tablespoon fresh flat-leaf parsley, chopped
2 teaspoons fresh chives, chopped

Remove the small crescent-shaped muscle from the side of each scallop, dry them thoroughly, and season (both sides) with salt and pepper.

Heat 1 tablespoon of the butter and olive oil in a large sauté pan over medium heat. Add the shallots and garlic and cook them until softened (2 to 3 minutes), but not browned.

Turn the heat up to high, add the scallops, and cook them for 1½ to 2 minutes, until browned. Reduce the heat to medium. Flip the scallops, add the white wine, cover the pan, and cook for 3 minutes. Transfer the scallops (minus the sauce) to warm plates.

Add the remaining butter, plus the parsley and chives, to the sauce and reduce briefly (1 to 2 minutes). Season with salt and pepper to taste. Pour the sauce over the scallops and serve them immediately.

Serves 3 to 4

Who Sells Seashells?

In 1833, Marcus Samuel opened a small shop in London that sold primarily antiques and exotic seashells. Years later, his son would expand the company to include the exportation of lamp oil. The company still exists today, though I believe Shell sells more gasoline than seashells these days.

Marinated Scallop Skewers

Stick 'em on a stick—what could be easier? If you like your scallops straight up, skip the marinade and go with a little olive oil, salt, and freshly ground pepper. If using wooden skewers, soak them in water to discourage any flame-ups on the grill.

1 pound sea scallops (16 to 20 per pound)
¼ cup soy sauce
2 tablespoons brown sugar
1 teaspoon cumin
1 teaspoon dry mustard
½ teaspoon paprika
2 tablespoons fresh green onions, chopped

Remove the small crescent-shaped muscle from the side of each scallop and dry them thoroughly.

Combine the soy sauce, sugar, cumin, mustard, paprika, and onions in a small bowl. Add the scallops, cover them, and marinate in the refrigerator for 30 minutes.

Pat the scallops dry and slide them onto skewers, 4 to 5 per stick, leaving a little space between scallops. *NOTE: Using two skewers per group will make them easier to flip.*

Grill the scallops over high heat for 1½ to 2 minutes per side. Serve them immediately.

Serves 4

Scalloped Ceviche

Heat is overrated. Bring on the lime juice! For those craving a little more variety, try 1 pound (total) of bay scallops, squid (mantle strips and tentacle clusters), and very small shrimp (uncooked; not cooked salad shrimp).

1 pound bay scallops
Juice of 6 limes (about 1¼ cups total), plus wedges for serving
1 tablespoon extra virgin olive oil
1 jalapeño chilie, seeded and finely chopped
1 ripe avocado, diced
2 medium-sized tomatoes, seeded and diced
2 tablespoons fresh cilantro, chopped
Kosher salt and freshly ground black pepper

Remove the small crescent-shaped muscle from the side of each scallop and dry them thoroughly. *NOTE: The little muscles are harder to find on bay scallops, but they do exist. If you miss a few no one will notice.*

Combine the scallops and lime juice in a glass or other nonmetal bowl and marinate them for 4 hours. The lime juice should cover scallops completely.

Drain the excess lime juice and pat the scallops dry. Toss the seafood with the olive oil, chilie, avocados, tomatoes, and cilantro in a large bowl and season with salt and pepper to taste.

Serve the ceviche on chilled plates with lime wedges and a sprig of cilantro.

Serves 4 to 6 as an appetizer

QUICK QUESTION

Is it true scallops explode in the microwave? First, a little science: Rather than warm foods with an outside heat source, microwave ovens generate microwaves (duh) that cause the water molecules in the food to repeatedly flip their electromagnetic orientation, bang into each other, and create a bunch of heat in the process. More water means more heat, and since scallops are full of water, some as much as 85 percent, it's possible to create a lot of heat. That's not bad, assuming enough of it can escape in the form of steam. If it can't…boom.

NUTRITIONAL INFO

Per 3.5 oz/100 grams (raw)

Sea Scallop		Bay Scallop	
Calories 87		**Calories** 80	
Calories from fat 7		Calories from fat 6	
Total fat . . . . 0.8 g		**Total fat** . . . . 0.6 g	
Saturated fat . . . . 0.1 g		Saturated fat . . . . 0.1 g	
Protein . . . . 16.2 g		**Protein** . . . . 14.8 g	
Cholesterol . . . . 36 mg		**Cholesterol** . . . . . 33 mg	
Sodium . . . . 87 mg		**Sodium** . . . . 161 mg	
Omega-3 . . . . 0.2 g		**Omega-3** . . . . 0.1 g	
Mercury . . . . . 0.05 ppm		**Mercury** . . . . . 0.05 ppm	

Chapter 7
Yellowfin Tuna
Fast Food

Tuna have always been in a hurry. Swim here, swim there, from New Zealand to Japan to San Diego and back again—this is a fish that does not slow down, not to eat, not to sleep, not for nothin'. Even the name means "to rush" in ancient Greek. So, what's the hurry? For starters, tuna need to keep swimming to stay alive. There's nothing like oxygen deprivation to keep a body moving. To that end, tuna were built for speed. Check out these standard features: hydrodynamic teardrop chassis, solar powered navigation system, recessed eye sockets, retractable fins, front and back—truly a marvel of underwater engineering. Which may explain why some models are so expensive. Twenty dollars a pound for yellowfin may seem steep, but top-quality bluefin can run more than $100—wholesale! At those prices, it's best to keep cooking to a minimum to preserve the fish's natural flavor. In fact, let's skip it altogether. Hey, 125 million Japanese people can't be wrong. Raw fish is nutritious, delicious, and fast, too! Just like tuna.

VITAL STATS

FIRST NAME: Yellowfin tuna (a.k.a. ahi, maguro, canned "light tuna")

SCI. NAME: *Thunnus albacares*

SIZE: Commercial average: 15-45 lbs; max: 400 lbs, 6 ft in length

LIFESPAN: 4-6 years; max: 7 years

RANGE: Tropical/subtropical waters, worldwide (except the Mediterranean)

CATCH: 1.1 million metric tons annually, worldwide (includes canned fish)

Right about now, you're probably wondering how that ruby-red Hawaiian beauty at the top of the priciest restaurant menus can possibly be the same fish that sells for a buck a can at the grocery store. Does stuffing tuna into a recyclable really reduce its value tenfold? No, not really. But cooking it does, or at least cooking it too much.

Yellowfin tuna, ahi to islanders and marketers looking for a name to distance it from the canned crowd, is best when treated like a steak—a very good steak. Sear it, grill it, make it medium rare if you must, but anything that pushes it past pink is a seafood sin. Yellowfin flesh firms up and dries out if cooked through, which is why it's not even considered the premier canned product (that would be albacore). If you can't stand the thought of undercooked anything, save your money.

On the other hand, served au naturel, yellowfin is a melt-in-your-mouth experience like no other. Sure, not everyone is ready for raw fish, which is why seared ahi has become so popular. A quarter inch of cooking means it's not raw, it's rare—a big difference for most fish-phobics. My mom absolutely loves seared ahi, but cut off the crust and she runs screaming from the room. This from a woman who prefers her steak vampire red. Whatever.

Why am I focusing on yellowfin? That's what you're going to find at the market. Bigeye, even when it's available, is sold under the ahi moniker and is indistinguishable from yellowfin to most palates. Albacore is starting to show up at some West Coast shops, but not in huge amounts. As for bluefin, assuming you could afford it, you couldn't buy it because what little is available is almost always sent to Japan. And unless you reside in a tropical paradise, skipjack only comes in a can.

seared ahi

In the Water
Red Rover

What makes yellowfin meat red? A lot of nonstop swimming. Tuna travel the oceans constantly, migrating great distances across the Pacific, Atlantic, and Indian Oceans. All that swimming requires a lot of oxygen, and thus, myoglobin, the iron-rich globular protein responsible for disseminating oxygen throughout the muscles and turning everything red in the process. Myoglobin also causes yellowfin flesh to turn brown once it's exposed to air, though that's not an issue with which the tuna are concerned.

Unlike most fish, tuna are effectively warm-blooded, capable of maintaining a temperature a few degrees warmer than the surrounding water, even at depths of several thousand feet. To keep a steady supply of oxygen hitting their gills, tuna swim with their mouths open, a trick that no doubt also helps them eat and run. It takes a lot of energy to keep a perpetual-motion machine going, thus a tuna may eat as much as a quarter of its own body weight a day to stay alive. With tuna reaching a top speed of near 50 mph, most of what it eats never sees it coming.

All species of tuna are prolific spawners. Larger females may release ten million or more eggs each time they spawn, which for yellowfin can be anywhere along their migration route, as long as the water temperature at the surface is at least 24° C.

When in Hawaii...

Yellowfin and bigeye are both marketed as ahi, the Hawaiian word for "fire." Albacore are called tombo, and skipjack are known as aku. I don't think Hawaiians have a word for bluefin, but they do catch a fish they call humuhumunukunukuapua'a, which, loosely translated, means "fish that grunts like a pig."

Tuna Tricks

Full-grown tuna don't have a lot of enemies—big sharks, toothy whales, us—but they do have a clever bit of camouflage, just in case. Look up at a tuna from below and its light-colored belly blends in with surface water. Look down on a tuna and its dark blue back is hard to distinguish from the depths below.

Tuna Varieties

Cod may be the catch that changed the world, but tuna is the fish that feeds it. The worldwide catch of tuna and tuna-related species comes in at over 5 million metric tons every year. In terms of tuna, the big five are:

bluefin

BLUEFIN TUNA (*Thunnus thynnus*): The biggest and generally considered the best in terms of flavor, the bluefin has been a mainstay in Japan since hand-rolled sushi hit the streets of Edo in the late nineteenth century. Topping the charts at 1,500 pounds and fifteen feet in length, bluefin are a sight to behold, one that is unfortunately vanishing. Due to a slower growth rate and intense demand, stocks around the world are diminishing. CATCH: 50,000 metric tons annually, mostly pole-and-line caught. PRIMARY USES: Bluefin's superior color, texture, taste, and fat content make it the top choice of the Japanese sashimi market, which is where nearly all are sold.

bigeye

BIGEYE TUNA (*T. obesus*): Widespread in tropical and subtropical waters, bigeye is commonly marketed as ahi and thus often mistaken for yellowfin. While very similar in color and texture, bigeye flesh usually contains more fat, making it more desirable to hardcore sashimi fans. CATCH: 256,000 metric tons annually, using purse seining and longline methods. PRIMARY USES: Sold fresh with larger bigeye now being sought to fill the gaps in the Japanese sashimi market left by declining bluefin stocks.

YELLOWFIN TUNA (*T. albacares*): This globe-trotting species is second only to skipjack in volume, but, when marketed as ahi, is generally the tuna of choice for most consumers. CATCH: 1.1 million metric tons annually, mostly by purse seining, some long-lining. PRIMARY USES: Most of the yellowfin catch is canned and sold as "light tuna." What appears in markets as steaks or loins comes from the longline catch, which better maintains the fish's quality.

yellowfin

ALBACORE TUNA (*T. alalunga*): Unlike its relatives, albacore prefers cooler waters, particularly those near Southeast Asia and the western United States. CATCH: 225,000 metric tons annually, using troll, pole and line, and longline methods. PRIMARY USES: The moniker "chicken of the sea" readily applies to albacore's white, mild-tasting flesh, nearly all of which ends up in cans labeled "white tuna."

albacore

SKIPJACK TUNA (*Katsuwonus pelamis*): Distributed throughout the world's tropical waters, skipjack make up more than 50 percent of the total tuna catch, despite being the smallest of the major varieties. CATCH: 1.5 million metric tons annually, most by purse seining. PRIMARY USES: In Hawaii, skipjack are popular in dishes such as poke, an island specialty of cubed, raw fish. The vast majority of the catch, however, goes straight into the can to be sold as "light tuna."

skipjack

On the Boats
Tradition, Traps, and Tuna

How do you catch something that never stops moving? Better yet, how do you find a fish that migrates hundreds, even thousands of miles each year, and doesn't leave a forwarding address? Set a trap.

Mediterranean fishermen discovered long ago that the best way to catch a tuna was to keep it moving, only in the direction you want it to go. During bluefin breeding migrations, long nets were used to intercept the tuna, and direct them through a series of chambers that ultimately led to the aptly named *camera della morte* or "death chamber." There they would be pulled from the sea by net and gaff in a bloody slaughter known as the *mattanza*. The practice, which survived centuries of technological advances and bad press, has faded in recent years as the number of Mediterranean bluefin has diminished.

Today, purse seiners catch the majority of tuna, most of which is skipjack and yellowfin destined for canneries. Many of the 150- to 250-foot vessels will stay out for months at a time, and when they finally return to port may be loaded down with more than a thousand metric tons of tuna. Various hook-and-line techniques are best for larger tuna, such as bluefin, bigeye, and older yellowfin. The more attention the fisherman can give each individual fish, the higher quality the catch will be, a very important consideration for fish destined for the fresh market. In the case of bluefin, speed is also an issue. Once the tuna is hooked, the fisherman has about ten minutes to get it out of the water and onto ice. If the giant fish continues to fight, its muscles will overheat, essentially "cooking" the flesh in the process. Japanese buyers will pay top dollar for fresh, high-quality bluefin, but not if it's damaged, even superficially. Proper handling is the difference between hitting the jackpot and barely covering expenses.

setting the trap, circa 1949

Seine in the Water

Giant nets, sometimes a mile long, are used to encircle the tuna before being drawn together at the bottom like a purse.

Tony Soprano, Mob Boss...Fisherman?

Gambling, drugs, tuna. Yes, the mob is in the fishing business due to ridiculously high bluefin prices. Mafia-owned fishing operations in the Mediterranean launder money, exploit fishing subsidies, and apparently provide some kind of special fish-related overnight accommodations. Or so I've heard.

Canned

Albacore was the first tuna to be canned in the United States, in 1903. By the 1920s, yellowfin, skipjack, and bluefin were also being canned.

Robotuna

The latest in futuristic crime-fighting fish? Almost. Modeled on a bluefin tuna, Robotuna was a robotic fish built by MIT researchers in order to study better means of underwater propulsion.

Dolphin issues

Tuna like to mingle. A school of tuna may contain a half dozen or more different tuna and tuna-like species, as well as other fast fish and marine mammals, including dolphins and porpoises. Fishermen caught on to this fact in 1950s, and soon began using the dolphins to track and catch yellowfin and skipjack tuna. By herding the dolphins, they could effectively direct the tuna right into their nets. The practice, known as "setting on porpoise," proved extremely successful, and by the mid 1960s, two thirds of all tuna were caught using this method. Unfortunately, so were a lot of dolphins.

Efforts to protect dolphins, including special nets and "backing down" techniques that allowed them to escape, were implemented throughout the 1970s and 1980s, but it was an act of environmental espionage that had the biggest impact. In 1988, biologist and activist Samuel LaBudde videotaped hundreds of dolphins dying in the nets of a tuna boat, often sacrificed to catch only a few dozen fish. The release of the tape turned the tide, and in 1990, the three largest tuna companies—Starkist, Bumblebee, and Chicken of the Sea—all agreed to purchase and sell only tuna caught using dolphin-safe methods.

Tuna ranchers

The latest trick in the quest to catch the tastiest, most sashimi-ready tuna is to send the fish to a fat farm. Tuna "penning" facilities in Australia, Mexico, and the Mediterranean take in wild-caught bluefin tuna and fatten them up on a diet of oily fish over the course of a few months to a year. The result is a tuna with much greater fat stores, but a taste that isn't quite up to par with true wild bluefin.

Tuna penning falls outside most fishing regulations since it's neither wild catch nor traditional aquaculture. Debate over whether the practice is environmentally sound has grown, but the higher prices will likely keep the number of ranches growing for the foreseeable future.

At the Market
Can't Judge a Fish by Its Color

While it's possible to spot an intact albacore now and then, you're never going to find a whole yellowfin at the market...unless you happen to live on that island paradise I mentioned earlier. But that's cool. Steaks and loins are all we need, and without my trusty tuna testing kit to take a core sample, I'd rather see the flesh up close and personal, anyway.

QUICK QUESTION

Has my tuna been tinted? Ruby-red flesh, traditionally a sign of quality and freshness, may actually be something else: a spray-on tan. Due to iron-rich proteins in its flesh, yellowfin turns brown as it ages. The process can be halted, even reversed, by spraying it with carbon monoxide. The treatment is harmless according to the FDA, but it does beg the question: are we being tricked into buying something that isn't as fresh as it appears? The gas does nothing to preserve freshness and although resellers are required to label the tuna as treated, some do not. The solution: find a fishmonger you trust and ask lots of questions.

How Much?

On January 5, 2001, a single 444-pound bluefin tuna was bought for $173,600 at the Tsukiji Market in Tokyo. That's $390.99 a pound. And now you all want to be fishermen.

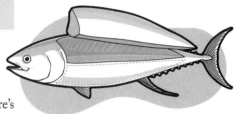

removing a tuna loin

What to buy

The Japanese have a saying: "Eat with your eyes." Good advice. Here's one of my own: "Buy with your nose." While you probably can't judge tuna by it's color (see "Has my tuna been tinted?"), you can buy it based on smell. For example, does it have any, and if it does, is it anything other than a mild sea breeze? Purchase accordingly.

That doesn't mean color isn't still an important factor for determining the quality of tuna. A bold, deep red is desirable; rusty brown, not so much. Hot pink tuna has definitely been smoking something and should be avoided. The flesh should also appear moist, but not wet. An oily, possibly rainbow-tinted sheen is normal for freshly cut tuna. Dry, bruised, or mushy flesh is not.

If you're in need of multiple steaks, ask the fishmonger for a whole loin or section and cut them at home. Even if you're only shopping for one, go ahead and ask for a fresh cut. That way you can get exactly the thickness you want. For me that means an inch and a half, but I really like tuna. An inch is plenty for most palates—thick enough to sear without cooking through, but not too thick to scare the neighbors.

Individually frozen tuna steaks have become quite popular in recent years, providing more markets the opportunity to offer yellowfin tuna. Unfortunately, much of the frozen product has been treated (again, see "Has my tuna been tinted?"), which means the quality is not up to that of fresh yellowfin. If it's cheaper (and it should be), frozen steaks are a good deal, but if you have the option, and don't mind paying extra, go with fresh.

Microcanneries

Similar to microbreweries, microcanneries are small, independent facilities that produce high-end canned tuna, often in direct partnership with fishermen. By using only troll-caught albacore ("white") tuna, and cooking it only once, they're able to provide a product that's more moist and flavorful than most big-name commercial brands. At the same time, limited processing means more nutrition makes it into the can. If you're counting your Omega-3s, this is the can to buy.

When in Japan...

Maguro is often used to describe any tuna, but in Japan it generally refers to bluefin (also called honmaguro). Bigeye is mebachi, albacore is binnaga, and yellowfin is kiwada. The Japanese further separate the tuna's flesh into the leaner tail meat, akami; the richer back meat, chu toro, and the richest, fat-saturated belly meat, oho toro, sometimes simply called otoro. If you're new to raw tuna, stick with the lean meat and work your way up to otoro. It's a bit of an acquired taste.

QUICK QUESTION

Am I being graded on this?   Tuna destined for the sashimi market are graded, fish by fish, based on texture, firmness, color, moisture content, and, most important, fat content. The best receive a "number 1" grade (often simply called "sashimi grade"), the next best a "number 2" grade. Sounds easy enough, but the difference in price between a number 1 and number 2 can be substantial. (Is there a number 3? Yeah, but you don't want that.)

If you're going to be cooking your tuna, don't buy a number 1. Even a simple sear is going to mask the qualities that define sashimi-grade tuna, so why waste the money?

Raw (but not wiggling)

If you're looking for tuna to serve raw, I highly recommend buying from a quality Asian market. Many fish markets now carry sashimi-grade tuna, but those that already cater to a sushi-loving clientele really know their stuff. Don't be shy. Walk right up to the fishmonger and demand the finest sashimi-grade tuna in all the land. When he hands you a small rectangular block of fish with a not-so-small price tag, don't be shocked. A little goes a long way when it comes to tuna sashimi.

What you see and smell in the market is what you'll get on the plate. Accept nothing less than the most impeccable piece of fish in the case. When buying for sashimi (sliced raw fish), a small 1- to 1½-inch thick by 2- to 3-inch wide block will suffice. The length depends on how much you need. Plan on each slice being about ¼-inch thick, but buy a little extra just in case. If you're going to be making sushi (raw fish combined with seasoned rice), a similar sized block is good for *nigiri sushi* (sliced raw fish on top of a small mound of rice), but *maki sushi* (raw fish and seasoned rice rolled inside of dried seaweed) doesn't need to be as perfectly shaped.

Bluefin Blues

If you really want to try bluefin (and can't hop on a plane bound for Japan), check with the local sushi concern—the best bars usually have a line on a little blue, and some will even order it for you.

In the Kitchen
Tuna Is a Rare Thing

Once you've brought your tuna home, cook it. That's a pricey piece of fresh fish you just bought, and it's not going to get any fresher. In fact, in just a few days, it's going to look a lot like a chocolate brownie. A fishy chocolate brownie. You don't want that. Cook it.

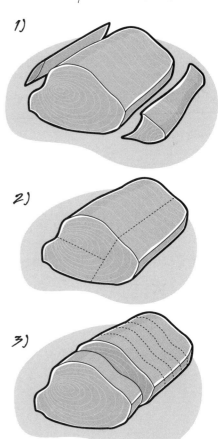

Tuna trimming

If you've already got your steaks, go ahead and skip to the cooking section, but if you've bought the loin, it's time to trim. For the prettiest presentation, a more even block shape will produce the best results. Granted, that requires trimming to shape your tuna, but you can always save the scraps for a tuna sandwich (a very expensive tuna sandwich).

Use single, even strokes when cutting, and try not to saw. Excessive back and force motion will only damage the fish's delicate fibers. As I mentioned before, thickness is up to you, but if you're cutting steaks, don't cut too thin. Thinner steaks (¾-inch or less) cook through too quickly. For a nice sear surrounding a red center, at least an inch of thickness is required.

The art of undercooking

Simple. Fast. Hot.

That's what you need to remember when cooking yellowfin tuna. Keep it simple by not trying to overpower the fish with a four-hour marinade or heavy pan sauce. A quick dip (say, 15 to 20 minutes) in soy sauce or other Asian-inspired flavors before cooking will add a little zing, but I prefer only the basics: salt, pepper, and olive oil. Boring, I know. The wasabi and soy come later.

Fast and hot go naturally hand in hand, the only trick being how to apply the heat. A heavy aluminum pan works fine, but a grill or cast-iron grill pan are better. For indoor applications, I especially like the grill pan, which provides a better sear than a regular pan. A flat surface cooks the steak too quickly; by the time the crust is perfect, the tuna is heated through. The grill pan is actually a less efficient way to cook, but in this case that's an advantage, since the center will stay rare. Plus it makes all those cool grill marks.

1)

2)

3)

Trimming the Loin

(1) Remove the dark bloodline and corner wedge. Discard the bloodline, but keep the wedge for tuna salad. (2) Cutting blocks. (3) Cutting steaks.

Safety First

Larger tuna rarely, if ever, carry the parasites sometimes found in other big fish, so feel free to cook them as little as you like.

Sashimi Cut

Tuna destined to become sashimi should be cut slightly at an angle (see above). This may render the first piece unusable, but—whoops, I ate it, never mind. For most applications a thickness of ¼-inch is appropriate.

Once the tuna hits the heat, the clock is ticking. For a one-inch-thick steak, it's only going to take a couple of minutes to sear each side. Beyond that, you're cooking it through. You can usually judge how far the sear has penetrated by watching the side of the steak, though it's usually a little less than what it appears. After removing the tuna from the heat, it'll continue to cook for a couple minutes, so don't be afraid to pull it early. If it's too rare, you can always toss it back on the grill.

The art of not cooking

Don't cook it.

I knew if I tried hard enough I could find an application that perfectly suits my "less is more" culinary mantra. Buy it, cut it, eat it. Oh, sure, you can arrange it on a plate if you want with a little wasabi, pickled ginger, and soy sauce. Rice? Well, yeah, if you want to make hand-formed *nigiri sushi*, you're going to have to have rice. Rolled sushi? For that you'll need some *nori* and a bamboo rolling mat. This is starting to get complicated. Let's look at some pictures instead.

1)

2)

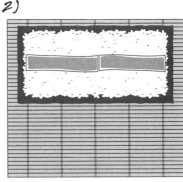

Nigiri Sushi

The basic hand-formed sushi is simply a small slice of raw fish laid over a bit of rice and then pressed together in the palm of one's hand. The secret: keep dipping your digits in lightly vinegared water so the rice won't stick to them.

Maki Sushi

There are many ways to make a sushi roll; this is the easiest.

3)

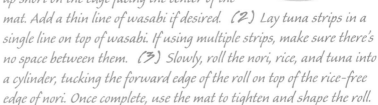

(1) Place a half sheet of nori (shiny side down) along the edge of a bamboo mat. Spread rice evenly over the surface, coming up short on the edge facing the center of the mat. Add a thin line of wasabi if desired. (2) Lay tuna strips in a single line on top of wasabi. If using multiple strips, make sure there's no space between them. (3) Slowly, roll the nori, rice, and tuna into a cylinder, tucking the forward edge of the roll on top of the rice-free edge of nori. Once complete, use the mat to tighten and shape the roll.

Tuna Recipes

For your friends and family who refuse to believe that raw fish is edible, seared ahi is the place to start. Remember, it's "rare," not raw. Sure, you can start medium rare. Eventually, they'll learn to love it your way (because that's the only way you're going to cook it). Once they've been converted to the dark (red) side, toss a tuna roll in front of them and see if they blink. Chances are they'll eat it without question. They're ready. To the sushi bar!

NUTRITIONAL INFO

Per 3.5 oz/100 grams (raw)

Yellowfin Tuna		Albacore Tuna	
Calories	108	**Calories**	172
Calories from fat	8	Calories from fat . . .	66
Total fat	0.95 g	**Total fat**	7.2 g
Saturated fat	0.2 g	Saturated fat	1.9 g
Cholesterol	45 mg	**Cholesterol**	38 mg
Sodium	37 mg	**Sodium**	51 mg
Protein	23.4 g	**Protein**	25.2 g
Omega-3	0.6 g	**Omega-3**	2.1g
Mercury	0.38 ppm	**Mercury**	0.35 ppm

HEALTH QUESTION

How do I play it safe? Preparing raw seafood at home can be a little unnerving for the chef wary of invisible (and other) critters joining the party. Fortunately, by following a few simple rules, most of the baddies can be avoided: (1) buy from a clean, trustworthy retailer; (2) handle your fish with the utmost care and make sure everything the fish touches has been thoroughly cleaned; (3) freeze it. Most parasites don't like the cold any more than the heat, so a week in the deep freeze (less than -4° F) will seriously ruin their vacation. *NOTE: Much of the product sold as sashimi-grade tuna has already been frozen for an extended period, so be sure to ask when buying so you don't end up freezing it again.*

Seared Ahi

Hot, fast, and rare. This is really the minimalist approach—no marinade, no spicy seasoning—just olive oil, salt, and pepper. This recipe calls for steaks, but can easily be applied to a tuna block (cut as shown in the illustration on page 79). See notes below.

2 thick (1½ inch) ahi steaks (6 to 8 ounces each)
Kosher salt and freshly ground black pepper
Extra virgin olive oil
Prepared wasabi (for dipping)
Soy sauce (for dipping)

Place a cast-iron grill pan in the oven and turn the heat up to 500° F. Once the oven hits the mark, transfer the very hot pan to a burner set on high. Or (for you grill-heads) preheat the grill by whatever means necessary. When it gets really hot, it's fish time.

Season both sides of each steak with salt and pepper, and add a very thin coating of olive oil—just enough to cover. Drop the steaks onto the heat and cook them until done to your liking. For rare, cook 1½ to 2 minutes per side, for medium rare, 2 to 3 minutes per side. *NOTE: If working with a block shape you'll also need to sear each side to even things out.*

Transfer the steaks to warm plates and serve them immediately with wasabi and soy sauce on the side. To serve a tuna block as an appetizer, rest it briefly (or a lot; serving it cold is perfectly acceptable), and then cut it into ¼-inch slices.

Serves 2

IMPORTANT NOTE: If you are cooking tuna on a flat surface, the fish will cook faster (over similarly high heat). For rare, cook each side for 1 minute, and for medium rare, 2 minutes.

"My Tuna Needs Help" Marinade

It happens to the best of us. We're in a rush and that ruby red tuna steak we bought at the market suddenly looks hot pink in the light of the kitchen. Never fear. A quick dip in this marinade will kick almost any tuna (or swordfish) steak back into game shape.

¾ cup soy sauce
2 tablespoons brown sugar
1 teaspoon wasabi powder

Combine all ingredients in a shallow nonreactive bowl. Stir until the sugar is dissolved. Add the tuna and marinate it for 30 minutes or up to 2 hours. If the marinade doesn't completely cover the tuna, flip the fish halfway through.

The Ultimate Fish Sandwich

This is quite simply the best tuna fish sandwich you'll ever taste. (Or, failing that, it'll at least be the most expensive, d'oh!) An albacore steak is a perfectly acceptable substitute, and for some may actually be preferable. And, yes, "barely medium" is what I meant to say. A rare tuna sandwich will end up cold, mushy, or both.

1 to 2 teaspoons prepared wasabi
3 tablespoons mayonnaise
1 teaspoon rice vinegar
1 tablespoon sesame oil
¼ teaspoon grated fresh ginger
Kosher salt and freshly ground black pepper
1 cup mixed salad greens of your choice
1 teaspoon toasted sesame seeds
2 sandwich-sized French rolls, split
Extra virgin olive oil
2 ahi (or albacore) steaks, each ¾-inch thick and 4 to 6 ounces
1 large tomato, cut into 4 to 6 slices
1 large red onion slice, separated into rings

Combine the wasabi and mayonnaise, stir it well, and let it stand for 30 minutes. Taste. Not hot enough? Add a little more wasabi.

Combine the vinegar, sesame oil, ginger, a pinch of salt, and a twist or two of pepper. Stir to dissolve the salt. Toss with mixed greens and sesame seeds.

Brush a little olive oil on each roll slice (inside only). Toast the rolls under the broiler until golden.

Preheat a heavy pan over high heat. Season both sides of each steak with salt and pepper, and add a very thin coat of olive oil—just enough to cover. Drop the steaks onto the heat and cook them until barely medium, about 1 to 1½ minutes per side.

Spread 1 tablespoon of the wasabi mayo over the bottom half of the roll. (Top, too? Hey, it's your sandwich.) Slide the steaks onto the bottom, top with tomato slices, onions, and greens. Serve with potato chips, french fries, or matching mixed greens.

Serves 2

Tuna Niçoise

Yes, this is a salad. And, yes, it's mostly just a bunch of precooked ingredients laid next to each other on a plate. (If you're missing a few, don't sweat it . . . unless it's the tuna.) Best of all, this is where you use those scraps of tuna left over after trimming your loin to size (not the bloodline, the good stuff). NOTE: In a pinch, I have substituted top-quality canned tuna. Keep it to yourself, okay?

2 tablespoons balsamic vinegar
2 teaspoons red wine vinegar
Kosher salt and freshly ground black pepper
2 teaspoons Dijon mustard
½ cup extra virgin olive oil
3 cups mixed salad greens of your choice
12 ounces cooked tuna, broken up
8 ounces slender green beans, blanched 3 to 4 minutes in salted water and chilled
8 to 12 very small red potatoes, boiled, chilled, and split
2 hard-boiled eggs, shelled and sliced
8 anchovies (canned), split lengthwise
1 red bell pepper, seeded and cut in thin strips
1 small red onion, thinly sliced
8 to 12 small cherry tomatoes (multicolored is nice), cut in half
¼ cup Kalamata olives, sliced

Combine the vinegar, a pinch of salt, and several twists of black pepper in a large, nonmetallic bowl. Stir until salt is dissolved. Add the mustard and stir to combine. Slowly drizzle in the olive oil, stirring constantly to combine. Taste the dressing on a green to check the seasonings and adjust accordingly. Pour about half of the dressing into a small container; leave the rest in the bowl.

Toss the greens with the dressing in the bowl to coat. Spread the greens evenly over 4 salad plates. Place ¼ of the tuna in the center of each pile of greens. In whatever manner you deem most aesthetically pleasing, arrange the green beans, potatoes, egg slices, anchovies, peppers, onions, tomatoes, and olives around the tuna on each plate. Some folks like it neat and rigid; others prefer the haphazard approach (yeah, that's me).

Drizzle the remaining dressing on top of the salads and serve.

Serves 4

No. 1 Super Best Tuna Roll

SUSHI SECRET No. 1: Keep your hands and your knife wet so the rice won't stick. SUSHI SECRET No. 2: Don't try to overload a half sheet of nori; if you want to add more stuff, use a full sheet or use ¼-inch-square tuna pieces. (Stuff = thinly sliced cucumbers, avocado, scallions, carrots, etc.) SUSHI REALITY No. 1: Your first roll will be a disaster; deal with it. NOTES: Nori is dried seaweed. It can be found at Asian markets and many non-Asian markets. Look for dark, tightly grained sheets. Wasabi is green Japanese horseradish, usually sold as a ready-made paste or as a powder that needs a little water to bring it to life. For a little variety, prepare a few rolls using cucumber and fresh chopped dill or avocado and lemon zest instead of tuna.

3 sheets nori, halved
Prepared sushi rice, as needed (see recipe)
Wasabi, as needed
6 ounces sashimi grade ahi tuna, cut into ½-inch-square strips
Small bowl of water for hand and knife dipping

Place a half sheet of nori (shiny side down) along the edge of a bamboo sushi mat. Get your hands wet and then grab a handful of rice, shape it roughly into a log, and place it in the center of the nori. Spread the rice evenly over the surface of the seaweed, coming up a little short on the edge facing away from you (near the center of the mat).

Using your finger, spread a thin line of wasabi along the center of the rice. Go easy; wasabi is strong. Lay tuna strips in a single line on top of the wasabi. If using multiple strips, make sure there's no space between them.

Grab the edge of the mat closest to you and slowly curl it away, rolling the nori, rice, and tuna into a cylinder as you go. The mat will need to be folded back a little as you roll, but continue to apply pressure so as not to lose the cylinder. The forward edge of the roll should tuck in nicely on top of the rice-free edge of the nori (and hopefully stick). Once the cylinder is complete, use the mat to tighten and shape it. See the illustration on page 80 for a clearer picture.

Unroll the mat and inspect your masterpiece. Set it aside and repeat the process using the remaining nori, rice, and tuna to create 5 more rolls. Moisten a very sharp knife and cut each in half, and then cut each half into 3 pieces for a total of 36 pieces. After each cut, wipe and remoisten the knife with a wet cloth.

Arrange the pieces artfully on a serving platter and serve them with soy sauce, wasabi, and pickled ginger.

Serves 6 to 8 as an appetizer

Sushi Rice

Be sure to use Japanese-style short-grain "sushi" rice. NOTE: *Kombu is dried kelp, which can be found in most Asian markets. If you can't find it, no worries; your sushi won't suffer sans sea kelp.*

1½ cups sushi rice
2 cups water
1 small piece *kombu* (optional)
3 tablespoons rice vinegar
2 tablespoons sugar
1 teaspoon kosher salt

Place the rice in a fine mesh strainer and submerge it in a larger bowl of water. Swish the rice around to loosen up some of the starch. Drain the milky water and repeat, 3 to 5 times, until the water is relatively clear.

Add the rice to a heavy, medium-sized saucepan. Add water and *kombu* (optional) and bring just to a boil over medium-high heat. Cover, reduce the heat to low, and simmer until the moisture is absorbed by the rice, about 20 minutes. Remove the pot from the heat and let it stand, covered, for 10 minutes.

Meanwhile, combine the vinegar, sugar, and salt in a small bowl and stir until the sugar and salt have dissolved.

Transfer the rice to a large bowl (ideally a presoaked wooden rice tub) and slowly fold in the vinegar mixture, a little at a time, until the grains have separated and taken on a glossy appearance. Gently fan the rice as necessary to bring it to room temperature. (Warm sushi rice is not cool.)

Left Coast Temaki Cone

Hand rolled for those without bamboo mats or hand-eye coordination. If you've got guests who like to get their hands sticky, this is the perfect "roll your own" appetizer.

5 sheets nori, halved
Prepared sushi rice, as needed (see recipe)
Wasabi, as needed
8 ounces sashimi grade ahi tuna
1 cucumber, peeled and cut into thin strips
2 avocados, peeled, pitted, and cut into thin strips
1 large carrot, peeled and cut into slivers
1 bunch fresh cilantro
2 lemons cut into wedges, plus zest

Pick up a sheet of nori and place a heaping spoonful of prepared rice in the left-most quarter of the sheet (for those holding nori with their right hand, reverse all the right-left directions). Spread the rice around to even it out top to bottom and then add a little wasabi with your finger (or a lot if you're nuts).

Arrange a strip (or two) of tuna plus a few pieces of cucumber, avocado, and carrot on top of the rice pointing toward the upper-left-hand corner of the nori. Don't overload it. Add a sprig or two of cilantro and sprinkle on a wedge's worth of lemon juice and a little zest.

Wrap the bottom left corner of the nori around the fillings and continue to roll, forming a cone shape in the process. The rice and fillings should peek out the open end. Repeat using the remaining nori and ingredients for a total of 10 cones.

Serves 5

NOTE: *In case you hadn't already guessed, yes, you can substitute other sashimi quality fish and fresh ingredients. Check out your local sushi bar for ideas. Have fun.*

Chapter 8
American Lobster
Crustaceanland

If you happen to be a lobster, there's no place you'd rather be than…Maine? Yes, Maine, that far-flung vacationland that most of us have only visited via Stephen King's worst nightmares, is home to millions of the undisputed king of crustaceans. Canada will no doubt try to claim its share, but this is truly an all-American crustacean. Look no further than the name, Homarus americanus—American lobster—the best-tasting, most awesome lobstrosity in the world! Spiny lobsters? Sure, the tails from down under may get bigger, but look at those dinky claws; our lobster could kick its ass. There's also a similar lobster across the Atlantic, Homarus gammarus, but he's a bit smaller than his stateside cousin. Truth be told, this is one American most Europeans wouldn't mind having over for dinner. (Hey, I said "most.")

VITAL STATS

FIRST NAME: American lobster (also Maine lobster, northern lobster)

SCI. NAME: *Homarus americanus*

SIZE: 1-2 lbs, but can grow to 40+ lbs

LIFESPAN: Most 5-7 years when caught, but may live to 100+

RANGE: Labrador (Canada) to North Carolina

CATCH: 182 million lbs in 2002 (U.S. and Canada)

Millions of years of erosion and tectonic redistribution created the Gulf of Maine, but a few oversized ice cubes turned it into lobster paradise. Ten thousand years ago, the last of the Great Ice Age glaciers began to recede, leaving behind a landscape of cracks, crags, and rocky debris. Overflowing with former glaciers, the Atlantic soon poured into the Gulf, creating the ideal habitat for the king of crustaceans.

Unlike the landscape, the lobster hasn't changed much in the past 150 million years. Were it available at Ruth's Chris, "Jurassic surf & turf" would look and taste very familiar…at least the surf part. Sadly, the fossil record has very little to say about the qualities of brontosaurus steak, but it does reveal that prehistoric lobsters were remarkably similar to their modern cousins: hard, chitin exoskeleton, fat tail, two front-loaded claws, and four pairs of happy feet. Sometimes evolution gets it right the first time.

In the Water
Bloodhounds of the Sea

Unlike practically every other critter on the planet, a lobster's eyes function using reflection rather than refraction. Such a system works well in low light conditions such as those found on the seafloor, but it's not great for discerning details. More important to a lobster is its ability to "see" with its nose, or more precisely, a small pair of antennules protruding from the head. A much longer pair of antennae provide a sense of touch, but it's the chemical sensors in the antennules that help the lobster hunt and socialize with fellow crustaceans.

Lobster "society" is actually anything but social. Truth is, they don't like each other. Those restraints fishermen put on a lobster's claws aren't just to protect your fingers, they're also to protect their investment. Given the chance, a tank full of lobsters will beat each other silly. Is a rubber band strong enough to do the job? You bet. A lobster's strength is in closing, not opening its claws.

Perhaps the only time lobsters do get along is when they choose to mate. A pair of lobsters will shack up for a short period (made possible by a male-mystifying pheromone released by the female) until the female molts. At this point, the male can either, (*a*) get busy, or (*b*) eat her. Most choose *a*. After mating, the female will hold onto the male's sperm, possibly for months, before fertilizing as many as 100,000 eggs. Once fertilized, she will carry her eggs on her tail for upward of ten months before releasing them to hatch in open water.

For most newborn lobsters, life rarely lasts more than two weeks before a hungry fish gobbles them up. Only about 1 in 2000 will survive long enough to be eaten by you or me.

Plague of Lobsters

Lobster is derived from the Old English loppestre, a modification of the Latin locusta, which is what it sounds like: a bug. Lobsters, like all crustaceans, are but a single scientific class removed from insects. This may or may not be something to bring up at the dinner table.

these legs were made for walking

QUICK QUESTION

Do lobsters swim? Not really. A contraction of the abdominal muscles can propel a lobster backward, but this is primarily an escape mechanism. On the other hand, lobsters are prolific walkers. On average, a mature lobster will migrate a couple of dozen miles each season, although some have been tracked covering hundreds of miles over mountainous terrain.

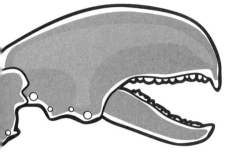

Double-Barreled

Although lobster claws (known as "chilipeds" in scientific circles) start out the same, one eventually develops into a crusher, the other a pincher or ripper. In case you hadn't guessed, the crusher is for crushing and the pincher is for annoying little brothers.

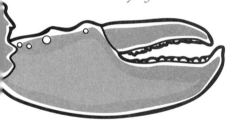

Shedders

Those lobsters lucky enough to celebrate a few birthdays grow by molting, a process in which the shell is shed and replaced with a larger coat of arms. By five years of age, most lobsters have molted twenty-five or more times. They'll continue to molt, about once a year, for the rest of their lives. This may sound like a sweet deal—who wouldn't like to step out of their skin for a little epidermal upgrade now and then—but for a lobster it's not an outpatient procedure. Molting is a gut wrenching (yes, literally) experience that requires the lobster to tear itself away from its old shell. Some lobsters don't live through the experience. Those that do survive find themselves defenseless until their new shell hardens, a process that can take weeks.

Mature lobsters shed in the summer, usually after spending a few weeks hanging out in the warmer waters near the shore. After molting, they make a break for deeper waters, often stopping for a snack along they way. On the menu are such seafood favorites as crab, mussels, clams, and the occasional small fish. They especially enjoy the millions of self-serve herring cocktails laid out by the landlocked locals. Whether or not lobsters realize they're walking into a trap has yet to be determined.

Learn the Lingo!

The smallest legal-sized lobsters, usually weighing around a pound, are called "chickens." "Quarters" weigh in around 1.25 pounds, "selects," 1.5-1.75 pounds, and "deuces," about 2 pounds. Anything bigger than 2.25 pounds is called a "jumbo."

On the Boats
The Lobstermen

Early American settlers didn't know how good they had it. Sure, there was that whole primitive-way-of-life thing, but consider this: Procuring a lobster dinner could be as simple as waiting for the tide to go out. After a storm, beaches were often littered with so many lobsters that farmers used them to fertilize their crops. Lobsters were so plentiful that most folks thought of them not as haute cuisine but rather as a last resort.

Today's fishermen have to do a little more work to catch a lobster, which may explain why they're not giving them away. Lobsters are caught using 3- to 4-foot-long vinyl-covered wire traps (also called

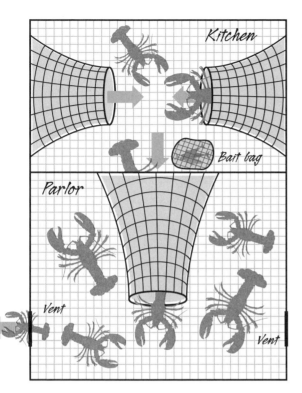

Kitchen

Bait bag

Parlor

Vent

Vent

Inside a Lobster Pot

A herring-filled bait bag hangs within the "kitchen," the first compartment of the trap, enticing lobsters inside. Two funnel-shaped openings allow easy entry into the kitchen, but make it very difficult for lobsters to back out. Another funnel leads into the "parlor" or "bedroom," a larger compartment where lobsters are free to hang out while others stumble into the trap.

Small rectangular vents in the parlor provide undersize lobsters with an escape hatch. The vents are secured using biodegradable rings so that if the trap becomes lost, larger vents will eventually pop open, allowing all lobsters to escape from this "ghost trap."

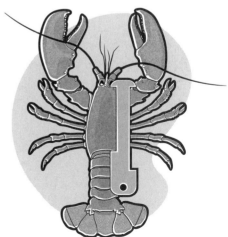

"pots") baited with herring and set on the ocean floor. Painted buoys mark trap locations, sometimes as many as eight on a single line. Traps are checked and fresh bait added every two to three days, even if it's just to "change the water" (hauling up an empty trap). Considering that these are usually independent fisherman working upward of 800 traps per cycle, that's a lot of water when the fishing's no good.

Buoys must be painted to match colors specific to each fisherman, which must also be displayed on the fisherman's boat.

Trapping Success

How effective are the traps? On a very good day, a single boat might haul in over a thousand pounds of lobsters. Since the early 1990s, there have been a lot of good days, especially for those fishing the waters off the coast of Maine. In 2002, over 60 million pounds of lobster were landed—three times the catch of only a decade earlier. Another example of overfishing? Not really. Lobstermen have long practiced conservation techniques to protect future harvests, beginning with minimum-size re-strictions in 1895. Today, a lobster must measure at least 3.25 inches and no more than 5 inches from the eye socket to the end of the carapace. Anything larger or smaller is thrown back. Females carrying fertilized eggs are also off limits, as are those bearing "V-notches." Fishermen are required to cut a notch in the tail of egg-bearing lobsters, a mark that will protect them even after they've released their eggs.

how to measure a lobster

THE BIG QUESTION

Will the big boom ever bust? Scientists have long predicted the demise of the big lobster hauls, but no one was prepared for the crash that occurred in Long Island Sound in 1999. Almost overnight, the lobsters up and died. What happened? Best guess: We did it.

Lobsters have a central nervous system very similar to insects, which means they're very susceptible to pesticides. When the area around Long Island Sound was sprayed to combat mosquitoes carrying the West Nile virus, some of the pesticide leached into the water, killing the lobsters. Even if a pesticide doesn't kill the lobsters outright, spraying can damage the immune system, making them more vulnerable to other diseases, such as the shell burn outbreak that has spread throughout much of the southern New England fishery.

In 2004, another theory was offered to explain the die-off and disease, which might also explain why the fishing got so good in the first place. Gradual temperature increases in the waters off southern New England (call it global warming if you must) pushed the lobster beyond its heat tolerance, making it more susceptible to disease. In Maine, where the waters are naturally cooler, the temperature increase actually spurred the lobsters to multiply even faster.

Can It

The market for lobsters was initially limited to New England due to lobsters' reluctance to travel. It wasn't until someone thought to stuff lobster meat in a can that all of America was able to enjoy it. Ironically, the success of the industry ultimately led to the canneries' demise. Size restrictions made it much more profitable for lobstermen to sell their catch to the fresh market, leaving the canners without anything to put in their cans.

Migration of the Lobstermen

Most of the lobster fishery lies within sight of the shore, although there is a small offshore fishery that expands as the lobsters migrate offshore during the winter months. Traditionally, lobstermen staked out claims where they would set their traps for a season, but many now follow the lobster. More than a few arguments have started because established fishermen felt overzealous outsiders were invading their turf. While most "gear wars" are limited to emptying traps and cutting lines, a few have escalated to damaging boats and violence between fishermen.

At the Market
Tanks for the Lobsters

One of the great culinary success stories of the twentieth century has to be the proliferation of lobster tanks in restaurants and supermarkets across the country. Whether you're living in Maine, Minneapolis, or Medford, Oregon, live lobster is just down the street. Of course, the freshest bugs are still found at the source, but with many retailers now offering overnight delivery coast to coast, even that gap is closing.

The height of the season usually falls between August and October, and that's when you find the best deals on fresh lobster. The summer demand is winding down, and with supply on the rise, many retailers are willing to make a deal. Rather than sell at a lower price, many lobstermen store their catch in huge saltwater ponds, called "lobster pounds," until the price goes back up later in the winter.

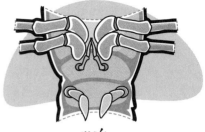

male

Buying

In terms of quality, there's really no "best" time to buy a lobster. Fresh lobster can be had year-round, although seasonal fluctuations can affect availability. Some folks wait for late summer soft-shell lobsters, preferring the slightly sweeter flavor and easy to open package. The main drawback is that soft-shells contain considerably less meat since the lobster has yet to fill out its new suit. Because transporting live soft-shells is difficult, it's rare to find a shedder outside of New England.

When buying a live lobster, start with the tank. Is it clean or green? If you can't see the bugs through the sludge, move on. The lobster itself should be feisty, not droopy. Never buy a "sleeping" lobster. How big depends on your appetite. Most eaters fall comfortably into the 1.25 to 2 pound range. Flavorwise, a bigger lobster isn't going to taste any different than a smaller one unless you happen to stumble upon a 10-pound giant. He might be a little on the stringy side. Bigger bugs do offer slightly better meat-to-weight ratio, although a more important yield factor is how recently the lobster molted. Ask to give the lobster a squeeze; if he feels a little soft around the middle, he's probably retaining more water than meat.

For the trip home, a cooler packed with damp newspaper and a sealed ice pack will do the trick. Lobster shipped overnight is often packed with seaweed, helping it retain a little more "flavor of the sea." If you live near a beach, try harvesting your own (just don't forget the ice pack).

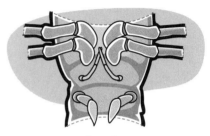

female

Boy or Girl?

To check whether your lobster is a boy or a girl, flip it over and look for the two tiny flippers at the top end of the tail. On a female they're soft and flexible; on a male they're hard.

Lobster Farms?

Despite numerous attempts, no one has yet found the secret to farming lobsters. What's the problem? They grow too slowly, order the most expensive feed on the menu, and would rather beat each other to a stumpy pulp than share a bedroom. So, if you don't mind waiting five years for a $60 one-armed lobster...

lobster in repose

HOW TO STORE: Lobster

LIVE: Keep live lobsters in the refrigerator, wrapped in a little damp newspaper, seaweed, or a damp towel. Properly stored they'll last 1 to 2 days. Do not place live lobsters on ice, in a bucket of water, or in the bathtub. Fresh water kills lobsters; unless you have a tank of circulating, temperature-controlled saltwater, stick with the fridge. Try to resist the urge to seal them inside a plastic bag. They're not going anywhere.

In the Kitchen

It's Alive

This might be a good time to remember that lobsters are simply over-sized insects. What do we do with bugs in the house? We squish 'em! Or in this case, we steam 'em. (Once cooked, promptly forget that insect analogy.)

Dispatching a lobster needn't be a trauma, but I understand it may be difficult for some novice chefs. Dropping a live lobster into a pot of boiling water is going to get a reaction from the lobster, and it doesn't appear to be a happy one. Here's what you do: just chill…your lobster. Chilling a lobster for about fifteen minutes in the freezer will slow its metabolism significantly, minimizing what (if any) pain it feels in the pot. Other "calming" methods such as rubbing the lobster's head or slowly heating the lobster generally prolong the critter's life rather than ease its suffering.

There are quicker ways to dispatch a lobster—splitting the head down the middle with a chef's knife works quite well—but if you're having trouble boiling a lobster, stabbing it in the head probably isn't for you.

Steaming versus boiling

Let's get this out of the way up front: Steaming is better than boiling. Consider: (*a*) Boiling a lobster requires a lot of water, and a lot of water takes a long time to boil. Steaming uses very little water. (*b*) Boiling dilutes the flavor by forcing water into a lobster and drawing flavorful juices out. Steaming does very little of either. (*c*) Keeping a constant temperature is more difficult with a large amount of boiling (or recently boiling) water. Steam is steam; the temperature remains the same. (*d*) Remember all that water? Who's going to clean that up? That's right, you are.

Tomalley, Too?

The tomalley (essentially, the lobster's liver and pancreases) is not really my thing, but lobster fanatics love this light green stuff, straight up or swirled into a sauce. Is it dangerous? Maybe. Because it filters toxins for a living, most experts advise against eating it. The bright red (when cooked) coral or roe sometimes found in female lobsters is a little more appetizing and can be served alongside the lobster. There are no safety concerns with regard to eating the roe. Dig in.

1-2)

Dismantling a cooked lobster

Ready to get a little messy? (Those bibs aren't just for show, bub.)

(1) Break off the claws and legs where they attach to the body.
(2) Twist off the thumb and then crack the claw. Carefully snap off the top of the claw and pull out the meat. (3) Remove the tail from the body with a twist. (4) Tear off the tail flippers and then push the meat through with a fork or finger. (5) Peel off the top of the tail to expose the dark intestinal tract. Get rid of it. (Incidentally, a clean intestine is a sign your lobster has been in the pound for more than a few days. Darker means fresher.) (6) Now, head back to those legs. Use a rolling pin to squeeze out every ounce of meat. (7) Finally, explore the body for leftovers. There's some good stuff near where the legs attach. (8) If it's a girl, there might be some coral, which you can eat if you like. I prefer to skip the tomalley (the green stuff), but some folks dig it.

3)

4)

5)

6)

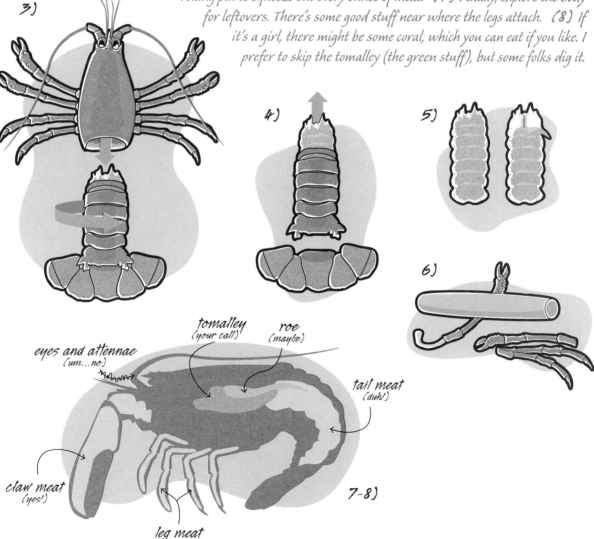

tomalley
(your call)

roe
(maybe)

eyes and antennae
(um...no.)

tail meat
(duh!)

claw meat
(yes!)

leg meat
(sure!)

7-8)

getting a grip on Mr. Lobster

Lobster Nutrition

Lobster is nearly fat-free and contains fewer calories and cholesterol than skinless chicken breast. It's also loaded with vitamins (A, B₁₂, E), minerals (calcium, phosphorus, zinc), and omega-3 fatty acids. It does have a relatively high sodium count, so keep that in mind if you're watching your salt intake.

QUICK QUESTION

Should I remove the rubber bands? There's no need to remove the claw bands before steaming (or boiling), but do snip them off before putting a bug in the oven or microwave. To avoid getting pinched, grasp the lobster around the carapace where it joins the tail. If he does manage to get a claw full of something he shouldn't, don't be afraid to relieve him of said claw. All's fair in lobster war.

I think if you ask most lobstermen they'd choose steaming, mainly because few have the time to wait for the pot to start bubbling. For me, it boils down to using the most consistent method for producing perfectly cooked lobster, which is steaming. If you prefer the idea of large pots of water, no problem, there's a recipe here for you, too.

The tail is going to curl as the lobster cooks. Some chefs advocate tying a chopstick to the underside of the tail to keep it straight. Good luck with that. If presented with a lobster whose tail is uncurled that you didn't see go into the pot kicking and screaming…walk away. It was probably dead long before cooking.

How about the microwave?

Yes, you can cook lobster in the microwave. In fact, if you're only cooking one, or are preparing a cold dish, I recommend it. Zapping a lobster effectively steams it inside its own shell, locking in more flavor than any other method. It also means fewer (i.e., zero) big pots to clean up.

Lobster also does well in the oven, although it requires a bit more work. I don't recommend broiling because it tends to overcook the meat. For you grill-heads, try steaming a lobster inside a pile of seaweed on top of the grill. Seriously, it's tasty, effective, and will make your friends think you're cool.

QUICK QUESTION

Does a lobster feel pain? Do you really want to know? Chances are they feel something, but since a lobster's nervous system is on a par with that of a grasshopper, it's probably not much. Lobsters don't "scream," by the way. That high-pitched sound you may hear is steam escaping from the shell as it cooks.

Lobster Recipes

Nobody seems to agree on the ideal cooking time for a lobster, be it steamed or boiled. Some chefs like to see a little translucence in the flesh, some not so much. Personally, I like my lobster just cooked through—opaque but succulent. Nailing the exact moment of ideal doneness is tricky, but the following chart should put you pretty close most of the time (without undercooking).

Weight	Cooking Time
1 to 1¼ pounds	12 to 14 minutes
1½ to 2 pounds	15 to 17 minutes
2¼ to 2¾ pounds	18 to 20 minutes
3 to 3½ pounds	21 to 25 minutes
4 pounds and up	7 minutes per pound

If you're cooking more than one lobster, these times still apply. The numbers refer not to total weight, but to individual weight. If you're cooking more than four lobsters at once, you might need to add a few extra minutes to the steamers. If you're boiling, the extra time will be built in, since it'll take a little more time to return the water to a boil (when boiling, the time starts after the water returns to a boil).

NOTE: Soft-shell lobsters require less time to cook. Subtract 20 percent from the total time if you managed to land a pot of softies.

NUTRITIONAL INFO

Per 3.5 oz/100 grams (raw)

American Lobster

Calories	90
Calories from fat	8
Total fat	0.9 g
Saturated fat	0.2 g
Cholesterol	95 mg
Sodium	296 mg
Protein	18.8 g
Omega-3	0.2 g
Mercury	0.31 ppm*

* from 1978 FDA test; recent tests have measured 0.15 to 0.25 ppm

Steamed Lobster

Debate no more! Steaming is the best. BONUS: For those who have to have it all, why not make a sauce out of the leftover steaming liquid? Simply strain it after use, reduce it in a pan with 2 to 3 tablespoons of butter or heavy cream (or both), add a few flavorful fresh herbs (cilantro, flat-leaf parsley, or chives), and season with salt and pepper.

2 cups salted water, dry white wine, or beer (amber or lighter)
4 live lobsters, 1¼ to 1½ pounds each
2 large lemons
Melted butter

Slide your lobsters into the freezer for 10 to 15 minutes to calm them down prior to cooking. NOTE: *If you aren't concerned about a little more movement in the pot, you can skip this step.*

Add the liquid to a stockpot large enough to comfortably hold the lobsters. Slice one of the lemons into wedges, squeeze the juice into the liquid, and toss the spent wedges in for good measure. Bring the liquid to a rolling boil over high heat.

Remove the lobsters from cold storage, rinse them off, and carefully place them, headfirst, in the pot. (No, you don't need a basket or something to keep them off the bottom of the pot.*) Cover the pot (tight) and steam for 15 minutes. NOTE: *For soft-shelled lobsters, steam for only 12 minutes.*

WARNING: *Steam is hot! Do not attempt to "get a good whiff" immediately after the lid comes off. Let the steam dissipate, and then stick your face in the pot. Better safe than scalded.*

Carefully remove the lobsters with a pair of tongs and drain them in a colander. If serving them hot, rinse under cold water briefly and plate as is or cracked for your guests' convenience. Serve them with the melted butter, the remaining lemon cut into wedges, and a big ol' bib.

Serves 4

Good Eats guru Alton Brown suggests using a single layer of river rocks to help redistribute the steam and heat the lobsters more evenly. Does it work? Sure. Is it necessary? Not really. Will your guests think you're nuts for putting rocks in your pots? Maybe. Check the local garden supply store for a bag of river rocks.

Boiled Lobster

The general rule of thumb is 1 gallon of water to boil 1 lobster, plus ¼ to ½ gallon more for each additional lobster. A 16-quart pot is a good size for cooking 2 to 4 lobsters.

½ cup kosher salt
1½ gallons water
2 live lobsters, 1½ pounds each
Melted butter
Lemon wedges

Add the salt and water to a large stockpot and stir to dissolve. Cover the pot and bring the water to a rolling boil over high heat.

When the water just starts to bubble (long before boiling), slide your lobsters into the freezer for 10 to 15 minutes. *NOTE: If you aren't concerned about a little more movement in the pot, you can skip this step.*

Once the water is rolling, remove the lobsters from cold storage, rinse them off, and carefully drop them headfirst into the water. Cover the pot and return it to a gentle boil. Once boiling, lower the heat, just enough to maintain a simmer, and cook for 15 minutes. *NOTE: For soft-shell lobsters, cook for only 12 minutes.*

Carefully remove the lobsters with a pair of tongs and drain them in a colander. If serving them hot, rinse under cold water briefly and plate as is or cracked for your guests' convenience. Serve them with melted butter, lemon wedges, and a big ol' bib.

Serves 2

Microwave Lobster

Hey, we already nuked a few Dungies, so you ought to be a pro by now, right? Oh, you skipped that recipe, huh? Never mind, then. Move along. For those still with me, think small; larger lobsters won't fit in the bag. NOTE: This is not the method to use if you're a big fan of tomalley. When microwaved, the stuff stays green and wet, making it less appetizing.

1 live lobster, 1 to 1¼ pounds
2 tablespoons white wine
1 lemon, cut in wedges
Melted butter

To calm your lobster down a bit, place him in the freezer for 10-15 minutes. *NOTE: Yeah, even if you aren't the squeamish type this will help keep the bug quiet.*

Remove the lobster from the chill, pull off the claw bands, and toss him into a heavy-duty microwave-safe plastic bag, along with the white wine and 2 to 4 lemon wedges. Seal the bag and place it in the microwave.

Microwave on high for 6 minutes for the first pound, plus 1 minute for each additional ¼ pound. (For example, a 1¼ lobster will take 7 minutes.) *NOTE: As with crab, there may be some flinching. Might be time to check your e-mail.*

When the beeper goes off, wait 5 minutes before opening the microwave. When you do retrieve the bag watch your fingers, as it will be hot. If you're serving the lobster warm, rinse it under cold water briefly before dismantling it. If serving it chilled, rinse it in cold water, drain it thoroughly, dismantle it, and refrigerate it until dinner.

Serve the lobster with melted butter, lemon wedges, and no bib. (You're eating alone, right? Feel free to make a mess.)

Serves 1

Grilled Lobster

Grilling a lobster isn't the most flavorful way to enjoy the big bugs (that would be steaming), but it may be the easiest way to convince the neighbors that you are the grill master.

4 live lobsters, 1¼ to 1½ pounds each
Melted butter
Kosher salt and freshly ground black pepper
Lemon wedges

Fire up the grill. We're looking for hot and even heat, so if you're using charcoal, spread it around. Meanwhile, slide your lobsters into the freezer for 10 to 15 minutes to calm them down.

Remove the lobsters from cold storage and kill them instantly by driving a chef's knife lengthwise through the head, splitting the front 2 inches of the body in two. *NOTE: For those who can't bring themselves to commit lobster homicide, bring 2 cups of water to a boil in a stockpot large enough to comfortably hold the lobsters. Slide the lobsters in headfirst, cover tightly, and steam for 1 minute. Remove from the pot and plunge in ice water to halt the cooking. Your lobsters are now dispatched.*

Once the lobster stops twitching (give it a few minutes), place it belly up on a large cutting board and split it from head to tail with a large chef's knife. Do *not* cut all the way through the back of the shell. Unfold the lobster like a book (the part you didn't cut is now your hinge). Remove all the nonmeat parts and discard them.

Place the lobsters, cut side down, on the grill and cook for 3 to 4 minutes, just until the meat is nicely marked (that's why you grill, right?). Turn the lobsters over and continue to cook for 10 to 12 minutes, until the meat is just cooked through.

Drizzle the lobster with melted butter, season it with salt and pepper, and serve with lemon wedges.

Serves 4 (or 8 if everyone agrees to share)

New England Lobster Roll

If you live near the New England coast, you already know the joys of the lobster roll. For those new to the sandwich, yes, it really is that simple. In fact, some cooks opt for an even simpler recipe using only lobster, mayo, salt, and pepper. What's the secret to the perfect roll? Use lots of lobster. One lobster per roll is about right. You'll get about a cup of meat, maybe a little more, from a 1¼-pound lobster.

2 cups cooked lobster meat, chilled
¼ cup mayonnaise
2 tablespoons minced celery
1 teaspoon lemon juice
Kosher salt and freshly ground black pepper
2 large split-top hot dog rolls (or other soft crust rolls)
1 tablespoon melted butter

If it isn't already, roughly chop the lobster meat into chunks and add them to a medium-sized bowl. Add the mayonnaise, celery, and lemon juice, and stir to combine them. Season the mixture with salt and pepper to taste. Chill briefly. NOTE: *The lobster salad may be prepared up to 3 hours ahead of time.*

Lightly brush the crustless parts of the rolls with butter. (If you're using a solid roll, cut a U-shaped section out of the roll so the lobster has a place to sit.) Toast the rolls under the broiler or on top of a griddle over medium heat. Don't overdo it; we're just looking for a light toast to keep the bread from getting soggy.

Fill the toasted roll with lobster and enjoy.

Serves 2

West Coast Meets East Coast Stuffed Lobster

Finally, a version of Clash of the Titans *that doesn't suck the life out of the room.* You don't have to use Dungeness crabmeat, but if it's available I highly recommend the combination. Besides tasting great, it's an excellent way to show off all that new knowledge you've gleaned by reading this book.*

2 cups salted water
2 live lobsters, 1¼ to 1½ pounds each
4 tablespoons unsalted butter
¼ cup onion, diced
2 tablespoons red bell peppers, finely chopped
2 tablespoons green bell peppers, finely chopped
½ pound cooked Dungeness (or other) crabmeat
1 cup butter cracker crumbs (yes, Ritz crackers)
1 tablespoon flat-leaf parsley, chopped
1 tablespoon creamy horseradish
1 tablespoon lemon juice
Lemon wedges

Slide the lobsters into the freezer for 10 to 15 minutes to calm them down prior to cooking.

Add the liquid to a stockpot large enough to comfortably hold the lobsters. Bring the water to a rolling boil over high heat.

Remove the lobsters from cold storage, rinse them off, and carefully place them, headfirst, in the pot. Cover the pot (tight) and steam for 4 to 5 minutes, by which time they should be bright red and partially cooked through. Carefully remove both (very hot) lobsters from the pot, and transfer them to a large bowl filled with ice water to halt the cooking. When cool, drain well.

Preheat the oven to 400° F. Place one lobster, belly up, on a large cutting board, and then split it from head to tail with a large chef's knife. Do *not* cut all the way through the back of the shell. Unfold the lobster like a book (the part you didn't cut is now your hinge). Remove all the non-meat and discard. NOTE: *If you want to use the tomalley and roe (if any), remove and set them aside. Remove the black vein in the tail (if visible).*

Melt the butter in a large sauté pan over medium heat. Add the onions and peppers (both colors), and cook for 2 to 3 minutes, until softened (the onions should be just translucent). Add the crabmeat, stir to combine, and then remove it from the heat. Add the cracker crumbs, parsley, horseradish, and lemon juice, and toss until most of the liquid has been absorbed. NOTE: *If you saved the tomalley or roe, add it now and stir to combine.*

Place the lobsters on a baking sheet and fill the open cavity with stuffing. Top the tails with a little stuffing, as well. Bake them for 8 to 10 minutes, then switch on the broiler and toast the topping until golden brown and crispy, 1 to 2 minutes.

Crack the claws, transfer all to serving plates, garnish with lemon wedges, and serve immediately.

NOTE: *Keep a few paper towels handy; chopping lobsters is messy.*

Serves 2

*You know, Harry Hamlin, Burgess Meredith, and bunch of crazy old Greek Myths? Come on, I'm not that big of a geek…am I?

Chapter 9
Catfish
Born-Again Bottom-Feeder

Once upon a time, wild chickens roamed the earth. And cows, lots of seriously free-range cows. Pigs? Must have been a few. Sheep? Absolutely. And catfish? Hmmm… No, we're not there yet. Wild catfish are plentiful, as any angler will tell you, but down on the farm there are probably more cats in the pond than the barn. Old MacDonald may not have had any fish on his farm, but there's little doubt his grandkids will. With a splish-splash here, and a splish-splash there, catfish have gone from a muddy-tasting Southern tradition to a high-quality seafood product available fresh, year-round, at every seafood counter in the country. And why not? Farm-raised cats taste better than wild, thanks to being raised in cleaner water and fed grain-based feed. These fish even have some table manners, having been trained to dine at the surface, rather than the bottom. Of course, if you subscribe to the theory that a little mud makes the meal, by all means grab a rod and reel, 'cause unless you caught it yourself, that cat came from a farm.

VITAL STATS

FIRST NAME: Channel catfish

Sci. name: *Ictalurus punctatus*

SIZE: 1-3 lbs farmed, can grow to 50 lbs in the wild

LIFESPAN: 1.5-3 years farmed, up to 20 years in the wild

RANGE: Central, Southern U.S., farmed and wild

HARVEST: 600 million lbs farmed annually, U.S.

The first catfish farms were primarily used to stock local lakes and rivers, but by the 1960s a few enterprising farmers were selling their "catch" to local markets with an eye on wider distribution. Fish farming flourished in the 1970s, after soybean farmers discovered that catfish was a much more dependable crop. Taking a cue from the poultry industry, cat farmers used streamlined growing techniques and highly mechanized processing facilities to turn a few million pounds into a few hundred million by the 1980s. Today, farm-raised catfish is the fifth most popular seafood in the United States, behind only shrimp, canned tuna, salmon, and fish sticks (pollock).

And on this farm he had some...fish

Certainly, much of the industry's success can be traced to its transformation of a bottom feeder with a bad reputation into a family favorite, but let's give the fish some credit. Channel catfish are extremely well suited to life on the farm. First and foremost, they don't require as much feed as other protein sources. Two pounds of catfish food will get you one pound of catfish, which is a little better than chicken, twice as good as pork, and almost four times as efficient as beef. The feed also happens to be largely grain-based, meaning it doesn't require other fish products to keep the cats happy.

Channel catfish are also fast growers and disease resistant, which allows them to live in relatively crowded ponds without getting sick. Since most don't mature until after reaching market size, it's easy to keep pond populations in check. And if a few fish escape into the wild, no sweat; even the environmentalists agree domesticated cats (the nonfurry kind) pose little threat to the native species thanks to eco-friendly farming practices.

The day may come when wild catfish are as hard to imagine as a flock of chickens pecking its way across the countryside. Before we forget, perhaps a look at the catfish in its natural habitat is in order.

In the Water
Wild Cats

Worldwide, there are more than 2,000 species of freshwater and marine catfish, averaging in size from a few pounds to over 500. In the United States, blues and flatheads may exceed a hundred pounds, but it's the smaller channel catfish that ends up on most dinner plates. Channel cats can be found in freshwater rivers, streams, lakes, and ponds between the Rockies and Appalachians, some as far north as the Great Lakes, although most call Southern waters home. Drab olive green or brown is about as colorful as a catfish gets.

Farming First?

Mississippi, Arkansas, and Alabama all claim to be the home of the first catfish farm in America. Who's right? Oh, sure, toss the writer in the middle of a Southern feud. No thanks.

PR Machine

It's unlikely catfish would be as popular as it is today without the help of The Catfish Institute, an association of farmers, processors, and feed manufacturers, who got together to champion their favorite finfish. Since the inception of the institute in 1986, catfish consumption has doubled in the United States.

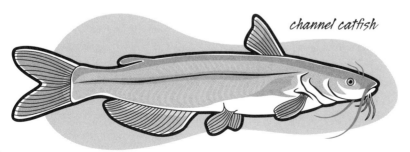

channel catfish

a deeply forked tale is distinctive of the channel cat

Giant Decline

Giant catfish weighing hundreds of pounds once roamed the Mississippi and Missouri rivers, but decades of excessive fishing and destruction of habitat (usually to improve navigation) have chased away most of the big cats.

Whiskers

Channel catfish are equipped with 4 dorsal and 4 ventral whiskers, technically known as "barbels." In addition to tasting their surroundings, barbels heighten the cat's sense of touch and smell.

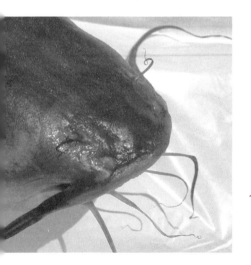

Taste sensation

Channel cats don't have scales, but they do have something else covering every inch of their body: taste buds. More than 25,000 buds, with concentrations on their whiskers and gill arches, allow the cat to track down lunch by taste. Small fish and mollusks top the menu, although cats are not adverse to a salad now and then. Young channels may dart to the surface to catch insects, but as they grow older, most prefer the relative calm of the sedentary lifestyle.

Nesting behavior

Cats are "cavity spawners," which means they'll only mate in dark, secluded spaces. In preparation for the big event, males build a nest, usually in a hole along the riverbank, although hollowed out logs and gravelly depressions will do in a pinch. After the female lays her eggs, it's the male's job to see that they hatch. This means fanning the eggs with his fins to aerate them and keep the nest free from waste buildup. After hatching, the male will defend the nest, usually until the last fry has gone off on its own.

(See, ladies, not all men are jerks…some of them are fish.)

On the Farm
Catchin' Fish on the Farm

If you happen to live in Mississippi, there's a good chance you already know something about catfish farming. Nearly 70 percent of the domestic harvest comes from ponds built in the Mississippi Delta, where abundant groundwater and acre after acre of flat, clay-rich soil provide the perfect landscape for fish farming. Toss in farms in Arkansas, Alabama, and Louisiana, and you've got 95 percent of the annual supply. That's well over 500 million pounds, or roughly 300 million catfish.

I know what you're thinking: *Now, that the kids are grown, we hardly ever use the pool. Maybe I could raise a few cats. How hard could it be?* Let's find out.

So you want to be a catfish farmer

The first thing you're going to need is a breeding pair (or two), ideally 4- to 6-year-old fish weighing in at 4 to 8 pounds. The top cats stay busy for 12 years, producing 3-4,000 eggs per pound of body weight each time they spawn, although production tends to drop off with age. To make your fish feel at home, it's best to build a special spawning container that

QUICK QUESTION

Is there a wild catfishery? Prior to the rise of the domesticated cat, a modest channel catfish fishery existed along the Mississippi and its tributaries. Ultimately, concerns of water quality and the popularity of farmed fish reduced the commercial catch to little more than a local novelty. Recreational catfishing remains very popular.

mimics the nesting behavior of wild catfish. After 2 to 3 days, take a peek. Are we egg-static? Next stop: the hatchery.

Catfish eggs require 5 to 8 days of incubation before hatching. Baby catfish are called "sac fry" due to the small yolk sac they carry around with them, which conveniently provides nourishment for the first 3 to 5 days of life. Once it is depleted, the fish naturally swim to the surface in search of food, and boy, are they hungry. Some demand upward of 12 feedings a day! Ah, the joys of parenthood.

After a few days, it's time to transfer the fry to a nursery pond, where they'll stay until they grow to fingerling size (3 to 8 inches). Remember, it's up to you to train the young fry to eat only floating feed. No bottom-feeders in this family.

In five to ten months, the catfish will be large enough to move out of the house and into a grow-out pond. Ideally, we're talking 10 to 20 acres of clay-based soil, surrounded by levees, and filled with 4 to 6 feet of fresh well water. Some farmers prefer smaller, deeper ponds, which use less water overall, but either way you'll need an alluvial aquifer to keep it aerated. (You know, so they can breathe.)

Finally, 18 to 24 months after playing catfish matchmaker, you've got a pond full of 1- to 2-pound cats. Time to harvest. Typically, weighted seines are pulled though the water by tractors on shore, while being directed by boats on the water. Large loading baskets collect the fish and transfer them to aerated tank trucks, which then deliver the fish to their final destination. Your work is done.

But the fish has one more stop: the processor. In 30 minutes or less, live catfish are stunned by an electrical current, cleaned by hand, sliced, and put on ice. A few lucky fish make it out unscathed, only to be shipped to markets that sell live catfish.

Dogfight

Never pick a fight with a catfish, or this case, his lawyer. Back in 1994, a longstanding trade embargo was lifted against Vietnam, allowing its products to be imported into the United States. One of

Fish Food

Catfish are fed puffed, high-protein food pellets made from a combination of soybeans, corn, wheat, rice, and various vitamins and minerals. No hormones are added. Larger farms use mechanical feeders to distribute the feed daily by blowing it onto the surface of the water.

Room to Roam?

Pond density varies from farm to farm, with some as low as 500 fish per acre, others as high as 10,000.

Taste Testing

Occasionally, farm-raised catfish develop off flavors due to naturally occurring bacteria or algae in the ponds. They're harmless, but not particularly appetizing. To ensure no funky fish make it to market, most farmers and processors employ catfish taste testers that check the quality of fish at ponds and processing plants.

QUICK QUESTION

How safe is farm-raised catfish?   Very. Domestic farm-raised catfish is subject to the Hazard Analysis and Critical Control Point Program, a regulatory system enacted to prevent food safety problems, and is inspected by the U.S. Department of Commerce at processing plants before being certified by The Catfish Institute.

those products was *basa* (*Pangasius bocourti*), a species of catfish farmed throughout Southeast Asia. In a just few years, Vietnamese imports managed to snag more than 20 percent of the domestic frozen catfish market. Guess who called his local congressman?

First to go was the name. Most basa was marketed domestically as catfish. A 2002 amendment to the Federal Food, Drug, and Cosmetic Act made it illegal in the United States to label any fish other than those within the family *Ictaluridae* as catfish, whether alone or as part of a longer name.

The big hit came in the form of an antidumping campaign, which claimed that unrealistically priced Vietnamese imports were driving down the price of domestic fish. The U.S. International Trade Commission sided with the local cats, slapping tariffs of up to 64 percent on Vietnamese catfish.

Were the Vietnamese dumping? Probably not. Is basa a catfish? Scientifically, yes. Did the wholesale price of catfish go up after the catfish lobby got what it wanted? Nope. Damn (mostly) free market economy.

At the Market
Smells Like...Chicken?

Fresh catfish smells, more or less, like raw chicken. No, really, it does. It's the feed. Think about it: A farm-raised cat has more in common with grain-fed, farm-raised chicken than it does with tuna or swordfish. If it smells like the ocean (or worse), it's either not a catfish, or it's spent a little too much time hanging around the other fish (neither of which is particularly desirable).

Thanks to speedy processing, most fish spend very little time out of the water before heading to the market. That means you should settle for nothing less than impeccably fresh catfish. The flesh should be slightly translucent white to off-white with subtle pink highlights. If it's yellow, skip it. Catfish flesh should be moist and springy to the touch, not dry

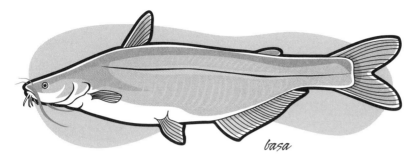

basa

Basa and Switch

On the whole, BASA is not a bad fish; in fact, it's pretty good eatin' if given the chance. It's not as firm as catfish, but does have a mild flavor and delicate texture. Unfortunately, much of what is imported into the United States is basa's cheaper, faster-growing cousin, SWAI (P. hypophthalmus). Swai, also known as "tra" or "China Sole," has a grainy texture after cooking that doesn't come close to matching farm-raised catfish.

and spongy. For whole fish, the eyes are the most important tell. Look for clear, protruding peepers, as well as a fresh scent and blemish-free exterior.

The product line

Most markets carry fillets, but closer to catfish country one can expect to find whole fish, steaks, fillets, and strips (usually sold as "nuggets"). Some markets carry live catfish, which they'll happily kill and clean for you, usually for free. Skinning whole fish may cost extra.

The frozen product line cover the same bases as the fresh—save for the live fish. Look for vacuum-packed IQF (individually quick frozen) items free of air pockets or excessive ice. There are also numerous "value-added" products, such as breaded nuggets and marinated fillets, which I know you have no interest in whatsoever.

In the Kitchen
Pump Up the Volume

The South has a long tradition of cooking catfish with all sorts of flavors, from the subtle (cornmeal) to the overpowering (Cajun spiced cornmeal). Some of the more potent flavors were most likely intended to cover up the muddiness of wild catfish. While that's no longer a problem with farmed cats, nobody said you had to put the loud flavors back in the box. Catfish will happily play with almost any flavor, and to whatever volume you crank it up.

Skin and bones

Catfish have large, easy to find bones, which can be removed without too much trouble. Even better, fillets and nuggets are usually bone-free, while steaks have but one.

Removing the skin is a bit tougher. Drop the knife and grab a pair of pliers—the only tool for the job. For steaks, leaving the skin on will

Skin It

Though you'll probably never see a whole catfish in your kitchen, here's a simple method for getting it ready for the frying pan should you have the need.

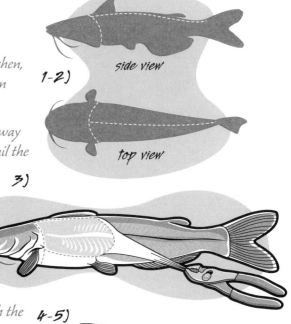

side view

1-2)

top view

3)

(1) Grip the head firmly and slice through the skin all the way around. Do not remove the head. (Fishermen sometimes nail the head to a piece of wood. Hey, whatever works, right?) (2) Make a slice along the back from the head to the tail. (3) Using a pair of pliers, grip the skin and pull it free on one side. Repeat on the other side. (4) Trim off the fins and tail. Watch out for the spines on the dorsal and pectoral fins. (5) Snap the neck (backbone) and you should be able to pull the head and viscera away from the body. Wash the body thoroughly under cold running water. (6) If you've got a small fish (less than 10 inches), go ahead and cook it as is. To fillet a larger fish, slide a thin knife beneath the fillet and on top of the spine. (7) Run the knife along the rib cage and spine all the way to the tail to remove the fillet. Repeat on the other side.

4-5)

help the fish hold its shape during cooking. Once cooked, the skin will peel away easily. For skin-on fillets, score the skin to keep the fish from curling.

Cornmeal cuisine

Lightly seasoned, catfish has a mild, sweet flavor that fries up nicely inside a cornmeal crust. Add some red beans and rice, a slice of cornbread, and half a dozen hush puppies and you've got yourself a sweet Dixieland dinner. Do not, under any circumstances, fry catfish using a flour-based fish-and-chips batter. Besides being a bit too moist, catfish (dead or alive) can smell Yankee cooking a mile away. It's cornmeal or no meal.

But this is the perfect fish to play dress up, so don't be afraid to try on a few other flavors (yes, even non-Southern favorites). Catfish is less flaky than most white meat fish, and has a tendency to cook quickly. Once the fish firms up and turns opaque (ideally, just before), get it off the heat. If your cat is wearing a coat, make a break in the thickest part to check whether the center is white all the way through. This is now your piece…or Blind Willie's. (Oh, like he's going to complain.)

Albino Cats

Though rare in the wild, some farmers are raising strains of peach-colored "albino" catfish.

HOW TO STORE: Catfish

FRESH: If you've brought home a pound or two of boneless catfish fillets, toss them in the fridge until you're ready to cook. A bed of ice is nice, especially if you're not planning on cooking them until tomorrow or the next day, just be sure the fish is safely sealed inside an airtight container of some sort.

FROZEN: If the big catfish cook-off isn't until next week, this fish is better sealed in plastic wrap and foil and stored in the freezer. Frozen fillets are best used within 2 to 3 months, although fish quick-frozen at the processor may last twice as long.

Catfish Hunter?

Baseball's legendary Jim "Catfish" Hunter got his nickname from Oakland A's owner Charlie Finley, who made up a story about Hunter stalking catfish in North Carolina, presumably with his fastball.

Fish in black

Here's my theory: the first "blackened" fish was done not by accident, as so many culinary comedians suggest, but by design as a way to prove some folks will eat anything as long as it's served at a fancy restaurant. *"Think they'll eat it if I burn the #!@$ out of it? Let's find out!"*

The rub, of course, is that burning a piece of fish beyond all recognition still tastes pretty good, especially if the rub happens to be a powerful set of spices. Traditionally, that means the likes of paprika, onion powder, thyme, garlic powder, oregano, chili powder, cayenne, salt, and black, red, and white pepper. When searing, I generally shoot for excessively brown, as opposed to black, but to each his own. For a less intense flavor, season only one side with the rub. Once blackened, flip it onto a separate, nonstick pan over medium heat to finish.

A few things to remember when blackening: (*a*) Use a cast-iron skillet. The key is the heat, and that nice, nonstick pan is not going to get there (and if it does, you're probably ruining it). (*b*) Blackened means burnt (more or less), so if you're not prepared to sear until it hurts to watch, don't do it. (*c*) Time to take down the No Smoking sign, turn up the fan, and crack a window. Don't forget to put the battery back in the smoke alarm when you're done.

QUICK QUESTION

What is catfish noodling? Simply put, catfish "noodling" is the art of fishing with your hands. Some folks call it "grabblin," others call it crazy. Here's how it's done: Stick a hand in a catfish nest and wiggle your fingers around. When the catfish chomps on your hand, grab on tight, and bring him up. If it turns out you stuck your hand in a snapping turtles den by mistake, call a paramedic.

NUTRITIONAL INFO

Per 3.5 oz/100 grams (raw)

Channel Catfish

Calories	135
Calories from fat	68
Total fat	7.6 g
Saturated fat	1.8 g
Cholesterol	47 mg
Sodium	53 mg
Protein	15.5 g
Omega-3	0.6 g
Mercury	0.05 ppm

Catfish Recipes

Outside the South, catfish rarely gets the respect it deserves. I know, you all have your local favorites, but give this cat a try. It's cheap, fresh, more flavorful than you've been lead to believe, and receptive to your more creative culinary whims. What could be better?

Pan-Fried Catfish

This is as simple as it gets, but it works. The buttermilk soak is traditional, but not really necessary. It was originally used to remove the muddy flavor of wild catfish, which isn't found in most farmed fish. I use it because I like buttermilk. Mmmm…buttermilk.

4 large skinless catfish fillets (6 to 8 ounces each)
Freshly ground black pepper
1½ cups buttermilk
1 cup yellow cornmeal
1 teaspoon paprika
1 teaspoon onion powder
¼ teaspoon cayenne
3 tablespoons peanut oil

Season the fillets with pepper and place them in a shallow bowl. Add the buttermilk and allow them to soak for 15 minutes.

Combine the cornmeal, paprika, onion powder, and cayenne in a separate shallow bowl. One at a time, dredge the moist fillets through the mixture and set them aside.

Completely cover a large sauté pan with oil and heat it over high until the oil sizzles at the drop of a hat (or a tiny piece of fish). Add the fillets and cook, 3 to 4 minutes, until golden. Flip and cook an additional 2 to 3 minutes. Serve immediately.

Serves 4

Fried Catfish Nuggets
with Hush Puppies

Dusted with cornmeal and fried in oil—this is Southern fast food at its finest. NOTE: I know it says "nuggets," but remember, in the catfish trade that means strips. Trim accordingly.

1½ quarts (6 cups) peanut (or other vegetable) oil
1 egg
1 cup milk
2 tablespoons all-purpose flour
Freshly ground black pepper
½ teaspoon ground red pepper flakes
2 cups yellow cornmeal

2 pounds skinless catfish fillets
Hush puppies (see recipe)

Heat the oil in a heavy 4-quart pot to 370° F. Preheat the oven to 200° F.

Combine the egg, milk, and flour in a shallow bowl and whisk them together until smooth. Combine the cornmeal and red pepper flakes in a separate bowl and set aside.

Cut the catfish fillets into uniform strips about 3 to 4 inches long. (Cut at an angle, they'll hold together better.) Season the fish with pepper and then dip each strip in the milk mixture. Next dredge each strip in cornmeal and shake off the excess. Don't do all the fish at once; work in batches that suit the size of your fry setup. (That means 2 to 4 batches in most cases.)

After dredging the fillets, carefully lower them into the oil using a fry basket or spider tool. Fry for 1½ to 2 minutes, then turn and fry them 1 to 2 minutes more, until golden. Transfer the finished pieces to a wire rack set over a baking sheet in the oven. Make sure the oil is at least 360° F before adding the next batch.

Serve the nuggets with hush puppies and tartar sauce (*see page 60*), Spicy Aioli (*see page 47*), or other hot sauce.

Serves 4

Hush Puppies

I love hush puppies! Deep fried cornbread—what could be better?

1½ quarts (6 cups) peanut (or other vegetable) oil
1½ cups yellow cornmeal
½ cup all-purpose flour
1 teaspoon baking powder
1 teaspoon kosher salt
½ teaspoon freshly ground black pepper
¼ cup red onions, finely diced
¼ cup red bell peppers, finely diced
2 large eggs, lightly beaten
½ cup buttermilk

Heat the oil in a heavy 4-quart pot to 370° F.

Combine the cornmeal, flour, baking powder, salt, black pepper, onion, and pepper in a large mixing bowl. Add the eggs and buttermilk and stir until thoroughly incorporated. *NOTE: If the batter seems overly dry, try adding water, 1 tablespoon at a time, to moisten it up. Do not add more than ¼ cup total.*

Carefully drop tablespoon-sized balls of batter into the oil and fry for 2 to 3 minutes, until golden brown. Stir occasionally to ensure even heating. *NOTE: Don't overcrowd the oil; cook 4 to 6 puppies per batch.*

Drain the hush puppies briefly on a rack over paper towels and serve them with catfish.

Blackened Catfish

Step 1: Turn off the smoke detector. Step 2: Open a window. Step 3: Burn, baby, burn. I highly advise using a cast-iron skillet for this recipe, as the high heat will mess with your fancy nonstick pan something awful. Also, don't use smaller fillets, which will overcook before they truly blacken.

2 tablespoons paprika
1 tablespoon garlic powder
1½ teaspoons dried thyme, crushed
1½ teaspoons dried oregano, crushed
1½ teaspoons freshly ground black pepper
½ teaspoon cayenne
½ teaspoon onion powder
¼ teaspoon kosher salt
2 large skinless catfish fillets (6 to 8 ounces each)
3 tablespoons butter, melted

Place a cast-iron pan in the oven and turn the heat up to 500° F.

Combine all the herbs and spices in a shallow bowl and mix thoroughly.

Once the oven hits the mark, transfer the *very hot* pan to a burner set on high. Wait 5 more minutes before adding the fish.

Coat the catfish with butter, both sides, and then roll the fillets in the blackening spices, getting as much as possible to stick to the fish. Turn the fan on high and gently set the fillets in the pan. You will now see some smoke. Don't panic. Cook the fillets for 3 minutes, flip them, and cook for another 3 to 4 minutes until the fish is cooked through. Serve immediately.

Serves 2

NOTE: *For less of a burn, sear the fillets on each side for 1 minute, and then transfer them to an oven preheated to 400° F. Cook them for 6 to 8 minutes, or until cooked through.*

Catfish Rolls

Usually a recipe like this is called "stuffed," but I think that's a little misleading. The fillets aren't stuffed with anything, but rather rolled around said stuff. NOTE: *If you're starting with fillets more than ½ inch thick, slice them in half horizontally. They'll roll more easily and won't be softball-sized when done.*

3 tablespoons unsalted butter
½ cup onion, diced
¼ cup red bell pepper, diced
1 pound cooked pink ("salad") shrimp

1½ cups fresh bread crumbs
Zest from 1 lemon
1 tablespoon fresh dill, chopped
Kosher salt and freshly ground black pepper
8 skinless catfish fillets, (6 to 8 ounces each)
Olive oil
Mom's Beurre Blanc Sauce

Preheat the oven to 350° F. Coat your largest casserole dish (or 2 smaller baking dishes) with nonstick cooking spray.

Melt the butter in a large sauté pan over medium heat. Add the onion and pepper and cook until softened, 3 to 4 minutes. Remove the mixture from the heat and add the shrimp, bread-crumbs, lemon zest, and dill. Season all with salt and pepper and stir to combine.

Season the fillets with salt and pepper, both sides. Place an even amount of the shrimp mixture on top of each fillet. Spread the mixture from end to end and then carefully roll up the fillets and place them, seam side down, in the casserole dish.

Drizzle the rolls with olive oil and bake them in the oven for 25 to 30 minutes, or until the fillets flake easily. Remove them from the oven and allow them to rest for 5 minutes.

Plate the individual rolls or serve them right out of the pan topped with Mom's Beurre Blanc Sauce.

Serves 8

Mom's Beurre Blanc Sauce

My mom is not a big fan of catfish, so she demanded I add this sauce to fancy things up a bit. Too French? Relax, it's mostly butter. By the way, this sauce goes well with almost any light, flaky white fish. Thanks, Mom.

¾ cup water
6 tablespoons white wine vinegar
¼ cup shallots, finely chopped
2 tablespoons whipping cream
1¼ sticks chilled unsalted butter, cut into tablespoons
¼ teaspoon white pepper
Kosher salt
3 tablespoons fresh chives, chopped

Add the water, vinegar, and shallots to a saucepan set over medium heat. Simmer until the mixture is reduced to about ¼ cup, 10 to 15 minutes. Add the whipping cream and turn the heat down to low. Add the butter, one tablespoon at a time. After each tablespoon melts, add the next one. Stir often.

Stir in the chives and season with white pepper and a pinch of salt. Taste the sauce—if it seems too acidic, add more butter.

Chapter 10
Oysters
Primitive Culture

"He was a bold man that first eat an oyster."
—Jonathan Swift

If I had to wager, I'd say Swift's bold man lived in a cave. Who else but a connoisseur of live crickets and raw dinosaur eggs would even consider an oyster edible in the first place? Compared to most prey, an oyster must have been easy pickings—no biting, no struggle— just one big, tasty gulp (after he got the damn thing open). No doubt, the forest fire buffet eventually introduced Joe Caveman to the wonders of barbecue, but one dish kept its cool: the oyster. Joe One-Bedroom Apartment may have given up on crickets and caves, but he hasn't been able to shake his oyster jones. Drawn from the foam, cracked open, and slurped straight from the shell, an oyster is more than food; it's a link to our prehistoric past. Try as we might, we can't escape our primal instincts any more than we can avoid dressing them up with fancy prose and anthropological hoo-ha. It's an oyster. You eat it. It's good.

VITAL STATS

FIRST NAME: Oyster (Eastern, Pacific, European, Kumamoto, Olympia)

SCI. NAME: *Crassostrea* and *Ostrea* spp.

SIZE: 2.5-5 in across the shell, Pacifics up to 10 in, Olympias as small as 1 in

LIFESPAN: Most 2-5 years when harvested, may live up to 50 years

RANGE: North American coastal waters, primarily Louisiana and Washington

HARVEST: About 35 million lbs (of meat) annually, U.S.

Americans have always been passionate about oysters, so much so that we've nearly loved them to death on several occasions. In New England, oysters were once so abundant ships had to be weary of their presence so as not to run afoul of their beds. Much like the lobster, oysters were seen primarily as a poor man's food, albeit a popular one. It was only after northern beds ran dry in the early 1800s that the bivalve's stock began to climb the social ladder. Southern oysters soon found their way north, as both food and seed to replenish depleted stocks. American oyster culture was born.

Out west, the native oyster played out nearly as quickly as the gold mines, thanks to a population that ate but failed to cultivate. Attempts to transplant East Coast oysters proved fruitless, but an import from Japan (*Crassostrea gigas*) took to the cold Pacific waters eagerly, soon becoming the dominant species up and down the coast.

The name game

The modern oyster is a marvel of careful cultivation and clever marketing. By branding their bivalves with local names growers have created a marketplace not unlike that of the wine industry. There are now hundreds of "varieties," each one with its own distinct flavor identity. Salty or sweet, fruity or metallic, firm or tender—an oyster is a combination of tastes and textures worthy of savoring on the tongue long after the last slurp has passed. It's an acquired taste for some, but one definitely worth picking up.

What makes an oyster taste like an oyster? Much like grapes, oysters reflect the environment in which they grow, meaning no two beds produce oysters with the same characteristics, even those of the same species. Water temperature, salinity, mineral and algae content, current, tidal flow, and method of harvest all have an effect.

Fortunately, choosing an oyster is not usually the endless label-reading horror that picking a bottle of wine can be. A little knowledge goes a long way, but a trip to the local oyster bar will take you even farther.

lunar landscape or lunch?

In the Water
Social Filters

Oysters are surprisingly social creatures, choosing to live in clusters, often stacked one on top of another like an underwater condo community. Waterwise, most do best in the relative salinity of a brackish bay or estuary where tidal ebb and flow provides a steady stream of nutrients.

Oysters are filter feeders, meaning they eat by extracting nutrients from the water. An adult oyster can filter upward of 50 gallons of saltwater a day during the summer months, making it a surprisingly efficient environmental cleaning machine. The huge oyster beds once found in Chesapeake Bay were capable of filtering the entire bay in less than four days. Through disease, habitat destruction, and overharvesting, it takes the current population about a year.

Hitchhikers

Tiny dime-sized pea crabs are sometimes found living happily inside live oysters, apparently with the consent of the bivalve. They're harmless.

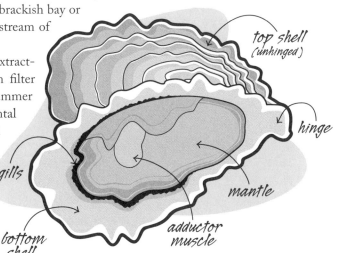

top shell (unhinged)

hinge

mantle

gills

adductor muscle

bottom shell

Oyster Bar

Pacific

A list of every oyster variety on the market today would be long and a little too close to free advertising for my tastes. An introduction to the five primary species seems a better place to start.

Originally a Japanese transplant known as the Miyagi, the hardy, fast-growing PACIFIC OYSTER (*Crassostrea gigas*) adapted quickly to the West Coast when it was introduced in the early twentieth century. Today, most cultured oysters in the United States are Pacific, most of them grown in the state of Washington. If given the chance, the craggy shell of a Pacific can reach ten inches, although most are harvested while the oyster is young and tender (3 to 6 inches). FLAVOR: Creamy and mild in flavor, often described as having a fruity or even melonlike aftertaste.

Eastern

The EASTERN OYSTER (*C. virginica*, a.k.a. the "Atlantic" or "American") is harvested from Maine to the Gulf of Mexico, primarily from wild beds. Easterns make up the largest part of the U.S. oyster market, although most are shucked and sold prepacked rather than served on the half shell. Look for a thick, deeply cupped, elongated shell usually 2.5 to 5 inches across. FLAVOR: Crisp and briny with a firm, meaty texture. Some tasters detect a slight, mineral aftertaste. Northern varieties tend to be firmer and are generally considered better for raw applications.

The round, flat EUROPEAN OYSTER (*Ostrea edulis*) is often marketed as the Belon after the most famous of its French varieties, although technically only those oysters grown in the Belon River estuary of Brittany should use the name. An easier way to identify a European is by its distinct flavor, one that is rarely appreciated by oyster novices (or some experts). FLAVOR: Complex and briny, with a strong metallic finish (some compare it to sucking on a penny).

European

If you're new to the half-shell game, this is the oyster for you. First cultivated in Japan, the KUMAMOTO (*C. sikamea*) was imported into the United States in the 1940s. Initially unpopular due to its slow growth, it has become a raw bar favorite in recent years. The deep cup of the Kumamoto holds a flavorful morsel similar to that of its Pacific cousin, but in a smaller, more accessible package (2 to 3 inches). FLAVOR: Sweet, buttery and fresh. The smaller size and less complex flavor make this a very popular oyster with beginners.

Kumamoto

If you can find it, the OLYMPIA OYSTER (*O. lurida*) is a taste of history. This tiny oyster once ruled the West Coast, but overharvesting and environmental damage wiped out the native stocks. Today, the "Oly" is cultivated near its namesake in Puget Sound and in very limited numbers because its growing cycle requires at least 5 years to produce an oyster barely large than a quarter. FLAVOR: Similar to the European, the Olympia oyster has a sweet, slightly coppery flavor—unique, but not for everybody.

Olympia

QUICK QUESTION

Are oysters an aphrodisiac? Are oysters the Viagra of the sea? Not really, although they do contain a lot of zinc, which supports the production of testosterone, the male hormone that makes men manlier. Oysters also have high levels of phosphorus and iodine, both of which may help increase stamina. Hey, anything helps, right?

Oysters in love

Warm water turns an oyster's thoughts to love, although exactly what he/she is thinking is anyone's guess. Oysters of the genus *Ostrea* (Europeans and Olympias) start out as males, change into females after spawning, and then continue to swap sexes after each successive reproductive cycle, apparently unable to make up their minds. *Crassostrea* oysters (Easterns, Pacifics, and Kumamotos) begin life as males, but after spawning, most switch sides and stay that way…usually.

Once the water temperature hits the magic number (around 68°F/20°C), males release hundreds of millions of sperm into the water, which either drift in the current until bumping into a free-floating egg (*Crassostrea*) or settle into the branchial chamber of a female (*Ostrea*) for an extra week or two of mothering. In warmer climates, it's possible for a female *Ostrea* to switch sexes and fertilize her…him…itself.

After three to four weeks of bouncing around the current, the salt-grain-sized larvae head to the ocean floor in search of a nice rock, shell, or other hard, relatively clean surface on which to settle. With a little dab of bio-cement, they become permanent fixtures, betting their futures on the menu offered by the local current. What most oysters fail to realize is their choice of homes may have already put them on a different menu.

Original Oyster Heads

The indigenous peoples of North America left million-count mounds of oyster shells on both coasts dating back thousands of years.

On the Beds and Farm
The Oystermen

The line between cultivation and wild harvest has blurred over the years, with many oystermen now tending to wild stock in order to improve its chances for survival, while farmers do everything they can to replicate traditional oyster beds and harvest methods. The collection of wild spat (oyster larvae) for reseeding natural beds has been an integral part of oyster farming for centuries. "Cultching," as it's known in the trade, gives the baby oysters a place to land where they can be raised until large enough to move to grow-out beds. When there's not enough spat to go around, oystermen turn to hatcheries to make up the slack.

Original Farmers

The Romans were the first to seriously cultivate the oyster, although some speculate the Chinese may have beaten them to it.

Most oysters are raised on shallow beds or suspended in the water in some form of off-bottom culture. Seed that is spread on the bottom grows up more or less the same as it would in the wild, albeit under the watchful eye of the oystermen. Off-bottom culture may include the use of rafts, floating lantern nets, and fences that look very much like a vineyard when the tide goes out. Better food circulation means suspended oysters will grow faster and fatter than their bottom-dwelling brethren. Unfortunately, they also develop weaker shells, which is why most are moved to bottom trays for a year or two to toughen up.

Bye-bye brine

When it comes time to get the oysters out of the water, most oystermen employ methods that have been around for hundreds of years. Long metal tongs and rakes are used to pluck clusters from the bottom, although in areas where oysters are exposed by low tide, most are handpicked. Small dredges may be used in deeper waters.

After harvesting, oysters are separated, cleaned, and graded. Some farms place their oysters in wet storage to remove sand and grit and allow for bacteria testing. Those that make the trip to the processor are generally shucked by hand, sorted, and packaged in their own juices. The shells are often returned to beds to provide homes for future generations of wild oysters.

At the Market
Take the Tour

While the best oyster bars might have a dozen or more varieties to choose from, even the better fish markets rarely carry more than two or three live options. What's an oyster junkie to do? Buy direct. Many growers and wholesalers now sell their oysters online, making it possible to sample oysters from either coast fresh from the brine in 24 to 48 hours. Prefer a face-to-face transaction? Check out your local farmer's market, where oysters have become a hot item in recent years. The best way to learn about oysters (besides eating them) is to talk to someone who deals with bivalves on a daily basis. For the truly seduced, it's worth making the trek to an oyster farm, many of which offer tours and tastings.

It's worth noting that many small oyster farms don't sell directly to the consumer, but rather to larger dealers who market them under regional names. In some cases, this means one "brand" may contain oysters from several distinct locales. If you're really into the idea of taste-testing oysters, it's worth researching the various brands and locations to know exactly what you're buying.

Location, location...

In choosing a suitable site for his farm, an oysterman must consider: the makeup of bottom, water depth, tidal action, whether it's sheltered from wind and waves, the potential for ice formation, local currents, temperature cycles, and external climate.

oyster rakes and tongs

Nutrition

Oysters are low in both calories and fat, and an excellent source of protein and heart healthy omega-3 fatty acids. They're also rich in vitamins A, B$_{12}$, C, and D, and contain generous helpings of calcium, copper, magnesium, phosphorus, potassium, iodine, iron, and zinc.

Good oyster, bad oyster

Oysters need to be kept cold, so if the market doesn't have theirs displayed on ice, take a pass. Buried in ice is equally offensive (melted ice = drowned oyster), as is storing sideways, which can result in a loss of liquid if the oyster opens up to take a look around. Bad smelling, broken, or overly barnacled shells should be avoided. And don't be afraid to ask an oyster how long it's been out of the water. It the oyster isn't talking (good, the shells should be closed), ask the fishmonger. Ten days or less is best.

Shucked oysters, usually packed in their own juices, come in a variety of sizes, both in terms of containers and oysters. Look for plump oysters in clear, not cloudy liquid, and be sure to check the pull date.

Summertime blues

Once upon a time, it was accepted wisdom that one should never eat a raw oyster during month that wasn't spelled with an R. Why? Back in the day, it had a lot to do with refrigeration, or the lack thereof, and a little to do with amorous oysters. Oysters spawn when the water warms up, becoming soft and gooey in the process. You can eat 'em, but…yuck. Fortunately, refrigeration isn't a problem anymore, and, thanks to science, neither is an oyster's love life (see "Triple Threat" sidebar).

There remains genuine concern surrounding a summertime bacterium called *Vibrio vulnificus,* which occurs naturally in a small percentage of warm-water oysters. While harmless to most eaters, it can be deadly to anyone with an impaired immune system. To play it safe, make sure those summer oysters are thoroughly barbecued before serving. For those who can't suffer the heat without a raw oyster, choose a West Coast variety. *V. vulnificus* doesn't grow in colder waters.

In the Kitchen
Eat It

If you intend to consume your oysters raw, I highly recommend doing so right now. Seriously, stop reading and go eat your oysters. I'll wait.

Done? Fresher is better, no? A live oyster can last a couple weeks out of the water, but why wait? It's not going to taste better tomorrow, especially on the half shell. Be impulsive, shop at the last minute, eat!

Shuck it

I believe it was Shakespeare who said, "Dude, the world's, like, totally my oyster, and I'm going to use this sword to pop its top!" Hmmm…maybe that was Jeff Spicoli. Either way, you're probably not going to need a

Safety First

The FDA's National Shellfish Sanitation Program monitors oysters from their growing waters, to processing plants, and on to markets.

Triple Threat

Perhaps not as revolutionary as sliced bread, the triploid oyster nonetheless deserves recognition as one of man's greatest achievements. By chemically shocking an egg to produce a third chromosome, an oyster can be rendered sexless and thus incapable of spawning. While all its buddies are losing their figures in the summer heat, a triploid remains plump and sweet.

Oyster Shucking

Raw oysters should be prepared at the last minute. No shucking three hours before your guests arrive. Any oysters accidentally mangled must be eaten immediately. (I don't make the rules, but I do enjoy them.)

(1) Grasp the oyster in your protected hand with the hinge toward you. For a slower, but safer method, set the oyster on a sturdy cutting board and hold in place with the protected hand. (2) Insert the knife at the hinge. (If the shell crumbles, try a different spot.) Using a side-to-side rocking motion, penetrate about ½ inch, and then pop the hinge. (3) Carefully slide the knife under the top shell, slicing through the adductor muscle. Remove top shell. Be sure to keep the oyster level so as not to lose the liquor. (4) Slide the knife under the oyster to cut through lower muscle. (For European-style oysters, leave the bottom muscle intact.) (5) Remove any bits of shell or mud. (Neither does much for the oyster's flavor or a fear of dentist's drills.) (6) Lastly, give it a smell. The nose is the last line of defense against a raw oyster gone bad, so use it!

1-2)

3)

4)

PULL ME
TO OPEN REMOVE TAB. SLURP TO EAT.
DO NOT EAT SHELL. DO NOT EAT PULL TAB.

Pull-tab Oysters

No, that's not a typo. A French aquaculturist has figured out a way to open an oyster like an old beer can. After anesthetizing the oyster, a stainless steel wire is looped around its adductor muscle and attached to a tab that sticks out the back end. When pulled, the wire slices through the muscle, opening the oyster. I'm not kidding.

sword, but an oyster knife helps. Look for a thick, medium-length blade (about 3 inches) with a slight upward bend at the tip to help the knife slip under the shell. Avoid thin blades, slick handles, and anything that costs more than $15. A screwdriver is not an option, nor is a can opener or a butter knife. If you're going to be shucking a lot of oysters, a thick, rubber-gripped glove is great for holding them still, but several layers of dishtowel do the job nearly as well.

If you need to open an oyster for something other than a raw application and a slight loss of flavor is not an issue, applying heat will do the trick. Steaming is a simple, no frills option, but you can also broil, bake, or even microwave the shells open. Just be careful; both the shells and the liquid inside will be hot.

Cooking oysters is evil

Never, ever apply heat to an oyster. Heat destroys the natural flavor, muting every environmental nuance that makes every individual oyster special. Would you bathe the *Mona Lisa* in fluorescent light? Play Mozart on a harmonica? Watch *The Matrix* in pan and scan instead of letterbox? Never!

To experience an oyster in all of its glory, it must be eaten raw on the half shell, preferably as cold as possible. Tradition dictates that raw oysters are served on a bed of ice, but if you're eating right away, you can skip the chips. If you've got guests, count on six oysters per person for a nice appetizer. Purists will tell you an oyster needs no adornment, but for the first-timer a squeeze of lemon or a dash of Tabasco helps the medicine go down.

Don't tell the boys down at the bar, but I like a light salsa fresca with overly salty oysters, especially if they're barbecued…oops.

Cooking oysters is divine

Okay, enough of that "cooking oysters is a sin" crap. Raw may be best, but a cooked oyster is nearly as tasty, especially when it's done right. Besides, this is what most folks do when they bring oysters home. Raw at the restaurant is fine, but at home a lot of us start worrying about bacteria and overproduced prime-time medical dramas. Fine. Cook 'em.

In their shells, oysters cook much like other bivalves—once open, they're done. Oysters on the grill (topped with that salsa I mentioned) are a knockout. On the half shell, oysters come with their own ovenproof platter, making them ideal for topping with numerous minced veggies, spices, cheeses, and other foodstuffs. Slide them under the broiler and in a few minutes you've got your own Oysters Rockefeller. Do keep an eye on them. Oysters cook very quickly, turning from plump and juicy to shriveled and tough in the space of about thirty seconds. The general rule of thumb: As soon as the mantle starts to curl, the oyster is done.

Oysters play well in soups and stews, especially when combined with their own liquor. Don't bother buying live oysters if you're going to be dropping them in a pot; fresh shucked oysters will do the job nicely.

Oh, my po' boy!

You might have a tough time convincing your food-phobic friends to try raw oysters, maybe even barbecued or broiled oysters, but toss 'em in a deep fryer and suddenly they're as irresistible as an open bag of potato chips. (The oysters, not your friends.) What's better than a bag of chips? A big sandwich, of course. Rolled in Cajun spices and cornmeal, nothing screams New Orleans like an oyster po' boy. Let's get to it!

NUTRITIONAL INFO

Per 3.5 oz/100 grams (raw)

Pacific Oyster

Calories	81
Calories from fat	20
Total fat	2.3 g
Saturated fat	0.5 g
Protein	9.5 g
Cholesterol	50 mg
Sodium	106 mg
Omega-3	0.7 g
Mercury	< 0.01 ppm

Eastern Oyster

Calories	68
Calories from fat	23
Total fat	2.5 g
Saturated fat	0.8 g
Protein	7.1 g
Cholesterol	53 mg
Sodium	211 mg
Omega-3	0.5 g
Mercury	< 0.01 ppm

curling mantle

Do I Chew?

Yes, you can chew a raw oyster. Don't be in a rush to slurp everything down. Nobody wants to give you the Heimlich.

Oyster Recipes

The general rule of thumb is six oysters per person as an appetizer, a dozen or more as a main course, depending on the size. Some crazies can put away a bushel in about the time it takes to shuck 'em, so know your audience before you buy.

The Unadorned Oyster
(on a Half Shell)

This really isn't a recipe. . . just a set of instructions for the obvious. (Hey, some people need directions for everything.)

36 live oysters
Crushed ice or shredded cabbage
Lemon wedges
Tabasco sauce (optional)
Mignonette Sauce (optional, see recipe)

Scrub the oysters under cold running water to loosen any dirt or broken shell bits.

Prepare individual serving plates or a large platter by topping them with crushed ice, rock salt, or shredded cabbage.

Shuck the individual oysters as instructed on page 112. *NOTE: If you find yourself spilling a lot of liquid, shuck the oysters over a bowl and pour the rescued liquor back into the oysters before serving.* Arrange the half-shell oysters on serving plates or a platter. Serve them with lemon wedges, Tabasco sauce, and Mignonette Sauce.

Serves 6 as an appetizer or 2 or 3 as a main course

Mignonette Sauce

Like pepper? Then you'll probably like this stuff. Don't like vinegar? Then you probably won't like this stuff.

2 tablespoons freshly cracked black pepper
2 tablespoons shallots, finely minced
1 tablespoon lemon juice
1 cup sherry vinegar

Combine all ingredients in a small bowl. That's it.

Barbecued Oysters
with Salsa Fresca

Kind of like hot dogs, oysters "pop" when you cook 'em. Well, they open up, which means they're ready to eat. In terms of toppings, there are really too many to mention, but just about anything you can dip a chip into or drag a piece of crusty bread through will taste good on top of an oyster.

48 live oysters
Salsa Fresca (see recipe)

Scrub the oysters under cold running water to loosen any dirt or broken shell bits.

Fire up the grill. The oysters need to be set about 6 inches above a very hot bed of coals, so adjust the grill as necessary.

Once the grill is hot, set the oysters on it, right side up, and cook them for 3 to 5 minutes, until the tops pop. Remove the oysters using tongs or an oven mitt (the shells will be very hot), and carefully remove the top and use an oyster shucker (or similar knife) to release the meat from the shell.

Once open, top the oysters with salsa, and enjoy. ALTERNATIVE: For those who want a little more heat, after topping the oyster with salsa, return to the grill for 2 to 3 minutes or just until the mantle starts to curl.

Serves 8 as an appetizer, 2 to 4 as a main course, or 1 really oyster-crazy guy.

Salsa Fresca

The key to good salsa? Good tomatoes. Go to the farmer's market and buy the best looking heirlooms you can find and I guarantee you'll never go back to store-bought. . . at least, not until the market closes for winter. Sigh. NOTE: *For less "heat" replace the jalapeño pepper with a small poblano pepper.*

3 or 4 large heirloom tomatoes, seeded and chopped
1 small onion, diced
1 jalapeño chili, seeded and *very* finely minced
2 tablespoons fresh cilantro, chopped
2 tablespoons lime juice
Kosher salt and freshly ground pepper to taste

Combine all ingredients in a small bowl. Salsa fresca can be made a day in advance and stored in the fridge.

Po' Boy Oy

The hardest part about making this sandwich is restraining yourself from eating the oysters right out of the fryer... not that there's anything wrong with that. In fact, if you want to stop short of making a "Po' Boy" and opt for "Oysters and Chips," I'm with ya. (See page 60 for chips recipe.) NOTE: Tradition dictates that this sandwich be made with a hot pepper sauce, but I'll leave the brand and intensity of the heat up to you.

1½ quarts (6 cups) peanut (or other vegetable) oil
1 cup yellow cornmeal
1 teaspoon paprika
½ teaspoon kosher salt
½ teaspoon freshly ground black pepper
½ teaspoon garlic powder
¼ teaspoon cayenne pepper
12 live oysters
2 8-inch soft French loaf (or similar roll)
¼ cup mayonnaise
1 cup shredded lettuce
1 large tomato, sliced
Hot sauce (your choice)
Juice of 1 lemon

Heat the oil in a heavy 4-quart pot to 370° F. Preheat the oven to 200° F.

Scrub the oysters under cold running water to loosen any dirt or broken shell bits. Shuck as instructed on page 112.

Combine the cornmeal, paprika, salt, pepper, garlic powder, and cayenne in a medium-sized mixing bowl. Mix thoroughly. Dredge the oysters through the cornmeal mix and gently lower them into the oil, 4 to 6 at a time, depending on size. Do *not* overcrowd the fryer. Fry the oysters for 2 to 3 minutes, until golden brown. Transfer the cooked oysters to a wire rack set over a baking sheet in the oven. Repeat the process with the remaining oysters.

STOP HERE IF HUNGER OVERCOMES YOU. To make Po' Boy, continue.

Split the loaf, but not completely through. Fold it open and spread the mayo on both halves. Add the lettuce and tomatoes, pile on the oysters, and top all with a dash or three of hot sauce to taste and a few squeezes of lemon juice. Serve immediately.

Serves 2

Baked Bills

The original name for this recipe (Oysters Rockefeller) was adopted because the recipe was said to be as "rich as Rockefeller." My only question is: What about inflation? Let's upgrade this baby to Gatesian proportions—at least in name (it's already rich enough, trust me). In a hundred years, when Bill Gates is as obscure as John D. Rockefeller, feel free to change the name to something else.

24 live oysters
Rock or coarse sea salt
4 tablespoons unsalted butter
¼ cup shallots, finely chopped
½ cup celery with leaves, finely chopped
2 large garlic cloves, minced
1 cup baby spinach, chopped
1 cup dry bread crumbs
2 tablespoon fresh flat-leaf parsley, chopped
½ teaspoon freshly ground black pepper
1 teaspoon Tabasco (or other hot) sauce
Pernod (or similar liqueur)
Lemon wedges

Preheat the oven to 425° F.

Scrub the oysters under cold running water to loosen any dirt or broken shell bits. Shuck as instructed on page 112.

Spread a ½-inch layer of salt over several pie dishes or a large baking pan. Arrange the oysters (on the half shell, liquor included) on the bed of salt. Set them aside. NOTE: If you don't have rock salt handy, crumpled foil will do the job just as well.

Melt the butter in a large sauté pan over medium heat. Add the shallots and celery and cook until softened, 4 to 5 minutes. Add the garlic and cook for an additional 2 minutes. Add the spinach and parsley, and cook until it is just wilted, about 30 seconds. Reduce the heat to low, add the bread crumbs, salt, and Tabasco, and cook for 2 minutes.

Top each oyster with an equal amount of the stuffing and a few drops of Pernod. Bake for 8 to 10 minutes, by which point the liquor should be bubbling. Serve immediately with lemon wedges.

Serves 4

Rocky Mountain Oysters?

No. I said no. Okay, but don't say I didn't warn you. They're fried bull's testicles. Happy?

Chapter 11
Red Snapper

Will the Real Red Please Swim Up?

I wouldn't buy that if I were you. Why? It's a conspiracy!
A plot, perpetrated by the fishermen, processed by the
wholesalers, and perpetuated by the man behind the
counter. I wouldn't be surprised if the fish were in on it.
I'm talking about red snapper, of course. Sure, the sign says
it's red snapper, but is it? How can you tell? Could be some other
snapper, or maybe even a rockfish. Do you really want to lay down a
bunch of clams for some phony fish? What? You think just because it's red and has red eyes
and tastes like red snapper that it must be red snapper? I suppose you think Roswell acted
alone, too, huh? What about aliens in the sewers? Alligator autopsies? Affordable health
care? Fine, if you want to buy an overpriced imposter, go right ahead. I won't stop you. Just
don't say I didn't warn you. Now, if you'll excuse me, I have other fish to fry.

VITAL STATS

FIRST NAME: Red snapper (a.k.a. American red snapper or northern red snapper)

SCI. NAME: *Lutjanus campechanus*

SIZE: Most 2-6 lbs, up to 35 lbs

LIFESPAN: Most 3-10 years when caught, up to 50 years

RANGE: North Carolina to Florida, Gulf of Mexico, South to the Yucatán

CATCH: 4.6 million lbs annually, U.S.

According to the United States Food and Drug Administration, *Lutjanus campechanus* is the only species that can be legally marketed as red snapper. To do otherwise constitutes fraud. Fair enough. *L. campechanus* is red snapper, after all.

It's also very tasty, very popular, and more often than not, very expensive. The fact that red snapper is not the most abundant fish in the sea has no doubt led some less reputable fishmongers and wholesalers to substitute other snappers in its place. Dressed down to nothing but a fillet, it's difficult to tell one snapper fillet from another—and there are others. Red snapper is but one of more than a hundred species of snapper fished worldwide. With more foreign fish hitting U.S. shores

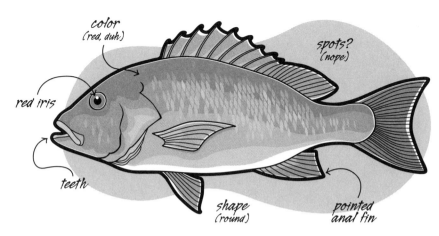

color
(red, duh)

spots?
(nope)

red iris

teeth

shape
(round)

pointed
anal fin

each year, it's easy to see how an importer might be tempted to simplify matters by using a more familiar name—a more sellable name.

But is this a big problem or simply a case of a few bad fish eggs? A 2004 study conducted by graduate students at the University of North Carolina suggested 77 percent of the red snapper sold at U.S. markets was not what it was claimed to be. Disturbing? You bet. Accurate? Well…

The reality of fake fish

Reports like the UNC study tend to use very small samplings and only test fillets. Whole fish are not tested, even though they represent a significant portion of the market. The question of whether the fillets were mislabeled on purpose or by mistake is also not generally addressed.

One of the more damning claims—that mislabeling may lead to inflated stock assessments—is dubious at best. It's possible the sight of red snapper at the market every week may lead the consumer to believe all is well, but faking out the fishery would require a dockside conspiracy that seems fairly unlikely.

It's safe to say there's a better than 1 in 4 chance of getting what you paid for if you buy red snapper. The fact that there's still chance involved at all is unfortunate. Who do we blame? I blame you. (Okay, me, too.)

The game of the name

It all comes back to the name. Red snapper is going to sell better than gray snapper or lane snapper or rockfish. The fishmonger knows this. It doesn't matter if the less expensive fish is comparable in quality, the customer is always right (even when we're wrong). Does this justify charging big bucks for faux red snapper? No. Should we be cautious when buying red snapper? Absolutely. Is it okay to ask for a DNA test before handing over the credit card? That's probably unnecessary.

Red Reality Check

Spotting a true red snapper is not as hard as you think…as long as it's still in one piece.

EYES: Just like the name, these babies are red.

COLOR: Care to guess? That's right, red on top, fading to pink around the middle and whiter toward the belly.

FINS: The most distinctive flipper on a real red is the anal fin, which is pointed rather than rounded.

SPOTS: Reds don't have them, except when they're young. A small (less than 12 inches) red might have a dark "thumbprint" on its side.

TEETH: All snappers have a mouthful, including densely packed villiform (hairlike) teeth and a few canines. (Where did you think the name "snapper" came from?)

SHAPE: Well-rounded, not too linear, triangular head—less obvious to the novice, but a pro can spot a red from its profile alone.

In the Water
Life in the Big Reef

Some fish prefer the relative quiet of the shallows, the seclusion of a rocky shoal, or the vast expanse of the open ocean. The red snapper is not one of these fish. The red is a city fish, preferring the hustle and bustle of the reef. Be it coral or rock, pipeline or pirate ship—if it's big and three-dimensional, a red snapper will call it home.

Most reds keep a place in the Gulf of Mexico where an abundance of natural and man-made structures provide plenty of underwater real estate. Everything a modern snapper could want is right at its fin tips, including shelter, a neighbor with which to socialize, and plenty of takeout. Daily reef specials include small fish, crustaceans, and mollusks. Yum.

Live long and prosper

Most red snappers are happy to spend their lives near the same reef, which for some may be as long as 50 years. Larger reds will sometimes leave the reef in search of a little more space, but not too far—you can take the red out of the reef, but not the reef out of the red.

The only time a red snapper does any serious long-distance swimming is when it's time to spawn. During the summer months, huge schools migrate to warmer, shallower waters, usually to the same spot every year. Come sunset, the snappers get busy, some as many as twenty-plus times in a single season. Sexual maturity begins at age two, but it's size that matters. Larger fish are able to produce significantly more eggs, as many as 9 million in one spawning event.

Once released, the eggs float in the current for a day before hatching. The tiny larvae grow quickly in the warm surface waters and after three weeks head for the muddy bottom. Most spend at least six months in the shallows, hanging out with the shrimp, before heading to deeper waters and a more metropolitan lifestyle.

On the Boats
Get Thee to the Gulf

The red snapper fishery has been a Gulf institution since before the Civil War. The first reds were pulled from the waters off Pensacola, Florida, in the 1850s, but as readily available ice made it possible to target deeper waters, fishermen headed to the snapper-rich waters off Mexico and Cuba. Today, all but about one percent of the domestic red snapper catch comes from the Gulf of Mexico.

red snapper on ice

Catching a fish that likes to hang around all manner of underwater obstructions is not as easy as dragging a net behind a boat. Most fishermen use bottom longlines outfitted with 10 to 40 baited hooks (ladyfish and squid are favorites). In shallow waters, handlines are more commonly used. Because red snapper tend to move in large schools, many fishermen use radar to spot the fish before dropping their lines.

Derby days no more

Until recently, the Gulf of Mexico red snapper fishery was managed derby style. Starting in February, monthly 10-day seasons opened and closed until two-thirds of the annual quota was caught, with the remainder picked up in October. As in other fisheries, the derbies resulted in more pressure on smaller boats, dangerous working conditions, lower prices for the catch, and little consistency at the market. One week there's plenty of reds, the next, nothing at all.

In 2004, the Gulf of Mexico Fishery Management Council made the decision to switch to an IFQ (Individual Fishing Quota) system in which each boat receives a personal quota that can be filled at any time during the season. That means fishing when the weather is good and the price is right. For the consumer, it should mean more consistent product at the market.

Blame the shrimp

Unfortunately, there's another very effective way to catch red snapper that doesn't fall under anyone's quota: shrimp trawling. The muddy flats where shrimp tend to congregate also happen to be popular with juvenile red snappers, many of which are scooped up in the shrimpers' nets. The resulting bycatch has been estimated at anywhere from 40 to 80 percent of the total juvenile stock in any given year. Not surprisingly, this has caused a bit of friction between snapper fishermen and shrimpers.

Not helping the situation is the fact that the National Marine Fisheries Service believes red snapper stocks in the Gulf of Mexico to be overfished. A plan to rebuild the stocks using annual quotas, size limits, trip limits, and seasonal closures was put into place in the midnineties. The fact that harvest numbers have been fairly stable for years has led some fishermen to question the restrictions, especially since many feel the shrimpers are the reason for the perceived overfishing.

To combat the bycatch issue, shrimp trawlers are now required to use bycatch reduction devices (BRDs) designed to give juvenile red snappers an escape hatch. Unfortunately, subsequent tests indicate most BRDs are not delivering on the promise of a 40 percent reduction in bycatch. Seems many of the little reds make their escape, only to turn around and go right back, believing the cavernous net to be a good place to hide.

swim bladder

swim bladder, inflated

Bladder Control

Like many fish, snappers use an inflatable swim bladder to achieve neutral buoyancy at different depths. When brought to the surface in a fisherman's net, it's not uncommon for the bladder to expand due to the sudden depth change, forcing the fish's stomach out through its mouth. Remarkably, many fish will recover if returned to the water immediately.

The TAC

The TAC, or total allowable catch, is the total harvest allowed for both commercial and recreational red snapper fishermen. The current TAC is 9.12 million pounds, with slightly more than half (4.65 million pounds) set aside for the commercial boats.

Homegrown

One way to improve your chances at nabbing an honest-to-goodness red snapper is to check the country of origin. If it's anywhere but the United States (or possibly Mexico), it's not a true red.

Caribbean red snapper

Second Place Red

This next best thing to a true red is its closest cousin, the CARIBBEAN RED SNAPPER (Lutjanus purpureus). Legally, this is the only other fish that can use "red snapper" in its name and cross state lines. Caribbeans are smaller and scalier than reds, but the most obvious difference is their yellow eyes. Most are imported from Caribbean and Central and South American waters.

What's the solution? The IFQ system should help ease some of the pressure on the fishermen and the red snapper stocks, but ultimately it's up to the shrimpers to reduce bycatch to a reasonable level. (No, it's not that simple, but let's pretend it is, at least for this chapter.)

At the Market
I See Red...Fish

Conspiracy theories aside, most fish markets are not out to con their customers. It's not good business. If the label says red snapper, it's probably red snapper (despite what your average know-it-all grad student says).

On the other fin, using a popular name to sell less familiar species is fairly standard practice, and (in most cases) there's nothing wrong with it as long as the price reflects the true value of the fish. Calling a rockfish "Pacific red snapper" to help sell it is fine; charging $12 a pound is not.

The best way to keep everybody honest is to buy whole fish. Red snapper is an excellent whole fish choice because it has a relatively good yield and a shape that works well in many pots and pans. Look for fish on or partially buried in ice. In addition to checking the signs (see "Red Reality Check"), look for bright skin, clear eyes, and a fresh sea scent. A dull appearance means the fish may have been improperly iced.

Even if you have no interest in cooking it head to tail, buy a whole fish and ask the fishmonger to do the dressing. You can always freeze what isn't used right away.

Tricky picking

Once the skins and fins have been stripped away, all snapper (and a lot of other fish) look pretty much the same, which is why most of the red snapper harvest is sold skin-on. It's easier to convince the customer that it's the real deal if they can see some skin. Several other snappers wear similar colors, but by far the most common crimson-skinned snapper is the true red. There's nothing wrong with buying a "red snapper" fillet sans skin as long as the price is right. If your fishmonger thinks no price is too high, try a different market.

Raw snapper flesh is pinkish with yellow tones and moderately firm to the touch. Moist and mildly scented is good; wet and moldy is not.

Don't expect to find much in the way of frozen red snapper, as there isn't usually enough to warrant freezing. Traditionally, seasonal closures in December and January meant reds found around Christmas were usually Caribbean reds, but with the new IFQ system in place, that may change. Imports from Mexico are available year-round.

The Usual Suspects

Though they don't quite match the rich, nutty flavor of the original, some of the best red snapper stand-ins come pretty close.

Coming in second in terms of overall domestic catch is the VERMILLION SNAPPER (Rhomboplites aurorubens), a slender, multicolored Gulf species. As

vermillion snapper

for the eyes, it's not their color, but very large size that gives them away. No one would mistake a YELLOWTAIL SNAPPER (Ocyurus chrysurus) for a red as long as it's still sporting its yellow and blue jacket and large, Y-shaped tail. Both vermillion and yellowtail snapper are similar in terms of taste and texture.

yellowtail snapper

Less common are the darker skinned GRAY (L. griseus) and MUTTON SNAPPERS (L. analis), neither of which looks much like a red snapper, at least not before processing. Bringing up the rear in terms of Gulf landings are the LANE (L. synagris) and SILK SNAPPERS (L. vivanus). Lanes don't look much like reds, but silks do. The only obvious difference is that silks have a bit more yellow in them, and are usually smaller.

A PACIFIC RED SNAPPER isn't a snapper at all, but rather one of seventy-odd rockfish species (genus Sebastes and Sebastolobus) that populate coastal waters from Alaska to Baja, Mexico. Only about a dozen are harvested regularly, any one of which can legally be sold as Pacific red snapper, but only on the West Coast in the state in which it was caught. Most are mild in flavor and semifirm in texture, making them a reasonable (though not ideal) alternative to reds.

In the Kitchen
Dressed for Dinner

Pacific red snapper

Dressing a whole red snapper (or other modest sized roundfish) is not for everyone, but it's definitely an experience that every would-be seafood chef needs to have at least once in his or her life.

First, get rid of the fins—top, back, and both sides, please. You'll need a good pair of kitchen shears for this. Yes, the tail, too. Scaling comes next and is best done inside the relative safety of a large plastic bag so the scales don't end up all over the kitchen. A fish scaler makes things a lot easier, but the back of a knife also does the job. Start at the back of the head and scrape the scaler back and forth across the length of the fish (1). When finished, run your fingers along the body to check for stragglers. Rinse thoroughly. (If you're going to be cooking the fish whole on the grill, leave the scales on. They'll add a layer of protection to keep the fish from sticking. Be sure to remove the skin before serving.)

1)

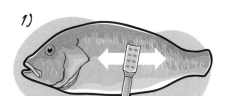

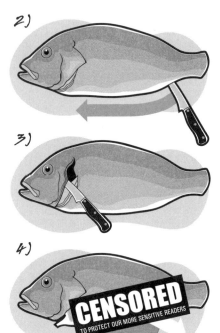

2)

3)

4)

CENSORED
TO PROTECT OUR MORE SENSITIVE READERS

Getting past the guts and gills is where most first-timers turn a little green. Honestly, it's not that big of a deal. If you're only interested in the fillets and have no intention of saving anything for making stock, you can skip to the filleting section. Whole fish that are going to stay that way throughout the cooking process need to be thoroughly cleaned. Using a sharp knife or kitchen shears, cut the belly from the small anal opening near the tail to the base of its head (2). Don't stick the knife in too deep or you'll slice open the guts. Yuck. Next, remove the gills by cutting along the edge where they attach to the body (3). Okay, ready? Reach in and carefully pull out the guts (4). You may need to trim the membrane holding the viscera in place. Finally, give everything a thorough rinse under cold running water to remove every last bit of viscera.

Fillet that fish

Filleting a fish from scratch (*see illustration*) is one of the more difficult tasks for the novice chef. Unfortunately, the only way to get better at it is to practice, preferably on a less expensive fish. Most fishmongers will be happy to do the deed if you don't feel up to it.

If you've cut your own fillets it's best to trim them down to size, say 6- to 8-ounce blocks, hopefully of similar size. Most markets tend to sell fillets already cut to size, but check to see if there are any pin bones. As for the skin, it hardly seems right to remove it, given how important it is to the purchase, but if you must, press down on the flesh with the palm of your hand and carefully slide a very sharp knife along the base of the fillet. For whole fillets, it may be easier to let the fish do the work. Grasp the tail end, get the knife started, and then pull the skin back toward you, shimmying it from side to side. Keep the knife as flat as possible.

Break out the island spices

Red snapper is lean and moist, with a mild, almost nutty flavor. The flesh is firm and slightly flaky. Simply put, it's good stuff.

Flavorwise, keep it light, fresh, and maybe a little exotic. Reds were made for tropical flavors, so here's your chance to break out that Caribbean cookbook gathering dust on the shelf. If you're cooking fillets, sautéing is best for those still in their skin. Be sure to score the skin a few times to keep it from curling. Skinless fillets are good for most methods, though they tend to fall apart on the grill.

No doubt you've figured out that I want you to cook a whole fish if you can find it. How? Stuffed with aromatic veggies, herbs, and spices, and roasted in the oven sounds good. There's simply no better way to get more flavor out of a fish...unless you happen to be grilling it. In that case, you'll have to watch out for sticky skin, but that's where a grill basket helps. If you can find them, banana leaves make a great makeshift steamer rig set right on the grill.

NUTRITIONAL INFO	
Per 3.5 oz/100 grams (raw)	
Red Snapper	
Calories	110
Calories from fat	24
Total fat	2.6 g
Saturated fat	0.5 g
Cholesterol	40 mg
Sodium	96 mg
Protein	20.2 g
Omega-3	0.6 g
Mercury	0.19 ppm

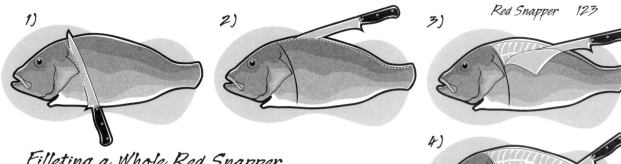

Filleting a Whole Red Snapper

(1) Start by making a cut along the diagonal of the gill cover, down to the backbone. *(2)* Moving from head to tail, slice through the back, keeping the knife level against the backbone. Don't go any deeper than about ½ inch. *(3)* Repeat, slicing deeper along the rib cage, folding back the fillet as you go. Long, even strokes will result in a cleaner, less "choppy" fillet. *(4)* When you get to the ribs, slice through them, and the rest of the fillet should come away easily. (You can also cut over the ribs, leaving them behind, but you'll loose a little meat.) *(5)* Turn the fish over, tail facing away. Make a cut across the base of the tail, then insert the knife and slide it back toward you along the backbone. *(6)* Repeat, slicing deeper along the rib cage, folding back the fillet as you go. *(7)* Cut through the rib cage and remove the fillet. (You may need to do a little trimming to release the fillet from the head.) *(8)* The ribs, a.k.a. pin bones, can be pulled out with a pair of needle-nose pliers, or (with larger fillets) simply cut away in a single strip.

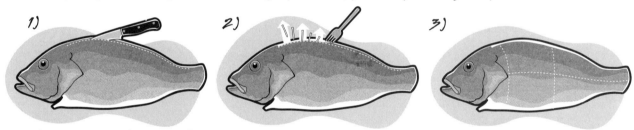

Carving a Cooked Red Snapper

Taking apart a whole roasted or grilled red snapper is a fairly simple matter, though keeping everything intact does take practice (and a little luck). Don't fret if your fish falls apart.

(1) To carve, start by making a cut along the back of the fish. *(2)* Remove the series of small bones running along the back, hopefully without doing too much damage to the skin. *(3)* Cut along the centerline from tail to head going as deep as the bone will allow. Cut the skin loose around the head (if necessary). If the fillet is fairly large, cut across the center, dividing the fish in half. *(4)* Slide a fish knife or a flat serving spoon under the top fillet (or fillets) and remove, preferably to a warm serving platter. *(5)* Repeat on the lower fillet, keeping an eye out for any stray bones. *(6)* Remove the backbone and head. If it doesn't lift out easily, slide a knife under the backbone to help release it. *(7)* Check the whole fish for stray bones, and then divide the bottom fillet into two (or four) sections mimicking the top fillet.

Red Snapper Recipes

The first three recipes given here are for whole fish, and each recipe contains a different set of interior flavorings—that is, the stuff you stuff inside the fish before cooking. Whatever you put in there is going to flavor the fish, subtly in most cases, so have a little fun. Feel free to swap flavors from one dish to another, experiment with your own (think citrus + herbs + spices), or drop them altogether (save for a little salt and pepper, maybe). You'll be surprised how good fish-flavored fish can taste.

Grilled Red Snapper

If you're going to be grilling a lot of whole fish, I highly recommend investing in a grill basket. It just makes things easier and it allows you to serve the fish with the skin still attached. Without a grill basket the skin will have been removed by (a) you, because you left the scales on to keep it from sticking to the grill and thus discarded it prior to serving, or (b) the grill, because you removed the scales prior to cooking and the skin stuck. Get a basket.

2 whole red snappers, 1½ to 2 pounds each
Extra virgin olive oil
Kosher salt and freshly ground black pepper
1 large lemon, sliced
2 limes, sliced

Fire up the grill. Set the grill about 3 inches from the heat. *NOTE: If cooking directly on the grill, move to about 4 inches from the heat.*

Remove the fins, gills, scales, and guts of the fish and rinse it thoroughly (*see directions on pages 121-122*). *NOTE: If cooking directly on the grill, leave the scales on.*

Season the fish inside and out with salt and pepper. Brush the fish with olive oil (inside and out) and stuff the body cavities with lemon and lime slices. Place both fish in a grill basket (or baskets) and grill them over high heat for about 10 minutes per inch of thickness at its thickest point. Flip the fish once and only once. When the fish are completely cooked through, the flesh just under the skin will be just starting to flake, but still seem moist.

Serve the snapper right off the grill to make an impression, or dismantled if you want to get to eating (*see directions on page 123*). *NOTE: If the fish was grilled with the scales on, carefully remove the skin prior to serving.*

Serves 4 to 6

Roasted Red Snapper

Pure, simple, and perfect for the chef who prefers to do less work up front, but doesn't mind showing off his dismantling skills at the table. If you can't track down a Meyer lemon, try using a combination of half regular lemon and half orange slices inside the fish.

1 whole red snapper, 2½ to 3 pounds
Kosher salt and freshly ground black pepper
Extra virgin olive oil
2 garlic cloves, minced
2 to 3 fresh thyme sprigs
1 large Meyer lemon, sliced

Preheat the oven to 400° F.

Remove the fins, gills, guts, and scales of the fish and rinse it thoroughly (*see directions on pages 121-122*).

Place the fish in a large baking dish and drizzle it with olive oil. Season it inside and out with salt and pepper, and stuff the body cavity with garlic, thyme, and lemon slices. Bake the fish for 25 to 30 minutes (about 15 minutes per inch of thickness at the fish's thickest point). To check for doneness, poke a small knife or fork into the thickest part of the fish along the back. The flesh should be moist but opaque, all the way to the backbone.

Remove the fish from the oven and carve it into fillets (*see directions on page 123*). Serve immediately.

Serves 3 to 4

Salty Snapper

Despite the fact that this recipe calls for 6 pounds of kosher salt, it does not taste salty. Well, maybe just a little, but that's the point. The salt adds just a hint of flavor while sealing everything else inside the fish so it can't escape. Be sure to show off the salt igloo to guests prior to cracking it.

1 whole red snapper, 3 to 4 pounds
Kosher salt and freshly ground black pepper
2 teaspoons fresh grated ginger
10 to 12 cilantro sprigs
2 limes, sliced
4 egg whites
½ cup water
6 pounds kosher salt
Lemon wedges

Preheat the oven to 400° F.

Remove the fins, gills, guts, and scales of the fish and rinse it thoroughly (*see directions on pages 121-122*). Season inside and out with salt and pepper, and stuff the body cavity with the ginger, cilantro, and lime slices. Set the fish aside.

Combine the egg whites, water, and salt in a large bowl and work with your hands to form a gritty paste that holds together when pressed between the palms of your hands.

Spread a ½-inch layer of salt on the bottom of a large baking dish or pan big enough to comfortably hold the fish. (Don't fill the pan all the way to the edge; just spread out enough salt for the fish to lie on.) Place the fish on the salt bed and bury it under the rest of the mixture. Use your hands to press the salt into place, completely sealing the fish inside. (If you run out of salt before getting to the tail, that's okay.)

Bake the fish for 35 to 40 minutes (or about 15 minutes per inch of thickness at the fish's thickest point). To check for doneness, poke an instant-read thermometer through the salt, well into the body of the fish (somewhere near the midsection). Once the temperature hits 135, remove the fish from the oven, show it off to your friends, and get to cracking. A few whacks from a small hammer and the salt will break like a shell. Pull off the salt, carefully transfer the fish to a platter, and carve it into fillets (*see directions on page 123*). Serve immediately.

Serves 4 to 6

Jerk Snapper

Okay, you bought skin-on fillets, which you're 99 percent sure are red snapper. Even if they're not, this spicy treatment will make the imposters taste good. You can use store-bought jerk seasoning or use the homemade version below. NOTE: Cooking a snapper fillet with the skin on will hold more of the moisture inside the flesh. If you prefer a firmer fillet, remove the skin.

4 red snapper fillets, skin on (6 to 8 ounces each)
Jamaican Style Jerk Seasoning (see recipe below)
2 tablespoons olive oil
Mango Salsa (*see recipe on page 61*)

Double-check the skin for any scales you (or your fishmonger) missed, and then make a series of short, shallow cuts across the skin (3 or 4) to keep the fillet from curling when it cooks. Flip the fillets and liberally sprinkle with the jerk seasoning on the flesh side only. Brush with a very thin coating of olive oil on both sides.

Heat a large nonstick sauté pan over medium-high heat. Once it is hot, add the fillets, skin side down, and cook for 3 to 4 minutes, until a little brown and crispy. Flip the fillets and cook them for an additional 3 to 4 minutes until opaque throughout. NOTE: *If you'd rather show off the non-skin side, cook it first, inverting the times.*

Serve immediately with Mango Salsa.

Jamaican Style Jerk Seasoning

2 teaspoons onion powder
1 teaspoon brown sugar
1 teaspoon cayenne
1 teaspoon dried thyme, crushed
½ teaspoon ground cinnamon
½ teaspoon ground allspice.
½ teaspoon kosher salt
½ teaspoon freshly ground black pepper
¼ teaspoon ground nutmeg

Combine all ingredients in a small bowl. Mix thoroughly.

HOW TO STORE: Red Snapper

FRESH: Whole red snapper will keep quite nicely in the fridge—up to a week if it's been cared for properly prior to purchase. The best option for home storage is in a large pan, directly on a bed of ice. Unless you've got a fancy, double-decker draining rig, you'll need to refresh the ice and drain the water at least once (preferably twice) a day. Fillets require less fuss, but aren't going to last as long. I'd suggest cooking on the day of purchase, but most will last 2 to 3 days in the coldest part of the fridge. On ice is fine, just not directly.

FROZEN: To freeze fresh fillets, give them a quick rinse, a thorough pat dry, and then wrap them tightly in plastic and foil. Frozen fillets are best used within a month. If you happen to find fillets commercially frozen, they should be good for 3 months.

Chapter 12
Swordfish
Errol Flynn of the Sea

This one's obvious, right? Look at that nose: it's a sword attached to a fish. Speaking scientifically, *Xiphias gladius* is a combination of Greek and Latin words that both mean sword. Heck, the first fisherman to land one probably didn't think long before proclaiming: "I caught me a swordfish!" But this hero of the high seas has had a rough go of it in recent years. Charges of overfishing and environmentally unfriendly techniques have dogged the fishery and convinced many chefs to remove what has long been a restaurant favorite from their menus. Worse, mercury, the bane of disco-era swordfish, once again made headlines as reason numero uno not to eat fish that live at the top of the food chain. Turns out, mercury is not an essential mineral. Who knew? To recap: Eating swordfish is not only bad for the fish, it's bad for the fisherman. Might as well skip this one altogether, right? En garde, monsieur, them's fightin' words!

VITAL STATS

FIRST NAME: Swordfish

SCI. NAME: *Xiphias gladius*

SIZE: 100-200 lbs, 4-6 feet in length (commercial catch)

LIFESPAN: 9-10 years, max

RANGE: Tropical and temperate oceans around the globe

CATCH: About 220 million lbs annually, worldwide

Once upon a time, it was simply our sword against theirs. Granted, ours had a rope attached to one end, but the fish had the entire ocean to hide in, so to most it seemed like a fair fight. Beginning in the early nineteenth century and continuing well into the twentieth, the majority of swordfish landings were done by harpoon. Yes, that's exactly what it sounds like: A guy stands on the end of a boat and throws a big pointy stick at fish in the water. A single fisherman might catch 15 or more on a good day. Not exactly shootin' fish in a barrel, but given this fish's ability to slash back, most fishermen felt it wise to take what they could get.

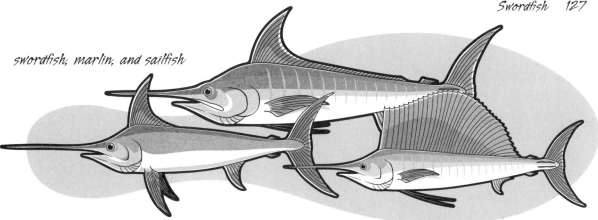

swordfish, marlin, and sailfish

Swordfish have long been defined by their Pinocchio-like appendage, from which—this is no lie—they derive a third of their overall length. From barely a millimeter at birth to a spectacular five feet in the record books, the sword of a swordfish is the longest of all billfish, a group that also includes marlins, sailfish and spearfish. The long, flattened oval spear caps a creature that can reach 14 feet in total length and weigh over 1,400 pounds.

Today, commercially caught swordfish rarely exceed 300 pounds, but remain impressive specimens of underwater rocket science. With their long, tapered bodies, swordfish are capable of reaching speeds that would earn them a ticket on most major highways. Estimates range from 60 to near 80 miles per hour, although, as of yet, no one has set up a radar gun on the Grand Banks to make it official.

In the Water
Slash and Grab

A highly migratory fish, swordfish are found throughout the tropical and temperate oceans of the world. Most choose to swim alone, preferring the nomadic life to that of the school. Swordfish especially like to hang out near the frontal zones where ocean currents collide, producing gradients in temperature and salinity, as well as breeding grounds for the numerous small fish and other critters swordfish like to call lunch.

A common misconception about swordfish is that they use their bills to spear their prey. Think about that for a moment: How exactly is Swordy going to get to his lunch when it's stuck on the end of his nose? Rather than stab, billfish swim vertically through a school of fish and slash with their swords, stunning or killing their prey, which they then gobble up at their leisure. Adult swordfish don't have any teeth, so a good slash-and-grab technique is paramount for successful fishing.

When Swordfish Attack!

In 1967, the Alvin, a 3-man deep-sea submersible, found itself the unlikely target of a swordfish's ire. The sub was exploring the seafloor near the Bahamas when the fish attacked, becoming trapped between two pieces of the sub's fiberglass outer hull. Unable to free itself, the fish soon found itself on the way to the surface. The crew cooked it for dinner.

Brain Heater

Swordfish prefer warmer waters, but have been known to dive in excess of 2,000 feet in order to find prey. To keep from getting an extreme case of brain freeze, swordfish are equipped with an extra layer of tissue to insulate their brains and prevent rapid cooling during deep dives.

QUICK QUESTION

How do swordfish spawn? At least once a year, swordfish give up the single life in order to spawn. Although very little is known about the mating rituals of the species, there is speculation that females prefer males with longer swords. (Insert your own "size matters" joke here.) After choosing a mate, the female releases more than a million eggs (possibly as many as 30 million), which her partner then fertilizes. After hatching, the newborn larvae stay in the sun-fed surface water, chowing down on zooplankton until they're big enough to dive for larger prey such as squid and small fish.

Not surprisingly, the world's best underwater fishing pole doubles as a defensive weapon when necessary. Ask any fisherman; when it comes to swordfish tales, the "one that got away" isn't always content with making his escape without a little payback. Numerous stories tell of fish that turned their spears on harpoon fishermen or their boats in an attempt to return the favor. Seems only fair, although whether such encounters were common or simply the exaggerated war stories of frustrated fishermen is not always readily apparent.

On the Boats
Swordfishing

Harpooning remained the dominant form of swordfishing long after most other fisheries had turned to more modern methods. That all changed in the 1960s with the introduction of longlining, a technique that used multiple baited hooks set along a long floating master line. How long? Forty miles was not uncommon, which meant a thousand or more hooks in the water. Better fishing gear and bigger boats enabled fishermen to land more swordfish, turning what was once a modest catch into a 100,000-ton per year worldwide haul. Today, North Atlantic fishermen go out on monthlong trips in hopes of catching 50,000 pounds or more. But more is not always better, especially for the fish.

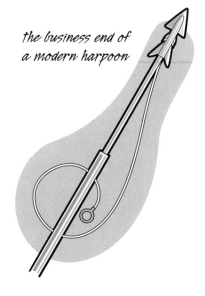

the business end of a modern harpoon

Gloom and doom

By definition, a sustainable fishery is one which takes what the sea offers, but leaves behind enough of a stock to keep future generations stable. Throughout the 1980s and into the 1990s, as more boats began to target swordfish in the North Atlantic (many from countries that were less than diligent about following established fishing guidelines), the

longlining for swordfish

average fish size dropped from the 250-pound markers of the 1960s to near 90 pounds by the close of the century. At that size, a high percentage of the catch would never have had the chance to spawn.

In its heyday, the swordfish harpoon fishery was stable because there was no way for fishermen to spear enough fish to do serious damage to the population. Smaller swordfish were not a target for the harpoons, so spawning proceeded without impediment. Long-liners aren't able to pick and choose their catch, thus juveniles are often hooked alongside their larger brothers and sisters. Catch and release would seem to be the way to go, but unfortunately the survival rate for young swordfish once they're on the line is low (less than 25 percent).

The fact that long-liners were an inherently more efficient way to catch fish wasn't a bad thing, but without some common-sense management, collapse was definitely in the future of the fishery. Fortunately, both the fish and the fishermen were more resilient than first believed.

Moon Fishing

For longline fishermen, the best time to catch swordfish is during a full moon. That's when the fish are most actively feeding, and thus are more likely to take the bait. Monthlong fishing trips are commonly coordinated to match the lunar cycles, which means the freshest swordfish hits the market soon after a new moon.

Glow-in-the-dark Bait

Swordfish apparently like to see what they're eating, so fishermen attach light sticks to the line near the bait. The light also attracts smaller fish, which in turn attracts more swordfish. On a single trip, one boat might go through ten thousand light sticks.

QUICK QUESTION

How do the fish stay fresh after being caught? Once landed, swordfish are dressed immediately, losing their heads, tails, and viscera in the process. They're then packed full of ice and stored in a specially designed hold surrounded by even more ice. Fishermen use saltwater ice, which is 4 degrees colder than regular ice, enabling them to keep fish cool and fresh for up to three weeks without any loss of quality.

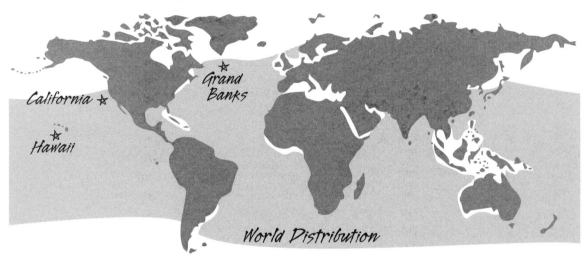

California ☆
Grand Banks ☆
Hawaii ☆

World Distribution

Swordfishing Grounds

Currently, the most popular spots for U.S. fishermen are the Grand Banks in the North Atlantic, the coast of California, and the waters around Hawaii. Fishing grounds off the Gulf of Mexico and the Southern East Coast are now only sparingly fished due to seasonal closures.

Rats on Deck?

No, fishermen don't have a pest control problem. A "rat" is simply a nickname for a swordfish that weighs less than 25 pounds. "Puppies" fall between 25 and 50 pounds, "pups" are 50 to 99 pounds, and anything over 100 pounds is known as a "marker."

Not so gloomy after all

Despite dire predictions of the species' demise, North Atlantic swordfish stocks recovered to near sustainable levels only three years after being labeled heavily depleted. In 1999, stocks were at 67 percent of what was considered healthy. By 2002, that number had risen to 94 percent.

Nobody was more shocked than the conservation groups who fought long and hard to get a ten-year plan in place to rebuild the population. How did the swordfish recover so quickly? Probably the most important factor was that swordfish reproduce and mature relatively quickly. When given a little room to roam, the population rebounded at a rate no one predicted. To that end, forcing fishermen to reduce quotas no doubt helped, but a bigger boost likely came from the closure of swordfish spawning grounds during the primary mating season.

It's not all good news. Seasonal closures and quotas have led many fishermen to give up on swordfish altogether. Even when the waters are open to them, fishing for swordfish isn't always cost-effective because wholesale prices are being driven down by product from foreign fleets. New international rules may ultimately improve the situation, but for now both the fish and fishermen remain on the road to recovery.

Swordfish and mercury

Several of the fish in this book have been affected by mercury issues, but none more so than the swordfish. In 1969, it was discovered that North Atlantic swordfish contained higher levels of mercury than most fish. Fearing industrial pollution, the United States Food and Drug Administration (FDA) banned the sale of swordfish with a mercury content of

0.5 parts per million (ppm) or greater, which, despite the qualification, effectively halted swordfishing for several years. It wasn't until tests done on preindustrial swordfish found levels of mercury similar to that of the modern catch that the ban was lifted and sales resumed. Ultimately, the FDA established a 1.0 ppm standard for mercury content in fish, which allowed most swordfish to slip under the radar. (The upside of the ban was that swordfish were given a breather, allowing their numbers to rise dramatically, so when the fishery restarted, there were a lot of big fish swimming around.)

Fast-forward to the new millennium and once again swordfish has become the poster child for mercury poisoning. New advisories issued by both the FDA and the Environmental Protection Agency (EPA) warn of the dangers of eating seafood with higher levels of mercury. The report flat-out recommends not eating swordfish. Of course, it also says: "For most people, the risk from mercury by eating fish and shellfish is not a health concern." Sounds fishy, no? What was generally glossed over was that the report specifically targeted pregnant women, women who may become pregnant, nursing mothers, and young children. Most folks saw the words "mercury" and "fish" and ran for the hills.

The good news is that eating fish, even swordfish, is not going to melt your brain. Yes, the mercury content of swordfish is higher than most fish, which means a swordfish a day should not replace an apple anytime soon. But once a month probably isn't going to hurt anybody.

At the Market
Domestic Fresh

Today, two-thirds of the swordfish consumed in the United States is imported, some of it from countries that continue to skirt the rules that domestic fishermen live by. The obvious solution would be to seek out only U.S.-caught fish, but this isn't always possible since there are no tracking or labeling requirements for swordfish. Even if the water of origin were stamped on the fish, that doesn't necessarily tell you who caught it since most of the U.S. Atlantic catch comes from international waters. What's a conservation-conscious consumer to do? Buy fresh.

Much of what arrives as fresh at the market comes from domestic fishermen, both from the Atlantic and Pacific swordfish fleets. That's not to say that frozen is always foreign, but if you want to maximize your chances for the most eco-friendly fish, ask for fresh swordfish.

Depending on the time of year and where you live, you may never see fresh swordfish at the market, but that shouldn't discourage you from

The Turtle Problem

In addition to catching swordfish, longlines also snag untargeted creatures—known collectively as bycatch—including several species of sea turtle. The numbers were high enough to force the closure of the Hawaiian swordfish industry for three years due to leatherback and loggerhead turtle bycatch. Fisherman are now required to use special circle hooks, which are much less likely to be swallowed by the turtles.

Restricted fishing, bycatch limits, onboard observers and dehooking equipment have also been employed to keep the turtles in their shells.

Swordfish Imports

In 2001, the leading exporters to the United States were Taiwan, Brazil, South Africa, Chile, Costa Rica, New Zealand, and Mexico.

trying the frozen product. Swordfish freezes quite nicely and is commonly sold as vacuum-packed frozen steaks that when thawed are almost as good as fresh. Often, frozen steaks will be thawed at the seafood counter and labeled "previously frozen," which is fine if you're planning to cook it on the day of purchase. If not, ask for frozen steaks.

Steak selection

When buying swordfish steaks (most likely all you'll ever see), look for firm flesh that is pale ivory to almost pinkish in color. Like all fresh fish, it should have as little smell to it as possible. Beyond that, the best way to judge swordfish freshness is to check the "bloodlines" that appear on the outer edges of the steak. Redder is better, in this case. If the lines have turned brown, the fish has probably been on land a little too long.

When buying multiple steaks, finding equal portions can be tricky. More important than overall size is thickness—make sure all you steaks are the same so they cook as evenly as possible. Anywhere from ½ to 1 inch is best. Any thicker, and the fish will most likely dry out before it cooks through.

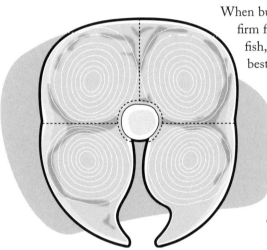

cross-section of a swordfish

In the Kitchen
The Key Word Is Steak

Okay, if you just plunked down a wad of cash on a couple of swordfish steaks, chances are you're out to impress somebody (good for you). Swordfish is a fine choice, mainly because it has a mild flavor that appeals to even non-fish fanatics, who view it as a fishy steak (I mean that in a good way). What do we do with steaks? Grill 'em, of course! Swordfish is especially nice grilled over a wood fire, which adds flavor to the dense, meaty flesh. So, fire up whatever flame or gas-powered device is handy and get to grilling. A few things to remember about cooking swordfish:

Moisture loss is the bane of swordfish cooking. This is a fish that tastes best when cooked through, so it is susceptible to overcooking. If that means slicing into the steak to know when it's done, so be it. That one's yours. Don't be afraid to pull a steak when the center is only almost done. In a few minutes it'll cross the finish line in fine form.

Swordshark?

Unscrupulous fishmongers will occasionally try to substitute shark for swordfish. Not cool. To avoid being duped, check the swirls. Swordfish steaks have circular rings that resemble the age lines of a tree; shark steaks do not.

HOW TO STORE: Swordfish

FRESH: Store swordfish steaks in the coldest part of the fridge, wrapped in plastic. If stored overnight, place on a bed of ice. Use within two days of purchase. *FROZEN:* Tightly secured in plastic wrap and foil, swordfish will keep for up to a month, three months if purchased already frozen. If the fish was thawed at the market, refreezing is not recommended, as it will damage the flesh.

Marinate for minutes, not hours. I've never quite understood why anyone would spend upward of $20 a pound for fish only to marinate it for hours. A short soak certainly accentuates the swordfish's flavor, but please resist the urge to drown your dinner with teriyaki.

Kebob bob bobbin' along. Swordfish is an excellent choice for making grilled kebobs because the firm flesh doesn't fall apart as it cooks. This is a good option for your fish-phobic friends since, depending on how the flesh is cubed, you can control the flavor intensity. Closer to the skin, swordfish flesh has a stronger flavor; closer to the center, the taste is milder.

Sauté, bake, or broil? Grilling isn't the only way to serve a swordfish steak, and any of these methods will produce a fine-flavored fish. Broiling is the next best thing to grilling, but it works best with slightly thinner steaks. Steaks more than ¾-inch thick will dry out before cooking all the way through. Sautéing swordfish adds a nice crust to the outside of the steak, but also works best with thinner steaks. Baked swordfish is good for any thickness, but benefits from a little added moisture. Herb butter? Hey, you're the boss.

Cutting Swordfish Steaks

A swordfish steak should require very little in the way of trimming, perhaps only the removal of the bloodline (avoid buying steaks with excessive bloodlines) and a thin strip of skin. Before removing the skin, take a moment to admire its texture. Notice anything different? That's right, no scales. Swordfish babies have 'em, but not adults. A fish with no scales? Madness!

Pseudoswords

Although it's usually harder to find, marlin makes a suitable swordfish substitute if you're at all concerned about overfishing. Albacore tuna makes a fair pseudoswordfish in a pinch.

NUTRITIONAL INFO

Per 3.5 oz/100 grams (raw)

Swordfish

Calories	121
Calories from fat	121
Total fat	4 g
Saturated fat	1.1 g
Cholesterol	39 mg
Sodium	90 mg
Protein	19.8 g
Omega-3	0.9 g
Mercury	0.97 ppm

fishermen's memorial in Gloucester, Massachusetts

Swordfish Recipes

Let's talk about grill marks. Grill marks are cool. Grill marks make fish taste better. Grill marks say: "I cooked this hunk of fish like a man." All true. But in the quest for the more photogenic crosshatch grill mark, some chefs are sacrificing the fish in the name of culinary vanity. Bad chefs.

For those who must mark their swordfish with the double cross, here's the trick: Cook side 1 for half the normal time, flip, cook side 2 for the full measure, flip, rotate ninety degrees, and cook side 1 for half of the normal time. Yes, that means only one side will be crosshatched. Serve that side up.

Grilled Swordfish

Okay, this is your showstopper: straight-up grilled swordfish with just a hint of garlic to tease the taste buds. Nothing more, nothing less, and very few things better. Don't bother grilling steaks thinner than ½-inch or they'll dry out (which also stops the show, but not in a good way).

4 swordfish steaks (6 to 8 ounces each), about ¾-inch thick
Kosher salt and freshly ground black pepper
2 large garlic cloves, crushed
Olive oil
Garlic Butter

Rub both sides of the steaks with garlic and season with salt and pepper. Brush on a thin layer of olive oil and wait 20 minutes before tossing on the grill.

Fire up the grill, with an eye on medium-high heat. Set the grill about 4 inches from the heat. *NOTE: A quick wipe of the grill with a towel dipped in vegetable oil just before adding the fish will help prevent sticking.*

Place the steaks on the grill and cook them for 3 to 4 minutes. Slip a grilling fork (inverted) underneath the fillet to raise it up, then slide a spatula beneath it and flip. Cook for another 3 to 4 minutes or until just pink in the middle (done, but still moist).

Carefully remove the steaks from the grill and serve them topped with a dab of Garlic Butter or Spicy Aioli (*see page 47 for recipe*).

Serves 4

Garlic Butter

When life gets you down, make garlic butter. Works for me.

1 large garlic clove, minced
¼ teaspoon kosher salt
¼ teaspoon freshly ground black pepper
4 tablespoons unsalted butter, softened
2 teaspoons fresh flat-leaf parsley, finely chopped

Place the garlic, salt, and pepper in a small bowl and crush them into a paste using the back of a spoon. Add the butter and parsley and stir the mixture until smooth.

Swordfish Kebobs

Instead of a "sword fish" it's a "fish on a sword"! Hey, I never said I was a comic genius. I did, however, say you should resist the urge to marinate, but I make an exception for anything on a skewer. If you prefer a more intense flavor, feel free to go over the time limit, say up to 4 hours. Overnight? You crazy kids...

¼ cup hoisin sauce
¼ cup soy sauce
1 teaspoon sesame oil
1 large garlic clove, minced
1 teaspoon freshly grated ginger
2 pounds fresh swordfish, skin removed
Kosher salt and freshly ground black pepper
1 red onion, quartered
1 red bell pepper,
1 green bell pepper,
1 pineapple, peeled, cored, and cut into 1-inch cubes

In a large nonreactive bowl (or plastic zip-top bag), combine the hoisin, soy, oil, garlic, and ginger. Cut the swordfish into roughly 1½-inch cubes, toss them in the marinade, and refrigerate for 1 hour.

Fire up the grill, with an eye on medium-high heat. Set the grill about 4 inches from the heat. *NOTE: A quick wipe of the grill with a towel dipped in vegetable oil just before adding the fish will help prevent sticking.*

Remove the swordfish cubes from the marinade and pat them dry. Slide them onto skewers between pieces of onion, pepper, and pineapple. Place at least 3 pieces of fish on each skewer. Brush the veggies with the marinade, if desired. *NOTE: If you're using wooden skewers, soak them in water for 30 minutes prior to grilling.*

Place the skewers on the grill and cook for 4 to 5 minutes. Flip to the opposite side and cook for 3 to 4 minutes. To test for doneness, slide another skewer into one of the cubes—it should slide in easily. NOTE: *There's no need to grill all four sides.*

Serve the kebobs immediately on a bed of steamed rice (I assume you can figure that one out on your own).

Serves 4

Cast-Iron Sword(fish)
with Tomato Basil Topping

The next time the weatherman blows it, pull out your cast-iron grill pan and try this basil-flavored fish. And no, that's not "marinating" in the oil mixture, it's just standing there . . . minding it's own business. Nothing to see here. Move along.

¼ cup extra virgin olive oil
2 tablespoons fresh lemon juice
1 garlic clove, minced
6 to 8 large basil leaves, chiffonade
Kosher salt and freshly ground black pepper
2 swordfish steaks (6 to 8 ounces each), about ¾-inch thick
Tomato Basil Topping (see recipe)

In a small bowl, combine the oil, lemon juice, garlic, and basil. Season the mixture with salt and pepper and blend thoroughly.

Place the steaks in a shallow bowl and coat them with the oil-and-basil mixture. Let them stand for 20 minutes at room temperature.

Meanwhile, place your cast-iron grill pan in the oven and turn the heat up to 500° F. Once the oven hits the mark, transfer the *very hot* pan to a burner set on high. Drop the steaks into the pan and cook for 4 minutes, flip them, and cook for another 3 to 4 minutes or until just pink in the middle (done, but still moist).

Transfer the steaks to warm plates, top them with Tomato Basil Topping, and serve immediately.

Serves 2

Tomato Basil Topping

This is basically just bruschetta without the crusty bread. Hmmm . . . maybe a swordfish steak sandwich on toasted sourdough? Interesting.

3 plum (Roma) tomatoes, seeded and diced
4 large basil leaves, chiffonade

1 small garlic clove, minced
2 tablespoons green onions, finely chopped
1 tablespoon extra virgin olive oil
1 teaspoon balsamic vinegar
Kosher salt and freshly ground pepper

Combine the tomato, basil, garlic, onions, oil, and vinegar. Season with salt and pepper to taste.

NOTE: *For those who skipped the squid chapter, chiffonade means "stacked, rolled, and cut into fine strips."*

Fisherman's Favorite

If you've ever eaten on a fishing boat, there's probably a decent chance you had fish served in a manner similar to this: slathered with mayonnaise and broiled. Fishermen love their mayo. Who can blame 'em? It's good stuff. Sure, there's a certain lowbrow quality to cooking an expensive piece of fish under a bunch of gooey fat, but that's part of the fun. Besides, once you taste the results, you might just swear off extra virgin olive oil forever. Or not.

6 tablespoons mayonnaise
1 tablespoon lemon juice
2 teaspoons fresh dill, chopped
Kosher salt and freshly ground black pepper
4 swordfish steaks (6 to 8 ounces each)
Lemon wedges

Turn the broiler to high and adjust the rack so that the fish cooks about 6 inches from the heat source.

Season both sides of the swordfish steaks with salt and pepper and arrange them in an oiled baking dish or on a broiler pan. In a small bowl, whisk together the mayonnaise, lemon juice, and dill. Spread half of the mayo mixture on top of the fillets, reserving the rest.

Broil the steaks for 5 to 6 minutes, making sure the mayo doesn't turn overly brown. (If it does start to discolor significantly, move the rack down a peg.) Flip the steaks, cover them with the remaining mayo, and slip them back under the broiler for 4 to 6 minutes, until cooked through.

Serve immediately with lemon wedges.

Serves 4

NOTE: *If you can't stand the idea of cooking with mayonnaise, replace it with the Spicy Aioli found on page 47. Your friends will think you're much more sophisticated.*

Chapter 13
Mussels
Fantastic Faux

*Faux fur, spray-on tans, composite roof
shingles, professional wrestling, Spinal Tap—
let's face it, sometimes fake is better than the real thing.
Take mussels, for instance. Farm-raised mussels grow five times faster, yield three times
the meat, and taste sweeter than their wild brothers and sisters. Because most are
grown on posts or ropes suspended in the water, they're free of the grit and sand found in
wild specimens, and can be harvested using environmentally friendly methods. About the
only thing wild mussels have going for them is a thicker shell, which is good for collecting
barnacles (and, one hopes, deflecting criticism). But perhaps fake is too strong a word.
There's nothing artificial about cultured mussels, they've simply been afforded the opportunity to be all they can be. Given the chance, who wouldn't take that?*

VITAL STATS

FIRST NAME: Mussel (blue, Baltic, New
Zealand greenshell, Mediterranean)

SCI. NAME: *Mytilus* spp., *Perna
caniculus* (N.Z.)

SIZE: Blue/Baltic: 15-20 per lb; New
Zealand/Mediterranean: 10-15 per lb

LIFESPAN: 12-24 months, cultured; up
to 12 years in the wild

RANGE: Worldwide coastal waters;
prime North American sites: New
England, Washington State, Canada

HARVEST: 1.5 million metric tons,
farmed annually worldwide

Once upon a time (1235), a shipwrecked Irish sailor named Patrick Walton built a makeshift volleyball net on a deserted French beach, and a few months later, the mussel farm was born. Seems Walton was trying to catch seabirds (yum), but discovered the poles he'd sunk into the tidewater were better at collecting mussels than cormorants. Walton soon had a series of wooden stakes planted just beneath the high tide line, a formation that would later become known as a *bouchot*.

Remarkably, Walton's method for growing mussels remains in use today, albeit on a much larger scale. Tens of thousands of poles dot the coastline of France, collecting mussels for a population that is nuts for the tasty bivalve. In fact, all of Europe is in love with the mussel to the tune of nearly 10 pounds per person per year—more than thirty times the American average. My personal intake hovers somewhere around the Euro number, so obviously some of you aren't pulling your weight. You're not alone.

It wasn't long ago that mussels were seen primarily as a nuisance to oyster and clam fishermen. Most Americans deemed them edible only as a last resort source of protein to be eaten during times of war or desperation. Fortunately, times change. Thanks in part to a rise in popularity of ethnic cuisine, mussels finally found a place on the menu in the later part of the twentieth century.

Today, a heaping bowl of steamed mussels is a restaurant favorite. They may not be the kitchen staple they are in Europe, but for anyone eager to take the next step up the shellfish ladder, mussels are the answer. Easy to buy, store, and cook, mussels offer a taste experience that's more complex than the average quahog, but doesn't require ordering anything "raw on the half shell" (not that there's anything wrong with that).

Mickey Mussel?

The origin of the word "mussel" comes from the Latin mus. Apparently, some Roman thought the bivalve's shape and size approximated that of a mouse.

In the Water
Don't Move a Mussel

In the wild, mussels populate intertidal areas, meaning some days they spend almost as much time out of the water as under it. Their twin shells remain closed while exposed to air, but once the tide comes in, they open, allowing tiny hairlike cilia to go in search of dinner. Being filter feeders, mussels draw in water continuously—anywhere from 12 to 24 gallons a day, depending on whom you ask—in order to collect nutrients from the sea. For a mussel, phytoplankton stew is the soup du jour, although just about any organic material might end up on the menu.

Main Mussels

If you've eaten mussels, chances are they were BLUE MUSSELS (Mytilus edulis). Blues account for more than 90 percent of those grown in the United States and Canada. The BALTIC MUSSEL (M. trossulus), a close cousin of the blue (some insist they're the same species), can be found in the Pacific Northwest. In terms of flavor, blues and Baltics are more or less the same. Subtle differences in taste or texture are a product of where they were grown, rather than the name they go by.

blues

The MEDITERRANEAN MUSSEL (M. galloprovincialis) is both larger and faster growing than its blue brethren, making it popular with farmers and fans of stuffed shellfish. In addition to more storage space, the NEW ZEALAND GREENSHELL (formerly green-lipped) MUSSEL (Perna canaliculus) also comes with a pretty green shell. Most greenshells are only available frozen in North America.

New Zealand greenshell

Although most of a mussel's existence is spent glued to a rock on the ocean floor, they don't begin life that way. When mussels spawn, they release sperm and eggs into the water, letting the current to do the work. Remarkably, it may take only five hours for a fertilized egg to develop into a swimming, larval mussel. Within a month, the tiny bivalve will have grown a shell and started looking for real estate. It might be a rock, a pier, even a fellow bivalve, but once a mussel finds the perfect home it secures itself via a cement-like substance secreted from a tubular appendage called the foot. Upon hardening, the black, threadlike cement, or byssus, looks like a set of whiskers, which explains why it's commonly called a "beard" by mussel purveyors.

On the Farm
Hanging Around

The *bouchot* technique (mussels on posts) is widely used in Europe, but in the United States and Canada, most mussels are grown on ropes. The principle is the same—give the mussels somewhere to settle and they will land—but the direction is reversed. Ropes hang down into the water from rafts or submerged lines, offering mussels the ideal vantage point from which to gather nutrients. Come harvest time, the ropes are pulled up by hand or machine and the mussels plucked from their perches.

A third option, referred to as beach or bottom culture, places mussels in a bed on the seafloor, more or less mimicking their natural habitat. It's a cheaper way to farm mussels, but the end product requires more postharvest processing to purge it of silt collected during growing.

Just add water

Mussel farming has been hugely successful in part because the mussels feed themselves. They eat whatever floats by, making them cost-effective and environmentally friendly. What's in the water also has an effect on the mussel's flavor. Prince Edward Island in Canada and Penn Cove in Washington State both have sheltered, nutrient-rich bays where mussels grow quickly, away from dangerous surf and most predators. Freshwater runoff makes these locations warmer and naturally less saline than other waters, resulting in a sweeter, plumper mussel.

One drawback to raising a filter feeder is that its diet is going to include any toxins, bacteria, or pollutants that happen to be in the water. To prevent any such nasties from reaching the public, farms are regularly monitored and their mussels certified by the National Shellfish Sanitation Program.

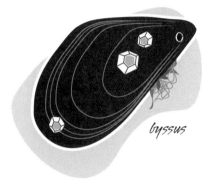

Stowaways

Some species of mussels have spread around the world by hitching a ride in the ballast of sailing ships bound for far-flung ports.

byssus

Suburban Shellfish

Even though young, rebellious mussels may strut around a bit, once they find a friendly community, most settle down to become good bivalves. Sure, it looks crowded, but by ganging up, mussels are able to offer each other protection from waves and better odds against being eaten (by non-human predators).

Rope Grown

Bare ropes are suspended in the water to collect spat (baby mussels) floating in the current. Some farms seed the water, while others depend on wild spat to populate their ropes. Once the mussels are big enough (around 15 millimeters), they're redistributed to allow each mussel room enough to grow big and strong. In many cases, young mussels are replanted inside long mesh socks, which offer a bit of protection and an ideal growing environment. Twelve to twenty-four months later, the mature mussels are harvested, processed, and shipped to market.

Where in the wild?

Despite the fact that cultured mussels are superior to wild in nearly every respect, there remains a modest fishery in New England that uses dredges and pump-driven suction gear to collect blue mussels from coastal waters. The easiest way to spot a wild mussel is to check the shell, which will be thicker and rougher than most farm-raised specimens.

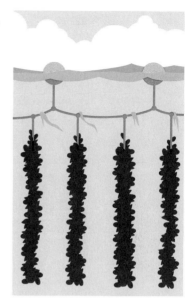

mussel rope culture

At the Market
Tag It and Bag It

Mussels are shipped to markets in a variety of forms, from 2-pound consumer friendly bags to 500-pound industrial-sized vats. Each container comes with a shellfish tag (sometimes called a "lot" or "bed" tag) that identifies both the date and location of harvest. In some cases there are two dates: one for the initial harvest, and one for when the shellfish were pulled from wet storage. If your fishmonger is kind enough to put this tag on display, it's worth a look.

a shellfish tag

Mussels are available year-round, but certain varieties are better at different times of the year. Because blue mussels spawn in the summer, their flavor, texture, and size are best in winter and spring. Mediterranean mussels are just the opposite, meaning they're plump and sweet in the summer. New Zealand greenshells are also available in the winter—our winter. They're actually cold-weather spawners, but the hemisphere change flips the seasons in our favor.

What to buy

If you have the option of buying either cultivated or wild mussels, buy the farm boys. They're worth an extra buck or two a pound. Choosing between different farms or varieties is more a matter of personal taste.

Male, Female, or...

When a mussel spawns, most of its energy goes toward reproduction, reducing its overall meat content by as much as 30 percent. To increase year-round production, as well as prevent fertilization of local stocks, some farms are now raising sterilized Mediterranean mussels. The mussels, called triploids, have an extra chromosome, and will never spawn, making them plump and juicy all year.

Color Coding

Mussel meat comes in two colors—orange and creamy white. Both colors taste the same, but one (the orange) comes from a female mussel, while the other (cream) comes from a male.

Sandy Mussels

If you've landed a bag of wild mussels that you can see are pretty sandy, an hour or two soaking in salted water (½ cup salt per quart) may help.

HOW TO STORE: Mussels

LIVE: Some sources recommend purging mussels in water along with a cup of cornmeal. This is not necessary. Most cultured mussels are clean enough already, and storing them in a bucket of fresh water will probably kill them. To repeat: *Storing mussels in fresh water will kill them.* Leaving mussels in a sealed, plastic bag will also hasten their demise. The best way to store mussels is in the refrigerator, in a bowl, loosely covered with a moist towel (the air is too dry without it). A little ice below doesn't hurt, as long as it's sealed in a plastic bag. Refresh the ice and remoisten the towel, as needed.

Out of the water, properly stored mussels will survive for 7 to 10 days. That's time from harvest or wet storage, not from when they're brought home. Most farmers are pretty good about getting their product to market quickly, but let's go with 5 to 7 days at home, just to be on the safe side.

Look for mussels whose shells are unbroken and mostly closed. If you get to handle them before purchase, tap any that happen to be open. Healthy mussels will close up shop in a hurry. In some markets, mussels are sold in 1- or 2-pound mesh bags, usually with some kind of identifying tag. With these, it's best to use your sniffer. Do they smell like a beach or a bog? Actually, I'm not sure what a bog smells like, but I assume it's unpleasant. I don't need that in my kitchen.

Online options

A surprisingly good option for finding high-quality mussels is the Internet. Many farms now sell direct to the public, meaning inexpensive, exceedingly fresh mussels can be had with just a few clicks. Not only does this give folks in Kansas a shot at the freshest shellfish, it also allows them to choose specific varieties and locales. Point and click.

In the Kitchen
Staying Alive

Thanks to cleaner cultivation techniques and postharvest processing, most mussels don't require more than a simple rinse prior to cooking. Still, it doesn't hurt to give each an inspection before it goes into the pot. The cold air of the fridge will have slowed their metabolism, but they should still clam up within 30 seconds. Any open mussels that continue to smile, even after handling, should be discarded. To check a closed mussel for life signs, try to slide the top and bottom shells in opposite directions. If they slip significantly, the mussel is dead.

Rinse each mussel under cold running water, and use a stiff brush to remove any unwanted artifacts. Some mussels have their beards trimmed prior to sale, but not removed. To get rid of the mini mutton-chops, simply grasp firmly and pull. Need help? A pair of pliers will get the job done. Home beard removal is usually a death sentence, so try to do it as close to cook-time as possible.

Despite all the warnings, your mussels aren't going to die at the drop of the hat. With proper storage and handling, it's unlikely there'll be more than couple of croakers in the bunch. If you do find an unusually high percentage of fatalities, be sure to mention it to your fishmonger.

Get steamed

Mussels are easy to cook. In fact, when I tell you how easy, you're going to wonder why you haven't been cooking them all of your life. Ready?

1. Steam mussels in flavorful liquid until open.
2. Enjoy.

It's just that simple. You'll probably spend more time setting the table. In addition to the mussels, you'll need a pot, something large enough to hold at least twice as many mussels as you've got, and the previously mentioned "flavorful liquid." What is that? If you're French, it's white wine, shallots, and parsley. If you're Italian, it might be olive oil, garlic, and tomatoes. If you're me, and no one's looking, it's beer and cilantro or dill. Honestly, it can be just about any combination of flavorful liquid, aromatic vegetable, and fragrant herb in the pantry. (Within reason, of course. Malt vinegar, red onion, and mint? I don't think so.)

Once steaming starts, a pound or two of mussels is going to take 4 to 8 minutes to cook, depending on size. Some individuals might hold out a little longer, but eventually they'll pop. If they don't, they were dead before they went into the pot. Toss 'em.

The rest of mussels are ready to serve, preferably in a bowl, accompanied by the flavorful liquid, which, thanks to your considerable culinary prowess, has been transformed into shellfish broth. Yes, the mussels helped a little by releasing their own flavorful juices, but if you hadn't turned on the heat, they'd still be sitting there (lazy bivalves). If you prefer your shellfish broth a little more saucy, go ahead and thicken it up with a little butter or cream before pouring it over the mussels. Don't forget the bread for dipping (I like French, but any crusty loaf will do). And fresh herbs? Absolutely! A sprinkling of fresh Italian parsley adds flavor and makes everything look very pretty.

Did I say pretty? I meant professional.

Why Alive?

Mussels are more than capable of defending themselves against bacteria and spoilage—while they're alive. Dead mussels have no such defenses, making them an inviting target for bad bugs. The solution: Cook 'em alive.

NUTRITIONAL INFO

Per 3.5 oz/100 grams (raw)

Blue Mussel

Calories	86
Calories from fat	20
Total fat	2.24 g
Saturated fat	0.4 g
Cholesterol	28 mg
Sodium	286 mg
Protein	11.9 g
Omega-3	0.46 g
Mercury	N/A

Protein Power

Think that steak has a lot of protein? Mussels pack in just as much, minus the saturated fat and 75 percent of the calories.

Mussel Recipes

There are two kinds of people in the world: those who love mussels and those who have never eaten mussels. Oh, sure, I suppose there are a few folks who claim not to like the tasty bivalves, but my guess is that they've just never had a good one. Since there's currently no "mussel reeducation facility" where we can send these people, it's up to you to learn 'em. You have your orders. Here are some recipes. Get to it!

Steamed Mussels

If you've never made mussels at home you're in for a treat. Few things are as easy or as flavorful. Don't worry if a few mussels refuse to open, even if all their brethren have already yawned. Remove those that have opened and give the stragglers a minute or two on their own. If they still won't open, toss 'em.

2 pounds live mussels
1 tablespoon unsalted butter
1 large garlic clove, minced
2 tablespoons shallots, minced
Freshly ground black pepper
¾ cup dry white wine
2 tablespoons flat-leaf parsley, chopped
French bread

Scrub and debeard the mussels, tossing any that are cracked or remain open after handling.

Place the butter, garlic, and shallots in a large saucepan (or pot) over medium heat. Season the mixture with pepper and cook until softened, 1 to 2 minutes. Add the wine, parsley, and mussels, cover the pan, and bring the liquid to a boil over high heat. Steam the mussels until the shells have opened, 4 to 6 minutes.

Transfer the mussels and cooking liquid to a large bowl. Serve immediately with bread for dipping. *NOTE: If the liquid seems gritty, carefully pour it into a separate bowl, leaving the grit behind, and then pour it over the mussels.*

Serves 3 or 4

ALTERNATIVE 1: Replace the wine with beer (something amber or lighter), the parsley with cilantro, and lose the garlic. After steaming, transfer the mussels to a bowl, but leave the liquid behind. Add 2 tablespoons unsalted butter, swirl until it is melted, and then pour it over the mussels (leaving any grit in the pan).

ALTERNATIVE 2: Replace the wine with coconut milk, the garlic with 2 teaspoons freshly grated ginger, and the parsley with fresh basil. Add the zest and juice of 1 lime, 1 tablespoon of chopped lemongrass, and ½ teaspoon of crushed red pepper flakes.

Bag-O-Mussels

After the folding, this recipe is even simpler than steamed mussels. You guys are getting off easy. Next book it's nothing but soufflés. NOTE: Don't overload the bag or there won't be enough room for all of the mussels to open. If you have 1½ pounds of mussels, make two pouches.

1 pound live mussels
1 cup fresh heirloom tomatoes, diced
2 tablespoons onion, diced
2 tablespoons fresh cilantro, chopped
Freshly ground black pepper
1 lime, cut into wedges
½ cup dry white wine

Scrub and debeard the mussels, tossing any that are cracked or remain open after handling.

Preheat oven to 425° F.

Toss the tomatoes, onion, and cilantro in a large bowl and season with pepper. Add the mussels, wine, and lime wedges (go ahead and squeeze the juice out of a few), and stir to coat.

To make the bag, begin with a piece of parchment approximately 15 by 24 inches. Fold it in half like a book. Fold the top edge of the book down twice (about an inch each time). Fold the bottom edge up twice. You should be left with an opening on the side.

Hold the parchment bag open over a large baking dish. Carefully pour in the mussel mixture and seal by folding the edge over twice in the opposite direction of the other folds. *NOTE: It helps to have an extra pair of hands holding the pouch edge so they don't unfurl.* Lay the bag flat and bake the dish for 15 to 20 minutes, by which time all the mussels should be open. (Discard any mussels that turn out to be closed.)

Transfer the unopened bag to a large bowl and open it at the table. Or if you're not trying to impress a date, open it on the kitchen counter and enjoy.

Serves 2 as an appetizer

Cast-Iron Mussels

What did I just say about easy? Hey, look! No flavorful liquid. This recipe can't possibly work, can it? You'd be surprised. (Okay, it's the mussels' own juices that help cook 'em. Hardly seems fair, but it tastes good.)

1 pound live mussels
Kosher salt and freshly ground black pepper
1 tablespoon fresh basil, chiffonade
Extra virgin olive oil

Place a cast-iron pan in the oven and turn the heat up to 500° F.

Meanwhile, scrub and debeard the mussels, tossing any that are cracked or remain open after handling.

Once the oven hits the mark, transfer the *very hot* pan to a stovetop burner set on high. Add the mussels in a single layer, cover the pan, and cook until the shells open, 3 to 4 minutes.

Transfer the mussels to a serving bowl. Drizzle them with olive oil, sprinkle on the basil, and season with salt and pepper. Serve immediately.

Serves 2

Mussels
with Roasted Tomato Salsa

Finally, a recipe that requires you to do a little work. No, I'm not saying you're lazy. I'm saying seafood is easy. That's kind of the point of this book. Interesting, tasty, and easy. Maybe I should say something about this recipe. Let's see. . .oh, yeah, the mussels! This recipe calls for the larger than average mussels, which gives you a good excuse to track down a few New Zealand green mussels. Chances are they'll be frozen when you find them—that's a good thing. Since they're already partially cooked, you can skip the steaming step and go straight to the stuffing and baking.

3 dozen very large live mussels
½ cup dry white wine
Roasted Tomato Salsa (see recipe)
Lemon wedges

Scrub and debeard the mussels, tossing any that are cracked or remain open after handling.

Preheat the oven to 425° F.

In a large pot, bring the wine to a boil over high heat. Add the mussels, cover the pot, and steam them until the shells have opened, 4 to 6 minutes. Discard any that refuse to open.

Discard the top shell of each mussel and then lay them flat on a baking sheet. Top each mussel with a spoonful of salsa. Bake 7 to 8 minutes, until bubbling on top. *NOTE: If frozen mussels are used it may be necessary to add a few minutes to the cooking time to heat them through.*

Serve immediately with lemon wedges.

Serves 3 or 4

Roasted Tomato Salsa

Roasting the tomatoes pumps up their flavor, making them rich and quite a bit sweeter, which contrasts nicely with the meaty mussels. By the way. . .yes, you could use this salsa as part of the flavorful liquid when steaming mussels.

1½ pounds plum (Roma) tomatoes, quartered
1 small onion, quartered and separated
6 large garlic cloves, peeled
Kosher salt and freshly ground black pepper
2 teaspoons dried rosemary
1 teaspoon ground red pepper flakes
½ teaspoon sugar
1 tablespoon lemon juice
2 tablespoons extra virgin olive oil

Preheat oven to 325° F.

Place the tomatoes (skin side down), onions, and garlic in a large nonreactive baking dish and season with salt and pepper. Roast for 1 hour. *NOTE: If the tomatoes start to burn before the time's up, cut the roasting session short.*

When the tomatoes have cooled, remove the skins and dice them. Dice the onion. Mince the garlic. Place all three in a large bowl and mix thoroughly. Add the rosemary, red pepper, sugar, lemon juice, and olive oil. Stir to combine.

Cover the bowl and allow the flavors to mingle in the fridge for an hour prior to use. Can be made up to 3 days in advance. (By the way, this salsa also makes a terrific pasta sauce. Simply reheat the sauce briefly and toss it with cooked pasta. Add a few steamed mussels? That's a fine idea.)

Chapter 14
Clams
Blue Collar Bivalve

Come low tide, you'll find them by the dozen, knee deep in the muck, mining for their supper. Armed only with bucket and shovel, the recreational clam digger is no threat to fish or fowl, but to the bivalve he is the harbinger of doom. Run, littleneck, run…something wicked this way comes. End times aside, what does it say about us that we're willing to dig a hole in the ground to find something to eat? Are we really that hungry, that desperate? Or is a clam simply that good? Sure, a clam isn't as exotic as an oyster, as elegant as a scallop, or even as trendy as a mussel, but what it lacks in pedigree it makes up for in accessibility. This is a bivalve for the masses. A bowl of steamers, a basket of fried strips, a cup of chowder—this isn't country club fare, this is side-of-the-road cuisine at its best. You don't need a membership to enjoy a clam, all you need is an appetite and directions to the beach. And maybe a shovel.

VITAL STATS

FIRST NAME: Clam (common varieties: hard-shell/quahog, soft-shell, Manila)

SCI. NAME: *Mercenaria mercenaria* (quahog), *Mya arenaria* (soft-shell), *Tapes phillippinarium* (Manila)

SIZE: Most 1.5-8 in across the shell

LIFESPAN: Most 4-8 years when harvested wild, 1-2 years cultured

RANGE: North American coastal waters, primarily Atlantic seaboard; Pacific Northwest; Canada

CATCH: About 125 million pounds annually, U.S.

For those who don't like sand in their shorts…or under their fingernails, or between their toes, or up their, um…well, anyway, it's okay to pay someone else to dig up a few clams. Just don't be surprised if your change comes back in shells.

Long before wooden nickels and two-dollar bills, clamshells were used as a makeshift currency in prerevolutionary America. The scarcity of metal coins had led early European traders to adopt polished clam and whelk shells as a substitute. It was Native Americans who first put wampum into circulation, albeit not intentionally. To them the strings of shells were best used as necklaces or belts, or possibly as a gift. The concept of money may have been new, but the locals caught on fast. By the mid-1600s, colonists and tribes throughout the Northeast were using wampum as legal tender, with the deep purple beads made from quahog shells having the most value.

Unfortunately, when the local currency can be found scattered on the beach, it's hard to base an economy on it. As coins became more plentiful, wampum's popularity waned. To honor its pecuniary past, the quahog was given the scientific name, *Mercenaria mercenaria*, which roughly translated means "pay up, you lazy colonist."

Today, the value of a clam is based more on what's inside than out. Sweet, tender, and occasionally chewy (in a good way), a clam is modest fare that's not out to impress as much as satisfy. Some folks call that boring. I call it comfort food.

In the Water
Gophers of the Sea

What does it mean to be "happy as a clam"? All evidence points to one thing: burying yourself neck-deep in the sand. Check almost any beach at low tide, and chances are you'll find "clam sign"—small holes in the sand that practically scream, "Hey, here I am!" If only they knew.

Most clams spend all of their lives tucked beneath the soft, sandy bottoms and mud flats between low and high tide in an area known as the intertidal zone. How low a clam can go depends on how far it's willing to stick its neck out. The neck, a.k.a. the siphon, acts as a subterranean snorkel that draws in nutrients and expels waste, all without exposing the clam to dangerous ocean conditions or predators (except those with shovels).

A man's clam

Clams grow faster in warmer waters, which is why quahogs from Florida tend to reach market size three times faster than their Northern brothers. The warmer water also gives the Southern boys a head start in terms of reproduction, which normally kicks into high gear after their first birthday. What about the Northern sisters and Southern girls? Ninety-eight percent of quahogs start out life as males. Fortunately, about half will change to females at some point during their lives (though probably not soon enough for the clams that don't).

Much like other bivalves, clams spawn externally, releasing their eggs and sperm to mingle freely in the current. In the two weeks a fertilized egg stays in the water column, it may drift fifty miles before settling on the seafloor. Once it touches bottom, the clam quickly adopts the subterranean lifestyle, using its tiny foot to burrow into the sand. Thus ends the aerobic portion of the clam's life (more or less).

Say what?

The name "quahog" (also spelled "quahaug") is derived from the Native American word "poquauhock," meaning "hard clam." (Which tribe? Algonquin, Narragansett, Wampanoag, Pequot…take your pick.)

Guess They Don't Retain Water

A 3-inch clam may filter upward of 6,000 gallons of water a year, from which it subtracts less than 4 ounces of food.

This Old Clam

The geoduck has a natural lifespan well over 100 years, a quahog close to 40. To check the age of a clam, count the growth rings on the outside of the shell, each of which represents one year of growth.

Clam Clan

Despite a lot of names, there are really only three categories under which the most commonly eaten clams can be found: HARD-SHELL, SOFT-SHELL, and OTHER.

Hard-shell clams

The most popular Atlantic hard-shell clam is the NORTHERN QUAHOG (Mercenaria mercenaria). Quahogs (pronounced KO-hogs) come in a variety of sizes, though the exact dimensions of a small, medium, or large 'hog varies from market to market. (In other words, the names are the same, but don't quote me on numbers.) The smallest (2 to 2.5 inches across the shell) are called "littlenecks," which are great for raw applications and steaming. Named for a bay on Long Island, littlenecks have sweet, tender meat, and are generally more expensive than larger clams. Some markets sell "middle-necks" or "top-necks," which are really just large littlenecks (2.5 to 3 inches). Next up the quahog ladder are the "cherrystones" (3 to 4 inches), which are more economical when it comes to steaming, but also fine for serving raw or stuffed. The largest quahogs are the chowders clams (4 inches plus), often simply referred to as quahogs. Chowders tend to be a little bland in the flavor department, making them perfect for chowder.

OCEAN QUAHOGS (Arctica islandica) are deepwater clams, primarily harvested for use in chowders. Small ocean quahogs picked up closer to shore are often sold using clever marketing names, such as "mahogany" or "Golden Neck," and are best served fresh from the steamer.

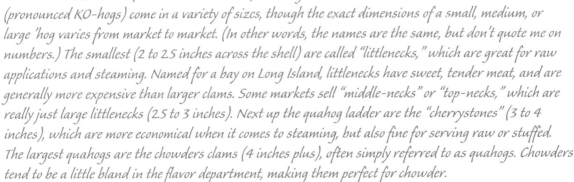

On the West Coast, a batch of PACIFIC LITTLENECKS (Protothaca staminea) will steam up much like their Atlantic cousins, though not as tender. More popular are the MANILA CLAMS (Tapes phillippinarium), which come in a variety of sizes, the smallest (1 to 2 inches) being best for steaming or raw applications. Manila clams have relatively thin shells, meaning there's more meat in a pound of Manilas than other hard-shell clams. Large PISMO CLAMS, a California classic, are rarely seen these days, thanks to hungry locals (both man and otter), but if you get the chance to try one, don't say no. They're tender and sweet.

Soft-shell clams

Soft-shell clams (Mya arenaria), popularly known as STEAMERS (also "fryers" and "longnecks"), can be found all along the Atlantic Coast from Maine to Maryland, and in some areas on the West Coast. The most distinctive feature of a softie is not its shell (which is fairly chalky and brittle), but its siphon. That ugly, little wormy thing hanging out is the reason why the soft-shell can never completely clam up. In terms of preparation, steaming is best way to cook a steamer (duh), but frying is pretty good, too. Raw? I don't recommend it.

Other clams

At 4 to 8 inches across, SURF CLAMS (Spisula solidissima), also known as "sea clams" or "bar clams," are too large to eat whole, thus most are chopped up for chowder or cut into strips to be fried. The surf clam harvest is the largest of any clam in the United States, more than half of which comes from New Jersey.

Varieties of RAZOR CLAMS (Ensis directus) are found on both coasts, though neither is in great supply. Seasonal harvests usually go straight to restaurants to be breaded and fried, though it's possible to find PACIFIC RAZOR CLAMS (Siliqua patula) in some West Coast markets in the late summer and fall.

razor

Finally, there are the GEODUCKS (Panopea abrupta) of the Pacific Northwest. While the name (pronounced GOO-ey-duck) may seem an accurate description, it actually comes from the Nisqually Indian word for "dig deep," which the geoduck does—up to 4 feet beneath the sandy bottom. A good-sized geoduck may weigh as much as ten pounds and sport a siphon more than two feet long. And, yes, folks eat 'em. They're quite popular in Japan, served raw or quick-cooked in a stir-fry. Pounded flat, the flavor is reminiscent of abalone.

geoduck

On the Boats and Farm
Digging in the Dirt

One would think that because clams tend not to move much, they'd be easy to catch. While there's more to harvesting clams than simply "digging in the right place," the success enjoyed by domestic clammers has made it look simple. The ocean quahog and surf clam fisheries harvest a combined annual total of more than 100 million pounds, well within the limits needed to maintain a healthy biomass. Most deepwater clams are collected using hydraulic dredges that pump jets of water into the sand to loosen them from their underground hiding places. Once a clam is out in the open, the dredge simply scoops it up.

Closer to shore, northern quahogs are harvested using rakes and tongs, with only a small percentage being brought in by dredge. Most soft-shell clams are harvested by hand using hoes and short-handled forks at low tide. Both quahog and soft-shell clam stocks are considered to be healthy.

amateur clam-digging tools

Red Menace

During warmer months, toxic marine algae can move into coastal waters creating a condition known as "red tide." Though harmless to the clam, a red tide can cause purulytic shellfish poisoning in humans who eat shellfish that have been feeding in contaminated waters. Areas where clams are harvested or cultured are monitored by state and local jurisdictions to ensure public safety. If you're planning a clam dig and don't know the status of local waters, check with state health services or fish and wildlife departments.

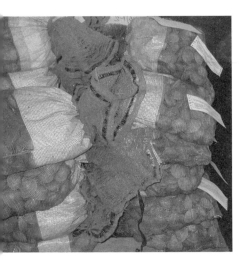

tagged and bagged quahogs

QUICK QUESTION

Are clam farms good for the environment? In general, clam farms are considered very eco-friendly. No additional feed is used, clams are harvested using bottom-safe methods, there's no competition with native stocks, and the addition of filter feeders actually improves the quality of the local waters by filtering out algae and plankton and reducing levels of nitrogen, phosphorus, and other suspended solids.

West Coast culture

Out west, 10 million plus pounds of Manila clams are harvested each year, most of which comes from shellfish farms in Puget Sound. The process starts with clam larvae weaned in tanks of nutrient-rich water, and then moves to floating nursery trays anchored offshore. Once the clams are about 12 millimeters across, they're removed from the trays and "planted" in the sandy bottom beneath a layer of sediment and protective mesh. When the clams reach market size, they're harvested by either hand or mechanical means.

At the Market
No Shovel Required

Remember all those clams I named a few pages back? Don't expect to find examples of each down at the fish market. A good selection would be two or three sizes of hard-shell clams, plus at least one soft-shell variety. If your market has more, give your fishmonger a hug.

The basic rule for buying hard-shell clams is this: the smaller the clam, the more tender it will be. Smaller is better for raw applications and steaming; larger is better for stuffing and chowders. Frying works both ways, depending on whether you're after strips or whole bellies. Soft-shell clams are best steamed or fried. Shucked clam meats can be found either fresh or canned; both are ideal for chowders.

The season runs year-round, but in most places spawning causes meat yields to decline during the summer. The best clams usually arrive in the fall and winter.

Bad clam

What constitutes a bad clam? Any of the following: a broken shell, a cracked shell, a gaping shell, a shell that refuses to close, a shell that rattles, a shell that sounds hollow when tapped, a limp siphon in a soft-shell, or a bad smell. Good clams smell briny-fresh, close when disturbed, and are heavy, but not too heavy (full of sand). Soft-shell clams can't close their shells, but the siphon will pull back slightly if touched.

As with any shellfish, bulk clams are required by the National Shellfish Sanitation Program to be distributed with a sticker that details everything you might want to know about their life history. The market doesn't have to display it, but they're required to keep it for 90 days in case there are any problems with the clams. (*See page 139 for an example of a shellfish tag.*)

Buying Raw

The best clams for serving raw on the half shell are the freshest clams, so don't be afraid to ask to see the bed tag if it's not posted.

In the Kitchen

Not Just Chowder Heads

Remember when I said there was no need to purge mussels since they were already clean? Same goes for hard-shell clams. Most cultured quahogs and Manilas go through some form of purging after harvest to rid them of any leftover grit and possibly their last meal. I do recommend a thorough rinse under cold water and a brief scrub with a stiff brush.

Soft-shell clams suck up a lot more mud than their closemouthed cousins, which means, regardless of whether they were store-bought or beach-caught, they're more likely to track dirt into your kitchen. The solution: Soak 'em. Give the clams a preliminary rinse, then toss them in large bowl or pot and cover with salted water (½ cup salt per quart). Store in the fridge for at least an hour. If the water looks especially muddy, change it out, and let the clams soak another hour.

Despite what your buddy from Ipswich told you, there's no need to add cornmeal or flour to the mixture. The clams will purge themselves just fine on their own. (Besides, do you really want to be eating clams full of cornmeal?)

HEY! If you purge them, be sure to *lift* the clams out of the water. Simply emptying the bowl into a strainer will result in much of the grit going right back into the clams.

Shucking

There are two ways to shuck a clam: the *right way* and the *dirty cheater's way*. The right way requires a clam knife (or other stubby, sturdy blade), a towel, and a little practice. The dirty cheater's way requires steaming or blanching clams briefly to get them to open up on their own. The former is required for any raw application. The latter is okay for certain cooked dishes where a small loss in overall flavor is not going to make a big impact. The choice is up to you.

HOW TO STORE: Clams

LIVE: Clams have a shorter shelf life than other bivalves, so your best defense against a quahog massacre is to use them within 2 days of purchase. Store live clams in a bowl covered with a damp towel or a few wet paper towels, preferably in the coldest part of the refrigerator. Clams spoil rather quickly after dying, so check for any expired clams before storing. Do not keep clams in a sealed plastic bag or submerged in fresh water or they will…well, you know. **FROZEN:** Clams can be frozen alive, either in the shell or shucked, but once thawed, the meat tends to cook up a little chewy (more than usual). If you plan on freezing your clams, it's actually better to cook them first.

1)

2)

3)

Hard-shell Shucking

Shucking a hard-shell clam requires protection, either in the form of a dishtowel or an oyster glove (or an oven mitt, sure).

(1) Place the clam in protected hand, right side up, with the hinge toward your wrist. (2) Carefully slip the edge of the knife between the lips of the shell, using the fingers of your protected hand to apply pressure. Don't go straight through. (3) Keeping it as flush as possible, slide the knife along the top shell to cut through the muscle that holds the clam in place. (4) Pry the shell open, and then slide the knife under the clam to it free from the bottom shell. Try not to spill any of the clam's juices.

Get steamed, part 2

Cooking clams is a lot like cooking mussels, but for those who skipped ahead, let's review:

1. Steam ~~mussels~~ clams in flavorful liquid until open.
2. Enjoy.

Yep, it's that simple. Granted, there are more varieties of clams and not all of them are ideal for steaming, but for small to medium hard-shell clams and soft-shell steamers, that's your master recipe. Five minutes is usually enough to steam a couple of dozen clams, give or take a few minutes for stragglers. Any longer and that low-fat, protein-rich meat will start to toughen up. If a clam isn't open after ten minutes, it never will. Chuck it.

What constitutes an appropriate "flavorful liquid?" How about beer? This is the blue-collar bivalve, after all. We don't need any fancy wine and shallots, or olive oil and garlic, or…actually, those sound pretty good, too. Okay, let's say anything that works for mussels works for clams, but a well-balanced beer adds a little something extra—call it beery goodness. Yeah, that sounds about right. Just don't go crazy with the hops unless you like bitter clam face.

That's Not a Steamer

In New England, a steamer is a soft-shell clam. Elsewhere, a "steamer" might indicate a softie, but it also might be a hard shell clam of some sort. Blasphemy!

QUICK QUESTION

Is it better to get muddy or sandy? Soft-shell clams fall into two categories: those that were harvested from mud and those harvested from sand. Muddy clams are usually less gritty, but sand clams tend to have more meat.

Soft-shell Shucking

Softies take less force to open, but you can use protection if you like.

(1) Slide the knife around the outer edge of the shell to loosen it. (2) Keeping it as flush as possible, slide the knife along the top shell to cut through the muscle that holds the clam in place. Remove the top shell. (3) Slide the knife under the clam to free it from the bottom shell. Remove the clam. (4) Pull or cut off the dark, leathery skin around the clam's siphon. (5) If the clam seems a little muddy, dip it in cold, salted water and pat it dry.

Clambakin'

A traditional clambake isn't so much a "bake" as it is a really big saltwater steam. Dig a large hole in the sand, fill it with rocks, and start a fire. Once the fire burns down and rocks are really hot, pile on the wet seaweed. Those funny little balls are full of saltwater, which turns into tasty steam when heated. Time to pile on the food: clams, lobsters, mussels, corn, potatoes, and pretty much anything else that happens to be lying around. Toss on a big piece of canvas or more seaweed to lock in the steam and in about an hour you'll experience seafood nirvana.

Clams also make an excellent addition to any backyard barbecue, assuming they're large enough not to slip through the grates. Toss a dozen cherrystones on the grill, cover with foil, and in a few minutes they'll be ready to eat. If it's raining outside, how about stuffed clams? Not your thing? How about fried clams? Everybody likes fried clams.

About that chowder...

Any seafood book worth its salt pork has to have a recipe for clam chowder, preferably in the traditional, New England style—none of that soupy, city stuff. Fine...but would that be Cape Anne or Cape Cod style? Thick or thin? How about clear? And what about Rhode Island Red? Did you think someone from Manhattan actually came up with a recipe for clam chowder? Silly reader.

There's only one rule when it comes to clam chowder: It has to taste like clams. Everything else is just there to support the name on the marquee. That means using good, fresh clams, and lots of them. Dig in.

NUTRITIONAL INFO

Per 3.5 oz/100 grams (raw)

Hard-Shell Clam

Calories	60
Calories from fat	9
Total fat	1 g
Saturated fat	0.2 g
Cholesterol	40 mg
Sodium	56 mg
Protein	9.2 g
Omega-3	0.2 g
Mercury	< 0.01 ppm

Soft-Shell Clam

Calories	65
Calories from fat	11
Total fat	1.2 g
Saturated fat	0.2 g
Cholesterol	25 mg
Sodium	N/A
Protein	10.7 g
Omega-3	0.2 g
Mercury	< 0.01 ppm

Clam Recipes

In general, anything you can do with a mussel, you can also do with a clam, so feel free to apply any of the basic recipes from the last chapter to a pound or two of littlenecks or Manilas. Granted, there are a few more varieties of clam, which gives your culinary muscles more of a chance to stretch. (Anyone who's tried to run around the block without warming up knows the importance of stretching.)

Steamed Clams

Here's your basic, blue-collar steamed clam recipe. Nothing but clams, butter, and beer. Oh, I suppose you could toss in some fresh herbs, maybe a little garlic or onion, but that's it. Lemon juice? I suppose...bacon? Now, why would you ever crumble 2 to 3 slices of crisply cooked bacon over steaming clams? That's crazy! Mmmm...bacon.

2 pounds live clams (the smaller the better)
1 cup beer (nothing too hoppy) or water
4 tablespoons unsalted butter

Scrub and rinse the clams, tossing any that are cracked or remain open after handling. *NOTE: For soft-shell clams be sure to purge them in salted water for an hour (maybe two).*

Place the beer and clams in a large pot, cover, and bring the beer to a boil over high heat. Reduce the heat to medium and cook the clams until the shells have opened, 2 to 4 minutes, depending on size. Transfer the open clams to a serving bowl with a slotted spoon. Give the stragglers a minute or two on their own. If they still won't open, toss 'em.

Swirl the butter into the cooking liquid and then pour it over the clams. *NOTE: If the liquid seems gritty, carefully pour it into a separate bowl, leaving the grit behind, and then pour it over clams.*

Serve immediately. *NOTE: For softies, remove the black skin from around the siphon prior to eating.*

Serves 2 or 3

Fried Clams

Hey, I bet you could use this recipe to fry mussels, too. I told you they were compatible. This recipe uses softies, but the same principle applies to hard-shell clams. Shucking your own clams is best, but buying preshucked clams is okay in a pinch.

4 dozen live soft-shell clams
1½ quarts (6 cups) peanut (or other vegetable) oil
1 cup corn flour
½ cup all-purpose flour
1 teaspoon freshly ground black pepper
1 cup evaporated milk
Tartar Sauce (*see recipe page 60*)
Spicy Aioli (*see recipe page 47*)
Lemon wedges

Rinse the clams and then place them in salted water (½ cup salt per quart). Soak for at least an hour. If the water is especially muddy, change it out, and soak for an additional hour.

Shuck the clams, making sure to remove the black leathery skin from around the siphon (*see page 151*). Dry the clams thoroughly. *NOTE: This can be done up to 2 hours in advance of frying. Store shucked clams in the fridge wrapped in paper towels.*

Preheat the oven to 200° F.

Heat the oil in a heavy 4-quart pot to 370° F. *NOTE: The deeper the pot, the better; clams have a tendency to splatter. A wire-mesh splatter guard helps, too.*

Combine both flours and pepper in a large bowl. Mix them thoroughly. Dip about a dozen clams in the milk, let the excess drain away, and then toss them in the flour to coat them. Shake off the excess flour.

Gently lower the clams into the oil. *CAUTION: There may be splattering.* Fry the clams for 2 to 3 minutes, turning them often, until golden brown. *NOTE: If the clams are overly large, reduce the number fried at one time so as not to overcrowd the pan.*

Transfer the cooked clams to a wire rack set over a baking sheet in the oven. Repeat the process with the remaining clams. Serve with lemon wedges and sauces for dipping.

Serves 3 or 4

Park on a Clam

It's common practice for surf clam processors to sell the leftover clamshells for paving driveways.

Stuffies

Time to break out the big boys. This recipe calls for linguisa, *but if you prefer a bit more heat you can use a spicier sausage, such as* chorizo. NOTE: *When buying the clams, be very particular about getting live specimens. When buying several dozen smaller clams, a few dead soldiers aren't a big deal; in this recipe a few clams is a whole serving!*

12 large quahogs
1 cup water
1 tablespoon unsalted butter
½ pound *linguisa* sausage, casings removed, and finely diced
½ cup celery, finely diced
¼ cup fennel, finely diced
3 shallots, minced
1 large garlic clove, minced
1 cup dried bread crumbs
Kosher salt and freshly ground black pepper
Lemon wedges

Scrub and rinse the clams. Place the beer and clams in a large pot, cover, and bring the beer to a boil over high heat. Reduce the heat to medium and cook the clams until the shells have opened, 4 to 8 minutes (the big guys take longer). Remove the clams using a slotted spoon, allowing their liquor to drain back into the pot in the process. Strain the cooking liquid and set it aside. Remove the clam meat from the shells, finely chop the meat, and set it aside.

Preheat oven to 425° F.

Melt the butter in a large sauté pan over medium heat. Add the *linguisa,* celery, fennel, and onion and cook, stirring often, until the sausage starts to brown, 4 to 6 minutes. Add the shallots and garlic and cook them until softened, about 2 minutes. Add the clams and half of the reserved cooking liquid. Bring it just to a boil and then remove from the heat. Stir in the bread crumbs until the moisture is absorbed. Add additional cooking liquid if the stuffing appears too dry. (It should be moist, but not soggy.) Season with salt and pepper.

Fill 12 of the best-looking shells with stuffing (if you have more, stuff more shells). Set the stuffies on a baking pan and bake 7 to 8 minutes, until just starting to brown. NOTE: *Aluminum foil may be used to help steady the shells if necessary.*

Serve immediately with lemon wedges. OPTIONAL: For a richer stuffie, top each baked clam with a dab of unsalted butter.

Serves 3 or 4

Clam Chowder
New England Style

There are more recipes for clam chowder floating around out there than any sane person would ever care to make. What I've put together here is a fairly simple chowder recipe that shouldn't offend too many folks. (If I've messed up the ingredient list to Aunt Sally's favorite, please accept my apologies.) NOTE: I'm making this with fresh cooked clams, but you could just as easily use 20 ounces of canned clams, including their liquid. I won't tell anyone.

4 pounds live clams (littlenecks, cherrystones, or Manilas)
1 cup water
4 ounces salt pork (or thick cut bacon), diced
¾ cup yellow onion, diced
¾ cup celery, diced
3 tablespoons all-purpose flour
2 cups fish stock or clam juice (or vegetable broth in a pinch)
1½ pounds red potatoes, peeled and diced into ½-inch cubes
2 cups light cream
1 cup heavy cream
Freshly ground pepper
Fresh parsley, chopped
Oyster crackers (optional)

Scrub and rinse the clams, tossing any that are cracked or remain open after handling.

Place the water and clams in a large pot, cover, and bring the water to a boil over high heat. Reduce the heat to medium and cook until the shells have opened, 2 to 4 minutes, depending on size. Remove the clams using a slotted spoon, allowing their liquor to drain back into the pot in the process. Strain the cooking liquid and set it aside. Remove the clam meat from the shells, finely chop it, and set it aside. Discard the shells.

In a large pot, slowly cook the pork over medium-low heat until the fat has been rendered. Discard the crispy bits, but keep the fat in the pot. Add the onion and celery and cook until they have softened, but not browned, about 5 minutes. Add the flour, stir to combine, and then add the reserved cooking liquid and fish stock. Whisk to remove any flour lumps. Bring the liquid to a boil, add the potatoes, reduce heat to medium low, and simmer until the potatoes are tender, 25 to 30 minutes.

Add the clams and both creams and bring the chowder to a simmer. If it seems overly thick, add additional cream to suit. Season the chowder with pepper, sprinkle with parsley, and serve with oyster crackers.

Serves 4 to 6 (or 8 to 10 as a first course)

Chapter 15
Shrimp
Saltwater Superhero

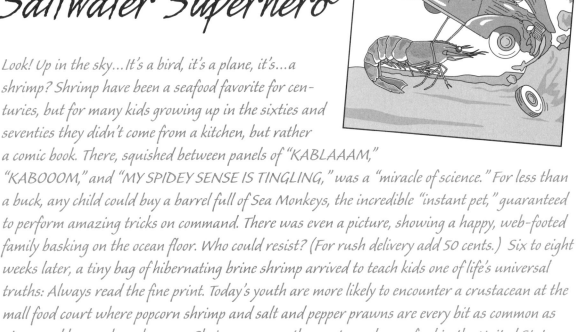

Look! Up in the sky…It's a bird, it's a plane, it's…a shrimp? Shrimp have been a seafood favorite for centuries, but for many kids growing up in the sixties and seventies they didn't come from a kitchen, but rather a comic book. There, squished between panels of "KABLAAAM," "KABOOOM," and "MY SPIDEY SENSE IS TINGLING," was a "miracle of science." For less than a buck, any child could buy a barrel full of Sea Monkeys, the incredible "instant pet," guaranteed to perform amazing tricks on command. There was even a picture, showing a happy, web-footed family basking on the ocean floor. Who could resist? (For rush delivery add 50 cents.) Six to eight weeks later, a tiny bag of hibernating brine shrimp arrived to teach kids one of life's universal truths: Always read the fine print. Today's youth are more likely to encounter a crustacean at the mall food court where popcorn shrimp and salt and pepper prawns are every bit as common as pizza and bacon cheeseburgers. Shrimp are now the most popular seafood in the United States, topping the charts with an impressive 4 pounds per person, annually. Do the math: That's more than a billion pounds a year. And they can't even leap tall buildings in a single bound.

VITAL STATS

FIRST NAME: Shrimp, a.k.a. prawn

SCI. NAME: Primarily *Penaeoid* (warm-water) and *Caridean* (cold-water)

SIZE: 3-13 in long

LIFESPAN: 4 months to 1 year (cultured); 1-4 years (wild)

RANGE: Coastal waters around the world, deeper northern waters

HARVEST: About 325 million lbs, domestic (all species)

Despite the obvious appeal of a caped crustacean, the shrimp industry hasn't had to rely on comic books to hook today's consumers. (If it did, movies about shrimp would make millions, but nobody would be eating them.) Our shrimp infatuation stems not from marketing, but availability. Shrimp are everywhere. Restaurants, fish markets, grocery stores—wherever there's fresh seafood, there's shrimp, and if there isn't, check the freezer section. Fresh or frozen, raw or cooked, peeled or unpeeled, there are plenty of shrimp to go around.

Where are they all coming from? North American waters are plentiful, but it's the imports that have made shrimp one of the most ubiquitous and affordable products in town. Billions of pounds are harvested worldwide, mostly in developing nations where shrimp prices bring a premium. Farms in South America, Mexico, Southeast Asia, and China have practically domesticated certain species, pumping out as many as three generations a year.

U.S. fishermen may only account for a small percentage of the overall harvest, but shrimp from the Gulf of Mexico are routinely rated the world's finest, thanks to a sweet flavor and a texture best described as "plump and crunchy." Unfortunately, because many markets sell by size rather than species, discerning a local from a tourist can be tricky, and even when names are front and center, they're not always helpful. Case in point: prawns.

The name game

Outside of bad-mouthing his favorite football club, the fastest way to rile up an English fishmonger is to tell him you like his shrimp.

"They're prawns, not bloody shrimp!"

Shrimp versus prawn—is there really a difference? The American answer is no, they're all shrimp. In certain parts of the country, larger shrimp and some freshwater varieties are called "prawns," but more often the name is simply used because it sounds better (or bigger). Across the pond, all shrimp are considered prawns, save for the smallest varieties, but down under, they've gone another direction, claiming all warm-water species (*Penaeoids*) are prawns, while cold-water species (*Carideans*) are shrimp. Can't we all just get along?

In an effort to clear up the confusion, the Food and Agriculture Organization of the United Nations has decreed that the difference is in the drink. Shrimps dig the salt, prawns prefer fresh. Sounds good. Of course, some species migrate between both, which means we need a third option. "Primp," anyone?

In the Water
Aliens at Sea

Contrary to every science fiction film every made, not all aliens come from outer space, inner space, or some far-flung underwater abyss. In fact, a quick check of the local lagoon will turn up a host of bizarre creatures, quite a few of them shrimp.

The average Gulf shrimp, for example, passes through numerous development stages on its way to becoming an adult, often appearing more alien than aquatic. This transformation occurs as larvae migrate from the

Snack Shells

Would you be surprised to learn that your potato chips contain shrimp shells? It's possible. Extracting the polysaccharide chitin from discarded Northern shrimp shells produces a substance known as chitosan, which can be used to reduce fat and calories in snack foods.

Same Sex Shrimp

Shrimp have separate sexes, but some species, such as the Northern pink, are hermaphroditic, spending half their lives as male, before permanently changing to female.

shrimp nauplius, zoea, and mysis

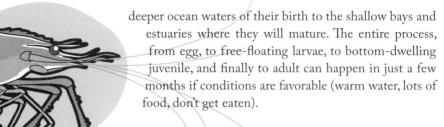

Freshwater Shrimp

The GIANT RIVER PRAWN (Macrobrachium rosenbergii), also known as the "Hawaiian blue prawn" is the most common variety of freshwater shrimp. Found wild in Southeast Asia, the river prawn is now farmed throughout the world (including Hawaii and a few Southern states). If you find a whole one, you'll know it by two very long blue legs and a blue tail. Flavorwise, freshwater shrimp taste great if treated like smallish lobster, but can also turn out bland and mushy, usually the result of improper freezing.

deeper ocean waters of their birth to the shallow bays and estuaries where they will mature. The entire process, from egg, to free-floating larvae, to bottom-dwelling juvenile, and finally to adult can happen in just a few months if conditions are favorable (warm water, lots of food, don't get eaten).

Shrimp posse

A shrimp body is made up of a "head" section, five sets of walking legs, antennae, and a segmented "tail" section that sports numerous pairs of small "swimming" legs. Like other crustaceans, shrimp are protected by a chitin exoskeleton that is periodically shed to allow room to grow. While the shell offers some protection, most shrimp venture out only during low-light hours in large, fishlike schools. The idea is not to overwhelm an attacking predator with superior numbers, but to scatter when confronted, giving the villain too many targets.

More proof that Monty Python had it right all along: *Run away!*

Crustacean courtship

Those males that stay alive long enough to further the species, must wait until the female molts before they can get busy. In species where the male is larger, he will choose a mate and defend her honor against interlopers. More commonly, the male is smaller, and thus must be more opportunistic about mating (lest he be eaten). Courtships begin and end in the time it takes a male to recognize he's stumbled upon a recently molted female. Most have just enough stamina for a quickie, before it's back to the hidey-hole. No comments, ladies.

A female shrimp can lay up to a million eggs at one time, most of which will hatch within 24 hours. In the case of warm-water shrimp, the eggs are released in the ocean current. Cold-water shrimp incubate their eggs along the underside of the female prior to release.

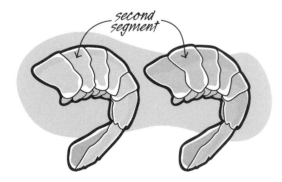

second segment

QUICK QUESTION

Is it hot or cold? Look at the shell. The second segment of a warm-water shrimp overlaps the third; in a cold-water shrimp, the second segment overlaps both the first and the third.

tiger

Saltwater Shrimp Varieties

*Many seafood counters simply sell "shrimp," a disservice
to the unique qualities of the dozen or so species (out
of 3,000 total) that reach consumers regularly.*

Warm-water shrimp

*Color-coded for your convenience (and confusion), GULF SHRIMP
are harvested, primarily wild, from the Gulf of Mexico and up the
Southeastern Atlantic coast. Gulfs come in WHITE (Penaeus setiferus),
PINK (P. duorarum) a.k.a. "hoppers," and BROWN (P. aztecus), with the
white being the most sought after for their sweet and firm meats. Pinks tend to be more
tender, browns less flavorful. The colors aren't always as clear-cut as the name implies. To make sure
you've got a white, check the tail; browns and pinks have a groove in the last tail segment not present in whites.*

Gulf white

*The PACIFIC WHITE SHRIMP (P. vannamei), often referred to as a "Mexican white" or an "Ecuadorian
white," is similar to a Gulf white, but since most are farmed they tend to be a little more mild in flavor. The
closely related BLUE SHRIMP (P. stylirostris) is often lumped in with Pacific whites, as it's similar in flavor and
texture (blues may be a bit more salty). Both species are farmed along the west coast of Mexico, with Pacific
farms stretching to South America.*

*CHINESE WHITE SHRIMP (P. chinensis) are often substituted for Gulf or Pacific whites, although the meat
tends to be softer and milder in flavor. Chinese whites are both cultured and wild caught, primarily in the
Yellow and East China seas. BLACK TIGER SHRIMP (P. monodon) are farmed throughout Southeast Asia,
with Thailand being the top producer. Tigers are dark-colored, usually bluish-black with darker stripes and
yellow markings. It's a pretty shrimp, if not the most flavorful. If you like mild, soft meat, this is your shrimp.*

Cold-water shrimp

Northern (pink)

*Wild NORTHERN (PINK) SHRIMP (Pandalus borealis and Pandalus jordani) are harvested
extensively from deeper Northern Atlantic and Pacific waters. The total harvest is in the
300,000-ton range, making it the largest shrimp fishery in the world. Due to their smaller size (the largest are
around 90 per pound), most Northerns are sold peeled and cooked, usually labeled "salad" shrimp. Both species
have a sweet, strong flavor and tend to be firm, though not as firm as most warm-water shrimp.*

*The largest of the cold-water species, the SPOT SHRIMP (Pandalus platyceros), is
often caught not by trawl, but by trap. They can be found along the Pacific
coast, with Alaska now delivering most of the harvest. In the shell, a spot
shrimp is pinkish orange and can occasionally be found with a clutch of roe still
attached under the abdomen. Spots are sweet and moderately firm.*

spot

*The ROCK SHRIMP (Sicyonia brevirostris) of Florida and the RIDGEBACK SHRIMP
(S. ingentis) of Southern California are generally sold peeled because they have a heavy shell
that's difficult to remove unless cooked. Rockies tend to be smaller, but what they lack in
size, they make up in flavor: sweet, plump, and almost lobsterlike.*

rock

not just a visual effect

Bycatch Blues

Where there's trawling, there's bound to be bycatch, and no one has seen it worse than the shrimpers (for more info, check out the Red Snapper chapter). As a result, U.S. trawlers are required by law to use one or more bycatch reducing devices that allow fish and other marine animals to escape without losing too many of the shrimp. Unfortunately, some foreign fleets are not as regulated as domestic fishermen, which has led to reports of bycatch as high as fifteen pounds for every pound of shrimp, most of which is simply discarded at sea.

On the Boats
Shrimpin'

According to *Forrest Gump*, all it takes to succeed as a shrimp fisherman is a boat, a surly, wheelchair-bound first mate, and an encyclopedic knowledge of shrimp recipes. Oh, and lots of special effects.

Non-Hollywood shrimpers prefer to rely on trawling and long hours to catch their namesake. Shrimp are brought up in long, cone-shaped nets, beheaded (usually), and put on ice. In the Gulf of Mexico, where the majority of the domestic harvest is landed, three-man crews may stay out for 4 to 6 weeks to fill their holds with whites, browns, or pinks. In artic waters, much larger factory trawlers catch, clean, cook, and freeze huge hauls of Northern shrimp minutes after fishing them out of the water. Out west, fishermen use traps to catch the popular spot shrimp. Just call 'em the little lobstermen. On second thought, don't do that.

Thanks to an ever-increasing global market, catching the shrimp is no longer the domestic shrimper's greatest challenge. Huge increases in imported product have forced many fishermen out of the business, and others to search for new markets to combat shrimp's international flavor. In 2002, domestic shrimpers accused several countries of dumping product, forcing them to sell their own shrimp at unreasonably low prices. The U.S. government ultimately responded by slapping tariffs on shrimp imported from Thailand, India, China, Vietnam, Ecuador, and Brazil. It should come as no surprise that all six nations are leaders in raising cultured shrimp.

Shrimp country

The boom in shrimp farming began in the 1980s, increased steadily throughout the 1990s, and now accounts for roughly 30 percent of the world shrimp harvest (and growing). More than half of all shrimp imported into the United States are farm-raised, usually warm-water species that are grown to market size in as little 4 to 6 months. Tiger shrimp were once the dominant import, but disease and higher labor costs have caused many farmers to switch to Pacific or Chinese whites.

There are different types of shrimp farms, from the small "backyard hatcheries" that let the shrimp do most of the work, to high-tech facilities that raise dense populations of formula-fed shrimp in climate-controlled tanks. Found primarily in the tropics, "extensive farms" draw wild larvae into tidal flats and simply constructed "shrimp pounds" where they're allowed to grow to market size. The crustaceans feed naturally, often sharing the space with shrimp-friendly farmed fish. The population density tends to be low, which is why many farmers opt for "semi-intensive farms" that use man-made ponds to grow larger numbers of hatchery or wild-caught larvae. Natural food is supplemented by special shrimp feed, and in most ponds the water is exchanged regularly. "Intensive farms" grow even more shrimp in less space by carefully controlling the environment through heavy feeding, waste removal, and water aeration. This approach requires more time and money to maintain, but produces a greater return on investment.

Unfriendly farms?

Many environmental groups contend that shrimp aquaculture in developing countries displaces traditional forms of farming (such as rice), exploits labor resources, and causes substantial habitat destruction, notably to native mangroves. While it's true the shrimp industry has changed the lives of many farmers and villagers, sometimes not always for the better, it has also added millions of jobs in areas where work is hard to find. As for the mangroves, it's now believed most of the damage was done not to clear land for shrimp ponds, but for wood.

Bottom line: Concerns about imported shrimp, both wild and farmed, are often exaggerated, but based on real problems. Fortunately, there's a simple solution: Buy domestic shrimp.

At the Market
How Big's a Jumbo Shrimp?

Here's where the fun begins.

Head down to the fish market—heck, make it the grocery store—and you're likely to find any combination of the following: whole shrimp, headless shrimp, peeled shrimp, cooked shrimp, peeled and cooked shrimp, shrimp with their tails on, shrimp with their tails off, and even "deveined" shrimp (I'll explain in a moment). Since I like to do my own cooking, I generally buy headless, unpeeled (shell-on) shrimp.

But wait, there's more! Do you want them fresh, thawed, or frozen in blocks, layer-packs, or individually quick frozen (IQF) bags? Fresh is best if you live close to the coast, but don't be afraid of the frost. Shrimp take to the freezer quite well, and most come to market in exactly that form. For convenience, buy thawed, but for the best, ask for a block of shrimp and thaw them out yourself. IQF shrimp are a fair compromise—buy them by the shrimp or by the bag and only thaw out what you need.

Nature's Wrath

Hurricane Katrina tore through the Gulf of Mexico in August of 2005 dismantling much of the region's fishing industry in the process. Nearly every commercial boat in Louisiana, Mississippi, and Alabama sustained damaged or was destroyed. Many fishermen lost their lives attempting to ride out the storm on their boats. In time, the boats, docks, and processing plants will be rebuilt, but the long-term environmental effects of the storm caused by polluted waters and debris-choked fishing grounds may not be known for years.

Peel Me

Quite by accident, J. M. Lapeyre discovered that when he stepped on a whole shrimp with a rubber boot it popped right out of its shell. Further experiments with the rubber rollers of his mom's washing machine led to the first shrimp peeler. Descendants of Lapeyre's invention now peel upward of 900 pounds per hour and can also cut and devein shrimp to any market style.

GRADING CHART

All sizes are for raw, headless shrimp

Name	Size
Extra colossal	Under 10
Colossal	Under 15
Extra jumbo	16/20
Jumbo	21/25
Extra large	26/30
Large	31/40
Medium large	36/40
Medium	41/50
Small	51/60
Extra small	61/70
Tiny	over 70

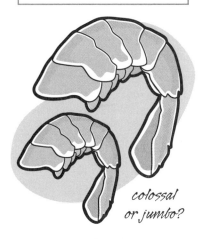

*colossal
or jumbo?*

To make it more confusing, shrimp come in different sizes and are given wonderfully accurate names such as "colossal," "extra jumbo," and "medium large." In theory, the names do mean something (see chart), but in practice, who can tell the difference between an extra large and a jumbo? Fortunately, most markets now display the "count," which is the number of shrimp it takes to make a pound. For example, 21/25 means there are between 21 and 25 shrimp in one pound of product. Simple enough. Of course, the numbers will vary depending on the state of the shrimp (whole, headless, peeled, and cooked), but overall it's a reasonable guide to buying shrimp.

Is bigger better?

You may have noticed there are a lot of "big" names on the grading list. Welcome to Shrimp Marketing 101: to sell small, spell big! A more substantial name must mean it's worth more, right? In fact, let's get rid of those little names altogether. Instead of "small" and "tiny," how about "cocktail" and "salad" shrimp? Now, you're learning.

But are the big boys worth the money? My taste buds say no. A mid-sized Gulf white may not look as impressive as a Texas-sized tiger, but the taste and texture are usually superior. You may not agree, but take a look at the price and I think you'll start to see things my way. If you do need to put on a show in a hurry, big shrimp are a worthy main attraction and will save you time in the kitchen.

Pickin' shrimp

Okay, you've decided on a pound of 21/25 Alaskan spot shrimp (raw, fresh, shell on)…whew…time to get critical. Are the shrimp of uniform size, color, and condition? Don't be afraid to ask for a count to see if the market's label is accurate. A few black spots are more of a cosmetic issue, but black rings or streaks should be avoided, as should broken or pitted shells (see "Are my shrimp on drugs"). How do they smell? Very little or fresh like the sea is good; an aroma of ammonia or rotten egg is not.

Scampi

"Scampi" is the Venetian word for Dublin Bay prawns, a.k.a. lobsterettes, langoustines, and langostinos. In the United States, scampi refers to shrimp cooked in butter and garlic.

QUICK QUESTION

Which shrimp tastes the best? A shrimp is a shrimp…except when it's a Gulf white—those are the best. I also like Mexican whites, and prefer Gulf pinks to browns. Cold-water shrimp tend to be smaller, but more flavorful; spot shrimp are excellent. Chinese whites are decent in a pinch. Freshwater shrimp are snazzy and pretty cool on the plate, but harder to find. What about tigers? Some folks dig 'em. I think they're pretty to look at, but bland.

In the Kitchen
Cook 'Em In Their Clothes

Shrimp taste better if cooked in their shells. The shells are full of flavor and offer the meat a modicum of protection from potentially dangerous flames or high heat. The shell also allows the cook to season liberally without overseasoning. When the shrimp is peeled, the seasoning travels from shell to finger to shrimp to taste bud. Obviously, it doesn't make sense to cook small shrimp for a stir-fry or pasta in their shells, but if getting a little messy is okay, leave 'em be.

Most shrimp benefit from a quick salt treatment, either in a brine or simply doused with the stuff. Both methods improve the taste and texture of shrimp, especially those that have been frozen. This will not make the shrimp taste salty…honest.

Bring on the desert heat

A shrimp is basically one big muscle, which means it's going to cook fast. As soon as the meat is opaque or the shell bright orange, the shrimp is done. For the largest shrimp, that might be a couple minutes for each side, but smaller, peeled shrimp can cook in thirty seconds or less. If you're concerned about undercooking, leaving the shells on will give you a little more wiggle room in terms of time.

A perfectly cooked shrimp has a pop to it, sort of a moist crunch. The best way to achieve this is with dry heat methods such as grilling, broiling, sautéing, or frying (technically a dry cooking method). Boiling or steaming a shrimp will usually turn it to mush. Here's your master recipe for basic broiled shrimp: Slip a couple dozen shrimp onto skewers, season with spices liberally, and slap on the grill or under the broiler; in a minute or two, turn them, wait another minute, peel, and eat!

Heads Up

Most markets don't sell whole shrimp, but if yours does, give 'em a try. Besides adding visual flair, the heads can be sucked of their juices or used to add flavor to sauces, soups, or stocks. When buying, be sure to buy enough (heads are about 40 percent of the total weight) and prepare sooner rather than later, since whole shrimp tend to spoil more quickly.

Brining and Salting

To BRINE a pound of peeled shrimp, dissolve ½ cup of salt plus ¼ cup of sugar in a cup of hot water. Add 2 to 3 cups of ice cubes and stir until cold. Add the shrimp and refrigerate, covered, for 20 to 25 minutes. Dry thoroughly before cooking. To SALT, simply add shrimp to a bowl, toss with enough kosher salt to coat, rinse, and repeat. Pat dry, and you're ready to cook.

Undressing a Shrimp

In an effort to cover all the bases, let's start with a whole shrimp and go from there. Feel free to join the demonstration where appropriate.

(1) Rinse whole shrimp, pat dry. Stop here for cooking whole shrimp. (2) Twist off head and save for cooking or freeze for later use. Stop here for cooking shell-on. (3) Using a pair of kitchen shears (or paring knife), trim shell along back to tail, exposing the black "vein." Remove the vein. Stop here for cooking shell on, deveined. (4) Remove the shell by peeling it back to tail, leaving one section intact. Stop here for cooking peeled, tail-on. (5) Remove tail. Stop here for cooking peeled, tail-off.

To shell without shears, simply remove the legs, "crack" the shell beneath the abdomen, and then pull it off. Some shrimp have sharp points on the tail and around the legs, so handle carefully.

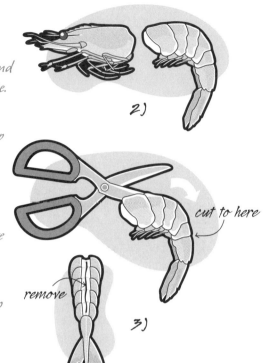

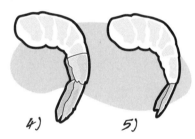

What the…Vein?

(Un)popularly known as the "mud vein," that dark tube is actually the shrimp's digestive tract. It's harmless, but most eaters squirm at the sight of it, so best to remove the vein prior to cooking. If it's clear, leave it be. If the shrimp are small (50 count or higher), it's usually not worth the trouble.

Get the big pot

There are, of course, exceptions to every rule, which is why shrimp boils are so popular in the South and elsewhere. There's just something irresistible about adding five pounds of whole shrimp to a huge pot of boiling spices. The trick of course is to cook the shrimp quickly, and then allow them to steep in the flavorful liquid…but not continue to cook. The solution? Ice. Pouring a bucket of ice cubes into the pot will stop the cooking, allowing the shrimp to soak up the atmosphere at their leisure.

Thicker fare, such as gumbo or jambalaya, are a terrific environment for a pound or two of shrimp of modest size. Since you can't go dumping a tray of ice cubes into the gumbo, it's best to hold the shrimp to the last fifteen minutes so as not to overcook them. Alternatively, shrimp can be added at the beginning, removed when cooked, and then returned just prior to serving. This method gets more of the shrimpy flavor into the mix…which is kind of the point, isn't it?

QUICK QUESTION

Can I cook cooked shrimp? I recommend only buying cooked shrimp if you plan to serve it cold, but if you must have the heat…less is more. Add cooked shrimp to a dish in the last stages of cooking to keep it from toughening up.

Shrimp Recipes

When cooking peeled shrimp, most chefs leave the tails on, even when the shrimp are to be eaten with a fork. Why? Because that's what everybody else does. This drives me nuts. I'm not going to eat the tails, I'm not going to pick them up by the tail, so what makes you think I want to poke and prod at them with a knife and fork just to remove the tail? Question authority, people.

Now, if you were to ask me if the tails add a bit of flavor. . . I'd say probably not, because, in most cases, they aren't cooked long enough to transfer anything substantial to the dish. Still, I'm glad to see you're thinking outside the box.

HOW TO STORE: Shrimp

FRESH: Give fresh or thawed shrimp a rinse, a pat dry, and then refrigerate in a closed container. They're best cooked on the day of purchase, but most will last 2 to 3 days. *FROZEN:* Properly frozen, shrimp will last 3 to 6 months. When it comes time to thaw them, the best place is in the fridge, overnight. The trick is to not let them sit in a pool of shrimpy water. Place IQF shrimp in a colander set inside a bowl to catch the drippings. A roasting pan with a rack works well for block shrimp, as does submerging the block in water, although you'll need to remove individual shrimp as they emerge from the ice. Once thawed, give each shrimp a quick rinse and then store it in the fridge until used.

NUTRITIONAL INFO

Per 3.5 oz/100 grams (raw)

Gulf Shrimp		Northern Pink Shrimp	
Calories 90		**Calories** 92	
Calories from fat 7		Calories from fat 8	
Total fat . . . . 0.8 g		**Total fat** . . . . 0.9 g	
Saturated fat . . . . 0.2 g		Saturated fat . . . . 0.1 g	
Cholesterol . . . . 96 mg		**Cholesterol** . . . 152 mg	
Sodium . . . . N/A		**Sodium** . . . . 140 mg	
Protein . . . . 19.4 g		**Protein** . . . . 19.4 g	
Omega-3 . . . . 0.3 g		**Omega-3** . . . . 0.2 g	
Mercury . . . < 0.01 ppm		**Mercury** . . . < 0.01 ppm	

Shrimp on a Stick

Indoors or out, nothing beats shrimp straight out of their shells. Sure, it's a little messy, but that's where the flavor comes from. Each successive shrimp tastes better than the last, thanks to all that shrimpy goodness sticking to your fingers. NOTE: You can dust the shrimp with just about any spicy mix or rub you happen to have lying around. Old Bay seasoning is fairly obvious, but I've never really found anything I like better. If I encounter impeccably fresh shrimp, I go the salt-and-pepper route, which not only highlights the crustaceans' flavor, but also allows me to call them "Salt and Pepper Prawns," which sounds much more impressive than "Shrimp on a Stick."

2 pounds raw shrimp, shells on, 21/30 range
3 tablespoons extra virgin olive oil
1 tablespoon lemon juice
Old Bay *or* kosher salt and freshly ground black pepper

NOTE: If you're using wooden skewers, soak them in water for 30 minutes prior to use.

Brine or salt the shrimp as directed on page 161. Rinse and dry them thoroughly. Devein them, but do not remove the shells.

Fire up the grill (high heat), setting the grates about 4 inches from the heat. If cooking indoors, flip on the broiler to the highest setting. Position the rack so the shrimp will be about 4 to 5 inches from heat.

Place the shrimp in a large bowl. Add the olive oil and lemon juice and toss to coat. Slide the shrimp onto the skewers and liberally sprinkle with Old Bay. NOTE: For a cleaner flavor, skip the Old Bay and go with simple salt and pepper.

Place the skewers on the grill (or under the broiler) and cook for 1 to 2 minutes, flip them, and cook for 1 minute more. Watch closely; shrimp are done as soon as they're opaque.

Serve the shrimp on their skewers with lemon wedges and plenty of napkins for messy fingers.

Serves 4 to 6

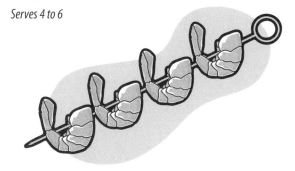

Tempura Butterflies

When it comes to deep-fried shrimp I prefer the light, airy qualities achieved by using a Japanese tempura batter. If you're making "popcorn shrimp" and you want to actually taste the tiny shrimp, this is the batter to use. In terms of veggies, I usually go with broccoli florets, trimmed green beans, and zucchini slices. If you're using denser veggies, such as carrots, be sure to cut the slices fairly thin (¼ inch) so they cook through. NOTE: If you don't have refined sesame oil, go with 6 cups of vegetable oil plus 1 tablespoon of either "pure" or "toasted" sesame oil.

1 pound raw shrimp, shell on, 16/24 range
4½ cups vegetable oil
1½ cups refined sesame oil
3 cups all-purpose flour
1 large egg, lightly beaten
1½ cups ice-cold water, plus a few ice cubes
1 teaspoon crushed red pepper flakes
1 pound of assorted vegetables cut into roughly equal pieces
Soy sauce (for dipping)

Brine or salt the shrimp as directed on page 161. Rinse and dry them thoroughly. Remove the shells, but leave the tails on. To butterfly, cut through the back to devein, cutting deeper but not all the way through.

Heat the oil in a heavy 4-quart or larger pot to 370° F. Preheat the oven to 200° F.

Sift 2 cups of flour into a medium-sized bowl. Combine the egg and ice water separately, and then add to the flour along with the red pepper flakes. Stir roughly with a chopstick (or a wooden spoon handle) until the batter is combined but still lumpy. Add a few ice cubes to keep it cold. Place the remaining flour in a separate bowl for dusting.

Dust a few shrimp and veggies in the flour, shaking off the excess. Dip them in batter and then lower them carefully into the oil using a fry basket or spider tool. Do not overcrowd the oil. Fry the pieces for 2 to 3 minutes, until golden. Transfer the finished pieces to a wire rack set over a baking sheet in the oven. Repeat the process with the remaining shrimp and veggies (making sure the oil is at least 360° F before adding the shrimp).

Serve the shrimp with soy sauce (at room temperature) or other dipping favorite.

Serves 3 or 4

Shrimp Boil

The way to get the best flavor in a shrimp boil is to use whole shrimp with the heads still attached. Don't worry; most folks are a little less intimidated by all the little faces if they're surrounded by a pile of potatoes and corn on the cob. Don't bother with plates, just spread everything on a clean, disposable tablecloth (the day's newspaper is traditional) and enjoy. NOTE: It helps to have a stockpot with a basket insert, but it's not absolutely necessary.

1½ gallons water
2 bay leaves
2 lemons, quartered
½ cup Shrimp Boil Seasoning (see recipe)
2 large onions, quartered
3 large celery stalks with leaves, roughly chopped
1 head of garlic, halved
4 pounds small red potatoes
6 ears sweet corn, halved
4 pounds raw shrimp, head on, any size
Lemon wedges

Add water, bay leaves, lemons, and spice mixture to a very large stockpot and bring to a rolling boil. *NOTE: The water shouldn't fill more than half of the pot.* Reduce heat to maintain a gentle boil and add the onions, celery, and garlic and cook for 15 minutes. Add the potatoes and boil (gently) until they start to soften but aren't cooked all the way through, about 10 minutes. Add the corn and cook for 5 minutes. Finally, add the shrimp, cover, and remove the pot from the heat. Steep for 15 minutes.

Drain the shrimp and spread them out on a disposable tablecloth or large serving platter.

Serves 6 to 8

Shrimp Boil Seasoning

Yes, you could simply use store-bought shrimp or crab-boil seasoning. If you just ran out, here's a reasonable scratch facsimile that'll keep you cooking.

4½ tablespoons cayenne pepper
1½ tablespoons allspice
2 teaspoons ground mustard
1 teaspoon freshly ground black pepper
1 teaspoon ground coriander seeds
1 teaspoon ground dill seeds
½ teaspoon ground cloves
½ teaspoon ground red pepper flakes

Combine ingredients and store in an airtight container.

Classic Shrimp Cocktail

Sometimes simple is best. This recipe is really more about presentation than cooking, so I've used a no-frills broil to prepare the shrimp, which will give you a clean, crisp flavor with as little hassle as possible. If you'd rather boil the shrimp. . .ah, what the heck. Go for it. I won't tell.

20 raw shrimp, shell-on, 16/24 range
1 tablespoon olive oil
1 tablespoon lemon juice
Cocktail sauce
Lemon wedges
Cilantro or flat-leaf parsley (for garnish)

NOTE: If you're using wooden skewers, soak them in water for 30 minutes prior to use.

Brine or salt the shrimp as directed on page 161. Rinse and dry them thoroughly. Devein the shrimp only if a black vein is visible. (Shrimp will look prettier without a split up their backside.)

Turn on the broiler to the highest setting. Position the rack so the shrimp will be about 4 to 5 inches from the heat.

Place the shrimp in a large bowl. Add the olive oil and lemon juice and toss to coat. Slide the shrimp onto skewers. *NOTE: For a cleaner presentation (no holes in the shrimp), don't use the skewers.*

Place the shrimp on a heated broiler pan and slide it under the broiler. Cook the shrimp for 2 minutes, flip them, and cook for 1 minute more. Watch closely; shrimp are done as soon as they're opaque. Remove the shrimp from the broiler and plunge them into an ice-water bath to stop the cooking. Drain and thoroughly pat them dry. Chill them in the fridge for 1 hour.

Place an equal amount of cocktail sauce in 4 shallow, wide-mouth glasses. Hang 5 chilled shrimp around the rim of each glass along with at least 1 lemon wedge. Garnish with cilantro or parsley.

Serves 4

Cocktail Sauce

No, it's not okay to use bottled sauce. Every one I've tried just seems to be. . . well, trying too hard. This quick recipe uses several store-bought items, but combined on the fly with a few fresh ingredients it makes for a surprisingly tasty cocktail sauce.

1 cup ketchup
1 tablespoon prepared horseradish
1 teaspoon Worcestershire sauce

½ teaspoon crushed red pepper flakes
1 tablespoon celery leaves, chopped
1 tablespoon lemon juice
Zest of 1 lemon

Combine all ingredients. Chill the sauce in the fridge at least 30 minutes prior to use.

Shrimp Scampi
with Pasta

Finally, I've included something for the garlic lovers in the house. If you don't absolutely love garlic, feel free to cut the amount in half and make up the difference in minced shallots. For a more traditional scampi, use parsley instead of basil. In terms of pasta, I like linguini, but you can use just about anything.

1 pound raw shrimp, shell on, 31/40 range
1 pound pasta
Kosher salt and freshly ground black pepper
3 tablespoons olive oil
4 large garlic cloves, minced
½ cup dry white wine
2 tablespoons butter
Juice of 1 small lemon, plus zest
4 to 6 large basil leaves, chiffonade
Extra virgin olive oil

Brine or salt the shrimp as directed on page 161. Rinse and dry them thoroughly. Remove the shells and devein.

Set a large pot of water over high heat. Once it boils, add a tablespoon of salt and the pasta. Cook the pasta until tender, 8 to 10 minutes. Drain it.

While the pasta is cooking, heat a large sauté pan over medium heat. Add the olive oil. Season the shrimp with salt and pepper and cook, just long enough to see pink all around, 1 to 2 minutes. Remove the shrimp from the pan. Add the garlic and cook, stirring often, until it's softened, but not browned, 2 to 3 minutes. Add the wine, butter, and lemon juice, bring them to a boil, and reduce, 3 to 4 minutes. Return the shrimp to the pan and cook them, stirring frequently, for 2 minutes.

Add the cooked pasta and lemon zest to the pan, toss to distribute the shrimp, and turn the scampi out into serving bowls. Garnish with basil and extra virgin olive oil.

Serves 3 or 4

Chapter 16

~~Chilean Sea Bass~~

Patagonian Toothfish

Pirate Fish!

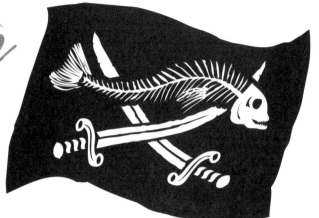

Yo ho, yo ho, a pirate's life for me! All right lads, how does a month or three on a rusty, water-logged factory ship working all hours in the middle of an Antarctic winter sound? Great, then you won't mind the occasional duck and cover when the local navy stops by for a visit. Don't worry, they've got a lot of ocean to cover, and even if they do catch us, it's only a big fine, jail time, and the seizure of the ship. Sink us? Aye, they might…but only if they feel like setting an example. Hey, where you going? Don't you want to know about the white gold? That's right…white gold, Patagonian pesos, Chilean sea cash—I'm talking toothfish, boys, and plenty of it. Enough to fill our holds ten times over with frozen fish stacked like cordwood. That'll fetch a fair price at the pier, it will. Aye, could be millions. Endangered? Perish the thought! The toothfish be as healthy as the growth beneath me fingernails. I may be a pirate, lads, but I'm no monster. Yo ho ho…

VITAL STATS

FIRST NAME: Patagonian toothfish (a.k.a. Chilean sea bass, Antarctic cod, mero)

SCI. NAME: *Dissostichus eleginoides*

SIZE: Most 20–40 lbs, up to 7 ft, 200 lbs

LIFESPAN: Most 6–10 years when caught, up to 45 years

RANGE: Southernmost waters of Pacific, Atlantic, and Indian oceans

CATCH: About 70 million lbs a year (legally); U.S. imports about 22 million lbs

Twenty years ago, no one had ever heard of Chilean sea bass. It didn't exist. There was a species called Patagonian toothfish that supported a small fishery off the coast of South America, but no one paid it much mind.

That all changed when a few chefs searching for the Next Big Thing happened upon the fish with the funny name and found it to their liking. Here was a fish worthy of their talents—snow-white flesh, extralarge flake, and enough built-in lubricant to make it nearly impossible to overcook. That the fish came from half a world away simply made it more exotic…and expensive (not necessarily a bad thing for the high-end restaurant trade). The only thing wrong with it was that

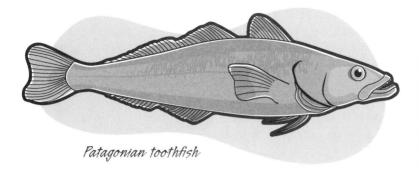

Patagonian toothfish

a Chilean sea bass steak in its natural habitat

name. "Patagonian toothfish" may have seemed apt to researchers who first encountered the toothy fish in whale stomachs in the 1950s, but to restaurateurs it sounded prehistoric. Thus, the Patagonian toothfish was rechristened the Chilean sea bass, and there was much rejoicing (in marketing).

The fish was an instant hit, despite the fact that very little about its new name was accurate. The toothfish was not a sea bass, nor was it confined to Chilean waters. Most of the South Pacific, Atlantic, and Indian oceans were teeming with toothfish. With demand on the rise, the fishery quickly expanded into the territorial waters of Australia, New Zealand, and South Africa, as well as international waters surrounding Antarctica. Ships scraping the bottom of North Atlantic fishing grounds headed south to partake of the new feeding frenzy. Areas previously deemed "unfishable" were suddenly "worth the risk," thanks to the promise of a million-dollar payday. The total toothfish harvest quadrupled in five years. The Chilean sea bass had arrived.

Guess what happened next?

Fish of doom

No fish has gone from revered to reviled quicker than Chilean sea bass. In 2001, toothfish was the "it" fish, the one the menu had to have, and the "Dish of the Year," according to *Bon Appetit* magazine. In 2002, it was the poster fish for all that was wrong with the fishing industry. Overfishing? You bet. Endangered species? Must be. Bycatch issues? Would you believe birds? To top it all off, this was the fish that made it profitable to be a pirate, again. Yo ho ho, indeed.

QUICK QUESTION

Where the heck is Patagonia? Patagonia is a region in South America located between the Andes and the South Atlantic, and includes parts of both Chile and Argentina.

Drink Up Me 'earties, Yo Ho!

"Yo Ho, Yo Ho (A Pirate's Life for Me)" was written by Xavier Atencio and George Bruns specifically for Disney's Pirates of the Caribbean ride.

The Other Toothfish

There are actually two fish in the toothfish fishery (say that five times fast), Patagonian and its southern twin, ANTARCTIC TOOTHFISH (Dissostichus mawsoni). Found only in the highest latitudes along the Antarctic icepack, Antarctic toothfish tend to be smaller, but are better suited to extremely cold water (they have an antifreeze chemical in their blood). Because the fishery is remote, only about 5 percent of the total toothfish harvest is of the Antarctic variety.

In 2002, the National Environmental Trust launched a national campaign urging consumers to boycott Chilean sea bass. As a result, more than a thousand chefs and restaurants turned their back on the fish they had made famous. Most cited concerns about the welfare of the fish and the legitimacy of the fishery as their main motivation. Ladies and gentlemen, the toothfish has left the building.

Bad fish or just fishy?

Is the Chilean sea bass fisherman really the scourge of the high seas, or merely a victim of a carefully choreographed campaign of eco-propaganda? Is the toothfish industry winning the battle against the pirates or on the verge of commercial collapse? And what about the fish? Is it in need of saving or better off sautéed?

As with most arguments about fishing, the truth is rarely found on the surface, but rather a mile or two beneath it.

In the Water

Deep Down Under

Patagonia toothfish dig the deep water. When they aren't popping up for a quick bite to eat, most can be found swimming closer to the bottom, anywhere from 300 to more than 3,000 meters beneath the surface. Most stocks are concentrated around continental shelves and islands where a steady diet of squid, fish, crab, and lots and lots of tiny pink shrimp keep them fat and happy.

Toothfish are the largest predator found at their depth in Antarctic waters, with older females approaching 200 pounds and 7 feet in length, males considerably less. Both have slender bodies packed with long, slow-twitch muscles, which provide them with short bursts of speed. Good for drag racing and snagging lunch, but long vacations are out of the question.

Stay Afloat

Toothfish have only lightly mineralized bones and plenty of lipids in their flesh, which help them achieve neutral buoyancy in the cold Antarctic waters.

Fish in the slow lane

Like most cold-water denizens, toothfish grow slowly, with females taking 8 to 10 years to reach sexual maturity (males do it faster in 4 to 6). When they do spawn, usually during the Antarctic winter, females release far fewer eggs than warm-water fish of comparable size. Depending on her girth, a toothfish will release 50,000 to 500,000 at one time. The relatively large eggs, (4 to 5 millimeters in diameter), float in the water column for up to three months before hatching, giving them plenty of time to be gobbled up by a hungry passerby.

Chilean Sea Cod?

In Chile, Patagonian toothfish is marketed as "bacalao de profundidad," or "cod of the depths." Don't be fooled. Toothfish neither looks nor tastes like cod.

Slower maturation, fewer eggs, and an increased potential for predation all point to one thing: Toothfish are vulnerable to overfishing. Pull too many out of the water at one time, and the species won't have the numbers to recover. Careful management is needed to ensure enough fish survive to support the fishery—easier said than done when the fishing takes place in some of the more remote corners of the planet.

On the Boats
Far Flung Fishing

The Chileans were the first to market toothfish in the United States, earning themselves naming rights in the process. They remain one of the primary harvesters, along with Argentina, Australia, New Zealand, South Africa, and France (in territorial waters). Roughly a third of the toothfish catch comes from international waters off the coast of the Antarctic continent.

Most toothfish are caught using longline methods, although a few of the smaller fisheries use trawls and traps. Large factory ships capable of holding a hundred or more tons of frozen fish make up the bulk of the fleet. Some stay out for months, often in weather conditions fit for neither man nor fish. Why? Twelve dollars a pound, if they're lucky. At its peak in the late nineties, the (legal) toothfish harvest was valued at more than a half billion dollars. Today, the total world catch averages 30-35,000 metric tons, which translates to between $250 and $300 million.

Management issues

Individual governments are responsible for regulating the fisheries within their own waters, but off the coast of Antarctica, a multinational commission calls the shots. Since 1982, the Commission for the Conservation of Antarctic Marine Living Resources (CCAMLR) has set policy for the region as part of an effort to conserve marine life in southern oceans. That includes setting annual quotas for the Antarctic toothfish harvest (about 15,000 metric tons for 2004-05), as well as implementing policies aimed at curbing illegal fishing and bycatch.

U.S. Toothfishery?

The United States does not actively fish for toothfish. Some boats have ties to domestic companies, but they aren't part of a U.S. fishing fleet.

QUICK QUESTION

What about bycatch? Odd as it sounds, the most significant bycatch issue on most toothfish boats is birds. It's the bait they're after, which unfortunately comes with a prize—a big hook. To protect seabirds, the toothfish industry has enacted a number of bird mitigation measures, including: setting hooks only at night, using bird-scaring devices, weighting lines to sink the hooks faster, and participating in seasonal closures at times when most birds are rearing their chicks. Through these and other measures, seabird bycatch has been significantly reduced.

It's generally assumed that vessels fishing illegally don't bother with the measures, meaning significant bycatch still exists, although to what degree is unknown.

The two primary controls enacted by the CCAMLR are the Catch Documentation Scheme (CDS) and the Vessel Monitoring System (VMS). The CDS requires that all shipments of toothfish be accompanied by documents certifying when and where the fish was harvested, as well as who caught it. U.S. Customs requires both CDS documentation and a valid dealer permit to import Chilean sea bass.

The VMS uses satellite-based tracking to keep tabs on all vessels fishing for toothfish. Each boat is required to report landing data every four hours, which is then used dockside to verify the catch.

Pirates of Patagonia

Despite the efforts of the CCAMLR, illegal, unreported, and unregulated (IUU) fishing remains the greatest threat to the stability of both the toothfish and the fishery. Unlicensed boats prowl toothfish waters flying flags of convenience and sporting names that change on a regular basis. Pirates use bribery, mislabeling, and forged documents to sell their catch, often in out-of-the-way ports to nations that don't require CDS documents. In some cases, these nations turn around and export the fish through traditional channels, effectively concealing the source. Are we talking about mob fishermen, here? We are. Several organized crime syndicates are thought to be involved in the toothfish trade from the deck to dock to distribution. (But you didn't hear that from me.)

High-Seas Pursuit

In 2003, an Australian customs ship chased a suspected poacher for 20 days through Antarctic waters before finally catching it with the help of British and South African ships. The ship was holding 85 metric tons of illegally caught toothfish, with a street value of about $1 million.

The numbers have been greatly reduced since the days when 50,000 metric tons or more were harvested illegally each year, but even at 6-10,000 metric tons, today's conservative estimates of the illegal catch remain high. Stepped-up patrols by fishing nations, notably Australia and France, have removed more than a few poachers from the pirate fleet, but not enough to discourage others from taking their place.

What do I tell my fish-hugging friends?

So, you've decided to eat the fish. Good for you. Here are a few comebacks to use when defending your choice.

1. Toothfish are not endangered.
2. Toothfish cannot be sold in the United States without documentation verifying they were harvested using legal means.
3. The Catch Documentation Scheme and the Vessel Monitoring System have made it possible to track and verify legitimate fishing in real time.
4. Increased patrols by France, Australia, and other nations have substantially disrupted pirate fishing operations.
5. Bird bycatch has been dramatically reduced by the numerous mitigation measures toothfishermen are required to use.

What do I tell my fish-hungry friends?

So, you've decided to save the fish. How very noble. Here are a few tips for enlightening the masses.

1. Toothfish may not be endangered, but slow growth and low fecundity make them more susceptible to overfishing.
2. Even elaborate paper trails can be forged. How can you be 100 percent sure that toothfish is legit?
3. The CDS and VMS are wonderful. Do the pirates use them?
4. It's a big ocean. For every illegal fishing operation that's sunk, how many slip through the net?
5. Unless it's a parrot, do you really think a toothfish pirate cares about birds?

Before Going to Market

In preparation for this book, I bought and prepared numerous toothfish fillets, most with great success and very little guilt. I was not accosted in the parking lot by the Save the Sea Bass Brigade, nor did I receive a Christmas card from the Toothfish Mafia thanking me for my patronage. That said, I doubt I'll be cooking Chilean sea bass at home any time soon. It's a tasty fish, but there are others I like better, both to cook and eat. If I'm being environmentally responsible by association, so be it.

Now, it's your turn: Save or sauté? If you're on the fence, cook a fillet and call it research. Whether you call it dinner or a crime against nature most likely will depend on how much you enjoy the result.

At the Market
Frozen from the Sea

Toothfish rule number 1: Ask for Chilean sea bass. Ask for Patagonian *anything* and you're likely to receive a blank stare. Toothfish rule number 2: It's frozen. If it says fresh, it's probably "refreshed," which means the importer or wholesaler thawed and filleted the fish before selling it to the retailer. More than 90 percent of all toothfish are FAS, or frozen at sea, which means they were caught, cleaned, and frozen within an hour or two of being pulled from the water. Due to the remoteness of the

Pirate Treasure

Want to make a quick $100,000? Inform on a few toothfish pirates. The Coalition of Legal Toothfish Operators (COLTO) has offered the reward for information leading to the conviction of those involved in illegal fishing activities in the Patagonian toothfish fishery.

Substi-toothfish

Halibut is a reasonable substitute for toothfish—one that's readily available—but for the closest approximation of toothfish try a sablefish.

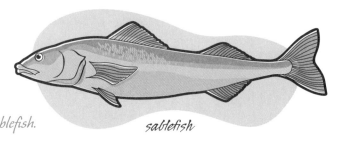

sablefish

SABLEFISH (Anoplopoma fimbria), a.k.a. black cod or butterfish (though it's neither a cod nor made of butter), is an oily, white-fleshed, slow-growing fish found in deep, cold waters. Sound familiar? Of the 25,000 metric tons harvested annually, about 75 percent comes from longline fishermen in Alaska, where the largest of the species (about 40 pounds) can be found. On the plate, sablefish has rich, white flesh that lacks the toothfish's large flake, but is surprisingly similar in terms of taste. Historically, most of the catch has been either smoked or exported to Japan, but the search for a sustainable toothfish alternative has brought more sablefish to domestic markets. The sablefish gets its name from its black, almost furry skin.

Hot Plate

Fish is best served right off the heat (no need to rest it like a steak), and nothing protects your efforts like a warm plate. Stick them in the oven or dishwasher, cover them in hot water, or wrap them in a heating pad— whatever it takes to kill the cold.

Jelly Toothfish

It's unlikely you'll encounter this at home, but most importers expect to lose a small percentage of their product to a condition that causes toothfish flesh to become soft and translucent, commonly known as "jellying."

fishery, some fish don't reach U.S. shores until weeks or even months after they were caught. Yes, that "fresh" Chilean sea bass you had at the fancy-pants restaurant may have spent three months out of the water.

Despite a long stay in the cold, FAS toothfish are usually superior to fresh because of the time it takes to get the fish through customs. It's true: Fresh toothfish do occasionally make the trip north, though your chances of encountering one are slim at best. (It should be noted that finding a fresh toothfish effectively guarantees it was caught legally. It's too much work for the pirates.)

Snow-white and shiny

Assuming you've found your fish (yeah!), here's what it should look like: bright, shiny, and opaque white. If it's creamy or translucent, it's not toothfish. Look for flesh that is firm and resilient, with a clean, mild fragrance, and no discoloration. Don't be surprised to find fillets more than 2 inches thick, usually skinned, although skin-on is better (more options to cook with).

If the flesh is still frozen, it should be bright white and blemish-free. If the fish seems overly moist, it may be suffering from excessive soaking. Some processors treat their fillets in a tripolyphosphate solution to reduce water loss, but the result is often an increase in water weight.

Chilean sea bass is available year-round.

Proof positive

If you're at all uneasy about buying a fish with a backstory like toothfish, talk to your fishmonger before buying. He may not have the documentation on hand, but someone in the market's chain of command does, and if they want to keep your business they should make an effort to prove their toothfish was caught legally (at least on paper).

In the Kitchen
Super Flake

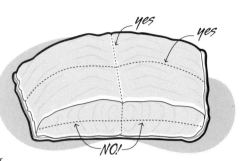

trimming toothfish

The most distinguishing features of toothfish fillet are its thickness and large tender flake. Daunting, yes, but you must resist the urge to turn a 2-inch-thick fillet into two 1-inch fillets. The larger size actually helps hold the fish together as it cooks, keeps it moist, and looks a heck of a lot more impressive on the plate. Cutting it down the middle to make 2-inch-thick square fillets is fine.

Skin on or off? That's up to you. If you leave it on, score it lightly a few times with a knife to prevent it from curling. And give the flesh a quick check for bones. Most fillets have a few pin bones, which sometimes can be difficult to remove without tearing up the flesh. The solution: cook 'em, and pull the bones prior to serving.

Overcook this fish

Finally, we come to the real villain in the toothfish saga: the fish itself. If the darn thing didn't taste so good, we wouldn't have to fret over eating it. Stupid fish.

Alas, it does taste good (kind of like a butter infused halibut), and due to a healthy dose of fat it's difficult to overcook. I've seared, broiled, and baked a fillet (yes, the *same* fillet) and still had it finish moist, flaky, and tender. This is especially helpful since judging the doneness of an overly thick hunk of fish that starts and finishes opaque and white can be difficult. What's the trick? Cheat. When the temperature at the center of the fillet hits 135°F, pull it. If you don't have a thermometer handy, get out the stopwatch. Fifteen minutes of cooking is sufficient for a 2-inch-thick fillet, although it'll probably still be moist and tender after twenty.

Double trouble

When it comes to cooking, toothfish benefits from a double bill. Searing the top (and bottom, if the skin has been removed) in butter or oil, followed by some finishing time in the oven, works wonders, as does a simple bake and broil. Both will result in a tender interior surrounded by a crisp, golden crust. Grilling is also an excellent choice, although it's best for skin-on fillets, which hold together better. Just don't get too fancy with the flipping, unless you want to see your flakes in the fire.

In terms of bonus flavors, don't go crazy. I generally stick with the basics—butter, olive oil, salt and pepper—although a thin soy glaze is nice once in a while. Overly flavorful sauces do little more than get in the way. Keep it simple.

Cooking Sablefish

Sablefish fillets tend to be much thinner and have smaller flakes, which means they're more likely to fall apart if overdone. They cook quickly and are ready as soon as the flakes around the edges pull away easily.

Omega, Too

Besides making it easier to cook, all that fat brings another bonus: omega-3s. At around 15 percent, toothfish have one of the highest concentrations of heart-healthy fatty acids found under the sea.

Toothfish Recipes

One of the best ways to get to know your fishmonger is to ask him or her about Patagonian toothfish (or Chilean sea bass, if need be). If the monger takes a step back, there's a good chance he's been asked this question before. After explaining that you're not on the environmental warpath (or are you?), you'll likely hear a strong argument either for or against the fish. Agree or disagree, it's always nice to see folks passionate about fish.

HOW TO STORE: Patagonian toothfish

FRESH: For fresh or refreshed fillets, a quick rinse and a pat dry are all that's needed before stashing them in the coldest part of the fridge. The high oil content means toothfish has a shorter shelf life once it's been thawed, so it's best eaten within a day or two. If the skin is still attached, it can be stored directly on ice, otherwise wrap the fillet in plastic wrap to prevent moisture loss. *FROZEN:* Do not refreeze toothfish. Even if the sign at the market said it was fresh, it has most likely been refreshed. For partially frozen toothfish, thaw in the fridge, preferably in a draining rig that keeps the fish away from melting ice.

NUTRITIONAL INFO

Per 3.5 oz/100 grams (raw)

Patagonia Toothfish		Sablefish	
Calories	184	**Calories**	195
Calories from fat	130	Calories from fat	138
Total fat	14.2 g	**Total fat**	15.3 g
Saturated fat	3.2 g	Saturated fat	3.2 g
Cholesterol	49 mg	**Cholesterol**	49 mg
Sodium	56 mg	**Sodium**	56 mg
Protein	13.2 g	**Protein**	13.4 g
Omega-3	1.3 g	**Omega-3**	1.4 g
Mercury	0.69 ppm	**Mercury**	0.22 ppm

Twice-Cooked Toothfish

The fish so nice we cooked it twice! At the market, look for full sides with the skin still attached and ask the fishmonger to cut off large 3-inch wide fillets. That should give you a very thick fillet, about 6 inches long, perfect for splitting into two 3-inch square fillets. *NOTE: If the fillets you landed happen to be considerably less than 2 inches thick, you can still use this method, but the oven cooking time will be shorter.*

2 large skin-on toothfish fillets, about 2 to 2½ inches thick
Kosher salt and freshly ground black pepper
2 tablespoons olive oil
1 tablespoon unsalted butter
Mango Salsa (*see recipe page 61*)

Preheat the oven to 375° F.

Check the skin for loose scales and remove any obvious pin bones from the fillet. Split each fillet into two thick squares, and make several short, shallow cuts in the skin. Season both sides with salt and pepper.

Set a large oven-safe sauté pan over medium-high heat. Add the oil and butter to the pan. Wait for the butter to melt, and then add the fillets, flesh side down. Sear for 1 to 2 minutes, until just starting to brown. Flip skin side down and sear for 2 minutes. Transfer the fish and pan to the oven and cook until the edges start to flake, 12 to 15 minutes. *NOTE: The internal temperature should be 135° F.*

Transfer the fillets to warm plates, top them with Mango Salsa and serve immediately.

Serves 4

Baked Toothfish
with Fennel

I know what you're thinking: fennel? Didn't he just tell us to keep it simple? True, fennel has a strong flavor, but I find it complements the oily flesh of the average toothfish quite nicely. (Maybe it's just me.) Be sure to save a few of the dill-like fronds to use as a garnish.

2 large toothfish fillets, about 2 to 2½ inches thick
4 tablespoons unsalted butter, plus extra for greasing
1 fennel bulb, roughly chopped
Kosher salt and freshly ground black pepper
½ cup dry white wine
Juice of 2 lemons plus zest

Preheat the oven to 375° F.

Cut off the skin (if any) and remove any obvious pin bones from the fillet. Split each fillet into two squares.

Melt 2 tablespoons of butter in a large sauté pan over medium heat. Add the fennel and sauté until softened, 3 to 4 minutes. Do not brown. Add the wine and lemon juice and cook for 4 minutes, allowing the liquid to reduce slightly.

Grease a large baking dish. Season the toothfish fillets with salt and pepper and place them in the dish. Dot the fillets with the remaining butter. Pour the wine and fennel over the fillets and bake until the fish is just cooked through, 18 to 20 minutes. *NOTE: The internal temperature should be 135° F.*

Transfer the fillets to warm plates, sprinkle them with lemon zest, and serve immediately.

Serves 4

Grilled Toothfish
with Soy Honey Glaze

Be sure to leave the skin on when grilling toothfish to help keep all those big flakes together. When it comes time to glaze, think thin . . . or thick. It's your call. The thicker the glaze, the more flavor there will be, but also more chance for the fish to stick. A quick wipe of the grill with a towel dipped in vegetable oil just prior to adding the fish will help discourage sticking. NOTE: For an even stronger flavor, fillets can also be marinated in glaze for up to 4 hours.

4 skin-on toothfish fillets (6 to 8 ounces each)
Freshly ground black pepper
¼ cup soy sauce
¼ cup honey
1 tablespoon chili oil
2 teaspoons sesame oil

Fire up the grill with an eye on medium-high heat.

Check the skin of each fillet for loose scales and remove any obvious pin bones. Make several short, shallow cuts in the skin.

In a small bowl combine the soy, honey, chili oil, and sesame oil. Season the fillets with pepper and brush them with the glaze.

Place fillets on the grill, flesh side down, and grill for 2 to 3 minutes. *NOTE: There may be flare-ups at first, as the glaze drips.* Carefully flip the fillets skin side down, and brush them with the glaze. Cook them until the edges begin to flake, 4 to 8 minutes, depending on the thickness of the fillets. *NOTE: The internal temperature should be 135° F.*

Serve immediately over steamed rice.

Serves 4

Sablefish en Papillote

Because it's not as thick as toothfish, sablefish works better in a pouch application. Just to make the meal complete, I've added a bed of corn and shallots. Don't skip the "milking" step as the moisture helps flavor the meal. NOTE: Depending on how the fish was trimmed, there may a series of bones running down the center of the fillet. Removing these without seriously damaging the flesh can be difficult. The solution: Leave the bones in with a warning to your guests about where to find them, or simply cut the center strip out of the fillet and push the two halves together in the pouch.

3 ears of sweet corn
2 shallots, minced
1 tablespoon flat-leaf parsley, chopped
Kosher salt and freshly ground black pepper
3 tablespoons unsalted butter
2 sablefish fillets (6 to 8 ounces each), skin removed
2 tablespoons dry white wine

Preheat the oven to 425° F.

Cut the kernels off of each ear of corn and then "milk" them by scraping down the cob with the back of a knife. Catch the juices in a bowl along with the kernels. Toss the corn with the shallots and parsley.

Fold two sheets of 12-by-24-inch parchment paper in half like a book. On each piece, make a bed of corn and shallots slightly to one side of the fold. Season the corn with salt and pepper and dot each bed with a tablespoon of butter.

Season the sablefish with salt and pepper and place each fillet on its own bed of corn. Sprinkle a tablespoon of wine over each fillet and dot it with a few dabs of butter. Secure the parchment pouch as directed in the illustration on page 37.

Place both pouches on a baking sheet and bake them for 15 minutes. Serve the pouches unopened for the full aroma or slice them open and plate the fish and corn without the bag for a cleaner presentation.

Serves 2

Chapter 17
Mahimahi
Popularity (No) Contest

STEVE MAHIMAHI
"Big Steve"

HONORS: 2006 Prom King, Captain of the Varsity Finball Team, Voted "Most Likely to Succeed," "Best Dressed," "Best Fins," and "Best Dancer."

Have a cool summer! Steve M²

This is the fish other fish love to hate. Growing up, mahimahi were always the most popular fish in the school. How could they not be? They're gorgeous! Beauty may only be skin deep, but if you've got the best skin, use it. Most mahimahi start dating long before the other fish even figure out there is an opposite sex…or what to do with it. Perhaps more insulting, mahimahi can eat anything, and no matter how fast or how large they grow, they always maintain their knockout figure. Did I mention they're the best athletes on the block? That shimmering blue green streak? Mahimahi. Even the name is cool—mahimahi—exotic, sexy, strong. What's the big deal about a name? Ask a flounder, dogfish, or monkeyface prickleback. It's all about the packaging, people.

VITAL STATS

FIRST NAME: Mahimahi (a.k.a. dolphinfish, dorado)

SCI. NAME: *Coryphaena hippurus*

SIZE: Most 5-25 lbs, up to 80 lbs

LIFESPAN: 2-5 years

RANGE: Tropical and subtropical waters worldwide

CATCH: About 3.3 million lbs a year, domestic; imports about 22 million lbs annually

ahimahi" is the Hawaiian name for dolphin. No, I'm not suggesting anyone chow down on Flipper. This dolphin is a fish—let's call it a dolphinfish—found in most of the world's warmer oceans. Who thought it wise to name a fish after Sea World's finest? It's possible the name came from the fish's habit of swimming alongside boats, much like its mammalian namesake. Another theory suggests "dolphin" may simply be a misinterpretation of the Spanish name *dorado*, which was in use when Captain John Smith first recorded catching the fish in 1627.

Whatever the origin, most restaurants and fish markets don't want anything to do with dolphin, but are more than happy to sell mahimahi. The FDA has gone so far as to make mahimahi the standard market name, although most fisheries continue to call it dolphin. (I'm guessing just to tweak environmentally fragile tourists.)

The Maltese fish

Fishermen in Malta have another name for dolphinfish, one they've used since Roman times: *lampuki*. Every year, from September to December, the lampuki migrate through the waters west of the island, providing a bounty of fresh fish for those able to catch them. Remarkably, most fishermen employ a technique nearly as old as the fishery itself called *kannizzati* fishing. In the weeks leading up to the arrival of the fish, fishermen build thousands of makeshift rafts out of wood planks, cork, and palm fronds, which are then anchored in the waters along the fish's migration route. Dolphinfish congregate under the rafts, making the fish easy targets for the fishermen.

Why do dolphinfish suddenly freeze in their tracks? Are they drawn to the underwater island aesthetic? (Palm fronds + flotsam = nouveau chic.) Perhaps they forgot where they were going. Or could it be they simply like looking at the only fish as attractive as themselves—other mahimahi.

In the Water
Pretty Fishy

Imagine a fish splashed in iridescent greens and electric blues, streaked with yellow and gold, dipped in silver, and finally handed off to Jackson Pollock's ghost for a little spot treatment. All of the neon in Las Vegas can't compare to the mahimahi in its natural habitat. Too bad you'll probably never get the chance to see it.

Dolphinfish may be one of the most beautiful fish in the sea, but out of it their color fades in about the time it takes to say: "Oh, look at the pretty fishy…well, it *was* pretty." The mahimahi gets its elaborate color palette from an array of tiny color cells in its skin called chromatophores. Underwater, these cells expand and contract, making the skin shimmer and appear to change color. When the fish dies, most of the color cells close up shop, turning a drab, dark gray in the process.

Grow fast and prosper

Most dolphinfish reach sexual maturity in just 4 to 5 months, wasting little time before pairing off to fulfill their fishy urges. Since they stick to warmer waters, spawning can take place year-round, although spring and summer see the most activity. Most females spawn several times each season, releasing upward of 1.5 millions eggs at a time. Once hatched, dolphinfish larvae grow quickly, quadrupling in size in just two weeks.

Meaningful Monikers

"Mahi" means "strong" in Hawaiian, which makes a mahimahi twice as tough as the average fish. "Dorado" translates to golden in Spanish, most likely named for the color, not the fish's perceived value.

dolphinfish

One Word or Two?

Is it "mahimahi" or "mahi mahi"? My spell-checker votes for the former, as do most Hawaiians. Score one for the spell-checker.

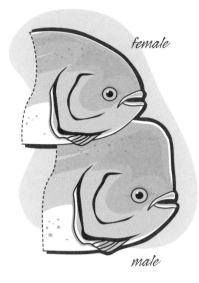

female

male

In order to maintain a metabolism that allows them to grow 3 feet in their first year, mahimahi need to eat a lot. Fortunately, they aren't picky about their diet, which includes small fish, shrimp, squid, crab, and whatever else the local waters have to offer (flying fish appears to be a favorite). Keen eyesight and a top speed approaching 50 mph keeps even the fastest prey on the menu.

Under cover

Mahimahi migrate seasonally, but like many species of pelagic fish, they're attracted to objects floating in the water—sargassum, storm debris, boats, and even floating rafts with palm fronds tied underneath. Schools of young dolphinfish are especially attracted to large masses of floating kelp. Why? No one has come up with a definitive answer, but the most prominent theory is that mahimahi are simply attracted to what they perceive to be shelter, and possibly a good source of food.

One interesting alternative theory suggests the fish may be using various floating natural and man-made objects as reference points from which to orient themselves in the vast emptiness of the ocean. The fact that fish will "orient themselves" to a piece of driftwood, leads me to believe most may be lost.

Bad-luck Banana

Hawaiian fishermen consider it bad luck to carry bananas on a fishing expedition. One can only assume that extends to monkey first mates and watching old Woody Allen films while at sea as well.

On the Boats
Bycatch This Fish

Not all bycatch is bad. Case in point: mahimahi. The commercial dolphinfish harvest began as simply an incidental catch of the swordfish and tuna fisheries. Its popularity justified giving mahimahi a targeted fishery, which today is made up primarily of boats using hook-and-line and longline techniques.

Domestically, the largest landings come from Hawaii, Florida, and the Carolinas. In Hawaii, the hook-and-line fishery dominates, with much of the carefully handled catch sold at auction to raw purveyors

Dolphinfish Double

The POMPANO DOLPHINFISH (*Coryphaena equiselis*) is often mistaken for a small female mahimahi thanks to its similar good looks. The primary difference can be found around the middle; pompano dolphinfish have a body depth greater than 25 percent of their length, making them fatter than the average mahimahi. Because the pompano dolphinfish occasionally schools with the common variety, it sometimes shows up at the market. Beyond that, there's no targeted commercial fishery because the fish tends to steer clear of coastal waters.

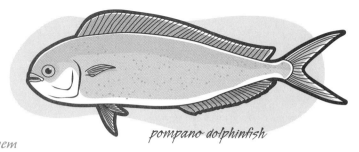

pompano dolphinfish

and high-end fresh markets. A little more than half of the Atlantic catch comes from fishermen using various hook-and-line techniques, including some not exclusively targeting dolphinfish.

Not just a passing FAD

Mahimahi harvests vary from year to year, not because the population fluctuates, but because water temperature does. Migrating mahimahi feed in warmer water currents, which normally take them into prime fishing grounds. Slight seasonal variations can send them off course, sometimes out of reach of fishermen using smaller boats not suited to deeper, offshore waters.

To help increase their chances for a successful harvest, fishermen around the world use fish aggregating devices (FADs), which, like the Maltese *kannizzati* rafts, exploit the mahimahi's attraction to floating objects. Modern FADs are made of fiberglass, steel, and polypropylene rope, and come equipped with radar and solar-powered lighting systems—a far cry from the wooden rafts and palm fronds used by traditional fishermen. Still, the concept remains the same: Float it, and the fish will come.

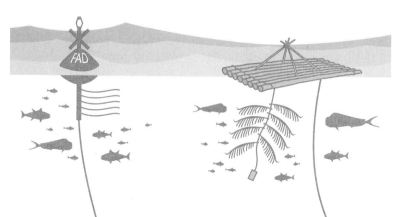

modern (left) and traditional FADs

Mahi Farms

A highly migratory fish may not seem like an ideal candidate for aquaculture, but don't tell that to the Australians. A single Aussie farm now produces more than 2000 metric tons per season.

Hawaiian Favorites

Mahimahi isn't the only oddly named Hawaiian fish that sometimes makes an appearance at mainland markets. Two equally tasty species to look for are ono (Acanthocybium solandri) and opah (Lampris regius). Ono, also known as wahoo, is a long, slender fish with lean, delicate flesh. "Ono" actually means "good to eat" in Hawaiian, which should tell you everything you need to know about this species. Opah has a beautiful, round body that is no doubt the origin of the fish's alternate moniker, moonfish. On the plate, opah is denser than mahimahi, making it an excellent substitute for those craving swordfish.

> ### QUICK QUESTION
>
> **Is bycatch a problem?**   Very little bycatch occurs in the hook-and-line fishery, but the longliners have had problems with sea turtles. Like some of the swordfish and tuna fisheries, mahimahi longline fishermen now use circle hooks (*see illustration, page 131*), and other measures aimed at limiting interactions with endangered species.

Doing just fine

While there's never been a scientific stock assessment of mahimahi, it's believed the populations in both the Atlantic and Pacific are healthy. Dolphinfish are inherently resistant to overfishing because they grow quickly, have a short lifespan, and mature early. In other words, these fish are ideally suited to commercial fishing.

To ensure the stocks stay healthy, measures such as set and catch limits, gear restrictions, and area closures are already in place in many areas. Both domestic fisheries (Atlantic and Pacific) have traditionally been managed under general pelagic fishing rules, but dolphinfish caught in the Atlantic and the Gulf will soon have their own management plan.

At the Market
Tourist Trap

Unless you live in Hawaii or Florida, it's likely the mahimahi at your local market is a tourist. Roughly 90 percent of the dolphinfish sold in the United States is imported, primarily from China, Ecuador, and Costa Rica. Most of the domestic catch goes to high-end restaurants, with only a small amount slipping through to the masses.

Even if you do spend Christmas among the palm trees, don't be surprised if your mahimahi burger arrived via a long boat trip. The imports are simply cheaper and more plentiful. Fortunately, they taste almost as good as the local boys and girls.

Both fresh and frozen product is available year-round, although seasonal landings tend to peak in the spring and summer (spring and fall in Hawaii).

Pretty in pink

For those lucky few who encounter whole fish, the usual rules apply—clear eyes, undamaged skin, and a clean, sea-breezy scent. Fresh steaks and fillets are far more common, usually running in the 1- to 1.5-inch-thick range. Do your best Elle Woods impression and demand the pinkest fish available. Beige and slightly translucent is okay, but brown is *so* last season. Depending on the cut, there may be a dark line (or spot on steaks) running along the center of the fillet. Redder is better (it is the bloodline, after all). If you're staring at a pale gray steak with brown spots, it's past its prime.

Vacuum-sealed frozen steaks have become very common in recent years. The quality tends to be good, although I'd avoid any that have been preflavored. Frozen flesh is usually lighter in color, but watch out for uneven coloring, excessive spotting, and air pockets in the packaging.

Some processors treat their fish with carbon monoxide (a.k.a. "taste-less smoke"), which helps the flesh maintain its pinkish glow. There's nothing wrong with this, unless it's used to turn an old or poor-quality fillet into a hot-pink beauty. Avoid "fresh" mahimahi that seems unnaturally pink or unusually affordable. (Mahimahi shouldn't be as pricey as swordfish or ahi, but in the ballpark.)

What's Your Sign?

Hawaiians born from February 19 to March 20 fall under the sign of Kaulua, which is represented by a pair of mahimahi, one facing toward the mountain, ("mauka"), the other toward the sea ("makai").

In the Kitchen
Take Me to Your Taco

Dark meat or light meat? When it comes to chicken I'm partial to white, but I'll definitely turn to the dark side for a mahimahi. The strongest flavor is found around the bloodline, where the meat is darker (redder). If your tastes tend to run a little milder, feel free to trim away, although I'd suggest giving it a try, at least once.

Dolphinfish skin is tough and, unlike some fish, isn't going to do anything for the flavor. For steaks, simply trim away the thin strip along the edge. For fillets, place your hand flat against the meat, and slowly slice along the bottom of the fish with a sharp knife. Fillets sometimes come with a strip of bones along the bloodline, which should be removed before cooking.

check for bones here

Pseudoswords

Most cooks compare the flavor of mahimahi to that of swordfish, which is fair enough. They're both firm, lean, steaklike fish, which take well to accent marinades, but I prefer mahimahi. It's firm, but not *too* firm—more like a steaky fish as opposed to a fishy steak. And whereas swordfish has a tendency to dry out quickly if overcooked, mahimahi is more forgiving. For friends who must have their fish cooked until it's *done*, mahimahi will make them happy *and* protect your reputation as a master chef.

Fish On

Mahimahi skin may not be tasty, but it does make a nifty fishing lure when dried. Back in the water, some of the old flash comes back, making it irresistible to fish that have a thing for bling.

Once the flesh firms up and shows a willingness to flake, get it off the heat and onto a warm plate. For thicker steaks, a peek inside with a paring knife may help. A little underdone in the middle is perfectly acceptable. Where should you cook it? Larger steaks are perfect for the grill. Smaller steaks and fillets do well under the broiler or sautéed. If you want to smash up a bunch of macadamia nuts for a crispy, Hawaiian-style crust…I have no problem with that.

Taco time

I do, however, have a problem with most fish tacos. Before I get to offending half of Mexico, let me say mahimahi is an excellent choice for making tacos. It begs to be marinated in lime, grilled, and flaked in a flour tortilla along with onions, tomatoes, cilantro, and a few chilies of your choice. Fruity tropical salsa? Sounds blasphemous, but go for it. Now, about those problems…

There are two styles of fish tacos: "Baja" and grilled. Baja-style tacos are made with lightly battered and fried fish, usually sea bass, cod, or other lean white fish. Done right, Baja fish tacos can be excellent, but I prefer the grilled variety, which allows the natural flavor of the fish to star, and doesn't require a pot of hot oil. My other fish taco "issues" are bit more subjective, so regard them with as much skepticism as you deem necessary.

Corn tortillas: I don't like 'em. I know, they're traditional, but to my tongue they distract from the flavor of the fish. Flour tortillas are more complementary, and don't require doubling up due to superior structural integrity. If you prefer corn, try the white variety, which has a milder flavor.

White sauce: Again, don't toss tradition in my face. A light Mexican *crema* (or crème fraîche) is fine, but the Stateside modification tends to be overly thick and (sour) creamy. Personally, I'm fine with salsa fresca, but if you feel the need to add additional flavors, think thin and light, like maybe a spicy tomatillo salsa. As for tartar sauce…That's just wrong.

Cabbage: Not on a grilled fish taco. Baja style…yeah, okay.

NUTRITIONAL INFO
Per 3.5 oz/100 grams (raw)
Mahimahi

Calories	89
Calories from fat	8
Total fat	0.9 g
Saturated fat	0.3 g
Cholesterol	86 mg
Sodium	128 mg
Protein	18.9 g
Omega-3	0.1 g
Mercury	0.24 ppm

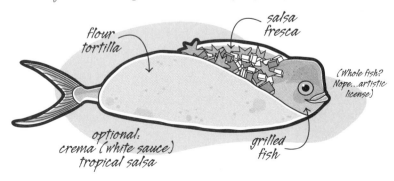

flour tortilla

salsa fresca

(Whole fish? Nope…artistic license)

optional: crema (white sauce) tropical salsa

grilled fish

Mahimahi Recipes

After a cursory glance at the following two fish taco recipes, you'll no doubt notice there's something missing: cheese. I have nothing against cheese. I like cheese. I like cheese on tacos. But on fish tacos? Not so much. There's something about the flavor and texture that just gets in the way of my enjoyment of the fish. (Exception that proves the rule: salmon. See Dill Salmon Wraps on page 15 for further proof.)

Of course, if you really dig cheese, grate to your heart's content. May I suggest a little pepper Jack?

HOW TO STORE: Mahimahi

FRESH: Mahimahi will stay fresh about ten days out of the water, but unless you were there when it hit the boat, don't plan on holding on to fresh steaks or fillets for more than a day or two. Store in the coldest part of the fridge, preferably on ice, wrapped tightly in plastic wrap (the fish, not the ice). **FROZEN:** Frozen product will last considerably longer, 3 to 6 months if commercially frozen. Thaw overnight in the fridge. If you need them for tonight's big luau, submerge sealed steaks or fillets in a bowl of water and pop in the fridge, or (to really speed things up) place in the sink under just a trickle of running water.

HEALTH QUESTION

Are there any health issues with mahimahi? Improperly handled mahimahi may produce histamines that can cause a severe allergic reaction known as scromboid poisoning. Fortunately, this is a very rare occurrence and can be easily avoided by not buying from the guy peddling fish out of the back of an old ice cream truck.

Grilled Mahimahi Tacos

You'll no doubt notice there's a brief rest included after grilling. The idea is to let slightly underdone fish finish on it own in a tight space (under foil) so it stays moist. You might not achieve the perfect grill marks, but no one's going notice. NOTE: Fajita-sized tortillas are smaller than soft taco tortillas, usually around 6 inches in diameter. I prefer the smaller tortilla, which gives me the illusion I have more to eat without actually having more to eat.

2 tablespoons extra virgin olive oil
2 tablespoons dry white wine
Juice of 1 lime, plus zest
1 garlic clove, crushed
1 teaspoon cayenne
½ teaspoon ground cumin
½ teaspoon crushed red pepper flakes
¼ teaspoon kosher salt
¼ teaspoon freshly ground black pepper
1 pound mahimahi steaks or fillets
6 flour tortillas (fajita size)
Baby spinach
Mango Salsa (*see recipe on page 61*)

Combine the oil, wine, lime juice, zest, garlic clove, cayenne, cumin, red pepper flakes, salt, and pepper in a glass dish (or zip-top bag).

Rinse the mahimahi and pat it dry. Add the fish to the marinade, turn to coat, cover, and chill for 1 hour. Turn the fish at least once. NOTE: For more intense flavor marinate the fish for up to 4 hours.

Fire up the grill, with an eye on medium-high heat. Set the grill about 4 inches from the heat. NOTE: A quick wipe of the grill with a towel dipped in vegetable oil just before adding the fish will help prevent sticking.

Remove the fish pieces from the marinade, pat them dry, and place them on the grill. Cook them for 3 to 4 minutes. Flip them and cook until not quite done in the middle, 3 to 4 minutes. NOTE: It's okay to cut into the flesh with a knife to test for doneness since you'll be breaking it up anyway.

Transfer the fish to a plate, cover it with foil, and let it rest until it's opaque throughout, 2 to 3 minutes. Flake the fish over the tortillas. Top them with baby spinach and Mango Salsa. Serve immediately.

Serves 2 or 3

Easy Mahimahi Tacos

Grilling and fancy marinades not your thing? No problem! NOTE: Mexican crema *is essentially the same as crème fraîche—light, tangy, and not as sour as sour cream. Check the refrigerated section of the supermarket for Crema Mexicana, somewhere near the salsas.*

Juice of 4 limes, plus zest
3 tablespoons extra virgin olive oil
2 mahimahi steaks or fillets (6 to 8 ounces each)
6 flour tortillas (fajita size)
1 white onion, diced
Mexican crema (or crème fraîche)
Salsa Fresca (*see recipe on page 114*)

Combine lime juice, zest, and 2 tablespoons oil in a glass dish (or zip-top bag).

Rinse the mahimahi and pat them dry. Add the fillets to the marinade, turn them to coat, cover, and chill for 30 minutes or up to 2 hours. Turn fillets at least once.

Heat a large nonstick pan over medium-high heat. As soon as the oil starts to ripple, add the fillets and cook for 4 minutes. Flip the fillets, and cook until not quite done in the middle, 3 to 4 minutes. *NOTE: It's okay to cut into the flesh with a knife to test for doneness since you'll be breaking it up anyway.*

Transfer the fish to a plate, cover it with foil, and let it rest until it is opaque throughout, 2 to 3 minutes. Flake the fish over the tortillas. Top the fish with a dab of crema, onions, and Salsa Fresca. Serve immediately.

Serves 2 or 3

GREAT. MY ONE SHOT AT PUBLISHING GLORY AND I'M A PUN. I NEED TO GET A NEW AGENT.

FISH TACO
EASY, DELICIOUS

TAKO THE OCTOPUS
CHEF, INTERNET CELEBRITY

LIVE BAIT

Mahi Macadamia

This surprisingly simple dish is (more or less) what made mahimahi a tourist favorite in Hawaii. NOTE: If you find yourself with exceptionally thick fillets, they can be finished in an oven preheated to 400° F to avoid overcooking the bottom of the fillet.

½ cup roasted macadamia nuts, finely ground
¼ cup unsalted butter, softened
2 tablespoons *panko*
2 tablespoons shredded coconut
1 tablespoon olive oil
2 mahimahi fillets (6 to 8 ounces each)
Kosher salt and freshly ground black pepper
Tropical Salsa (see recipe)

Stir the nuts, butter, *panko,* and coconut in a small bowl until thoroughly combined.

Remove the skin and bones from the fillets (if any). Season both sides with salt and pepper. Spread the nut mixture evenly over the tops of the fillets.

Heat olive oil in a large nonstick sauté pan over medium-high heat. Add the fillets, nut side down, and cook until lightly browned, 2½ to 3 minutes. Flip the fillets and cook them until opaque throughout, 3 to 5 minutes, depending on thickness.

Transfer the mahimahi to warm plates and serve it topped with Tropical Salsa.

Serves 2

Tropical Salsa

This is a fruitier version of the Mango Salsa I've used elsewhere in the book. It really makes this dish special, so don't skip it.

1 whole mango, peeled, pitted, and chopped
½ cup pineapple, diced
1 kiwi, peeled and diced
2 tablespoons red onion, finely chopped
2 tablespoons cilantro, chopped
¼ teaspoon red pepper flakes
1 tablespoon lime juice plus zest of one lime
Kosher salt and freshly ground black pepper

Combine the mango, pineapple, kiwi, onion, cilantro, red pepper flakes, lime juice, and zest in a small bowl, and season with salt and pepper to taste. Store the salsa in the fridge for up to 3 days.

Grilled Mahimahi Burger

One of my favorite things is a really good fish steak sandwich. Mahimahi is especially well suited for such an endeavor thanks to its meaty but moist texture. NOTE: *If it's raining outside, the fish can be just as easily sautéed.*

4 mahimahi steaks (or fillets) (4 to 6 ounces each)
Kosher salt and freshly ground black pepper
Olive oil
4 thin slices of pineapple
4 thin slices of red onion
Lettuce leaves
4 large sesame seed hamburger rolls
Lime Aioli (see recipe)

Fire up the grill, with an eye on medium-high heat. Set the grill *about 4 inches from the heat.* NOTE: *A quick wipe of the grill with a towel dipped in vegetable oil just before adding the fish will help prevent sticking.*

Remove the skin and bones from steaks (if any). Season both sides with salt and pepper and brush with olive oil.

Place the steaks on the grill and cook them for 3 to 4 minutes. Flip them and cook until not quite done in the middle, 3 to 4 minutes. Transfer the steaks to a plate, cover them with foil, and let them rest until opaque throughout, 2 to 3 minutes.

Place the pineapple slices on the grill and cook to the desired doneness, flipping them once. NOTE: *It may be necessary to place the pineapple on the grill before removing the fish in order to achieve the desired results. The onions may also be grilled.*

Brush the inside of the rolls with olive oil and grill them briefly. To build burgers, place a leaf or two of lettuce on the bottom, followed by the mahimahi, a dab of Lime Aioli, a slice of grilled pineapple, and a slice of onion (or only a few rings). Top with toasted bun and enjoy.

Serves 4

Lime Aioli

Unless you really like aioli, this recipe will make enough sauce to top 6 to 8 burgers (about ½ cup).

2 large cloves garlic, peeled
1 egg yolk
¼ teaspoon kosher salt
Freshly ground pepper, to taste
1 tablespoon lime juice, plus zest of 1 lime
6 tablespoons extra virgin olive oil

Crush the garlic into a smooth paste (using a mortar and pestle or a spoon and small metal bowl). Transfer it to a mixing bowl, add the yolk, salt, pepper, limejuice, and zest, and whisk to combine ingredients.

Add a small amount of the olive oil and whisk until absorbed. Continue to gradually work in oil until the sauce forms a smooth emulsion. Adjust the seasonings as desired.

Baked Mahimahi

It occurs to me that I rarely make a sauce to go with fish. Why? When a fish is done I want to eat it. Letting it sit for a few minutes while I concoct a sauce with the pan drippings seems an unusually cruel thing to do to a perfectly cooked piece of fish…unless, of course, I was to undercook the fish slightly, thereby allowing it to finish cooking off the heat. Yes, that might work. NOTE: *For a more intensely flavored fish, marinate the fillets in the white wine and fruit juices for 15 minutes prior to cooking.*

4 mahimahi fillets (6 to 8 ounces each)
Kosher salt and freshly ground black pepper
Extra virgin olive oil
¼ cup dry white wine
¼ cup pineapple juice
Juice of 1 lemon plus zest
Juice of 1 lime plus zest
Tropical Salsa (optional, *see recipe on page 184*)

Preheat the oven to 400°F.

Remove the skin and/or bones from the fillets (if any) and season both sides with salt and pepper.

Spray a large baking dish with cooking spray. Lay the fillets in the baking dish and drizzle them with olive oil. Add the white wine and pineapple, lemon, and lime juices to the dish. Bake the fillets for 12-15 minutes, or until they're not quite done. They should be firm and starting to flake, but still a little "pink" in the middle.

Remove the fillets from the pan and set them on a warm plate, loosely covered with foil. Carefully pour the pan juices into a small saucepan, stir in the zest, and bring to a boil over medium high heat. Cook until the sauce is reduced by half, about 4 to 5 minutes.

Transfer the fillets to serving plates and top them with reduced sauce and Tropical Salsa (if desired).

Serves 4

Chapter 18
Tilapia
The Once and Future Fish

Ladies and Gentlemen, presenting the King of Fish, the one, the only…tilapia. (insert sound of crickets chirping) What, you've never heard of tilapia? Small fish, rarely more than a pound or two, firm fillets, mild flavor…Nothing? But it's the King of Fish! Well, historically speaking, I suppose it's more the fish of kings. When ancient Egyptians stocked the pharaohs' tombs, it was with tilapia. When a certain biblical savior needed to feed a few thousand followers, he turned to tilapia for the assist. Even Elvis was a fan, as evidenced by his fondness for fried peanut butter and tilapia* sandwiches. These days, tilapia is the fish poised to feed the world. When farmers needed an edible critter willing to live in muddy water on a diet dominated by pond scum, tilapia happily volunteered. A few million metric tons later, it's the fish on everyone's lips. No, you won't find it at fancy-pants restaurants, but that's probably a good thing. This is a fish of the people, grown by the people, for the people. Hmmm…maybe tilapia should run for president.

*Might have been "peanut butter and bananas." My notes are a little fuzzy.

VITAL STATS

FIRST NAME: Tilapia (a.k.a. St. Peter's Fish, cherry snapper, sunfish)

SCI. NAME: *Oreochromis* spp., plus numerous hybrid species

SIZE: 1-2 lbs farmed (2 ft max in wild)

LIFESPAN: 8-10 months farmed, up to 12 years in the wild

RANGE: Native to Africa, farmed worldwide

HARVEST: 1.6 million metric tons worldwide (and growing)

The fish that would be king first appeared in the fresh waters of Africa, most likely originating in the Nile River. Egyptian paintings and hieroglyphics depict tilapia being farmed in small ponds as far back as 2000 B.C. Known in Egypt as *bolti*, tilapia was considered a symbol of rebirth and was often associated with Osiris, the god of fertility and eternal life.

Linking tilapia and fertility makes sense; after all, this is a fish that knows how to multiply. According to the parable of the "loaves and fishes," Jesus transformed five loaves of bread and a pair of fish into a feast for 5,000 followers. Could those fruitful fish have been tilapia? The

Sea of Galilee is thought to have been full of tilapia at the time, making it the most likely catch of St. Peter and his pals.

Tilapia's ascension to the throne domestically is a more recent event. The first varieties imported into the United States were most likely aquarium fish. In the 1960s, a few species were introduced in California and Florida as a way to combat algae, but the fish ultimately proved to be more of a pest than the plant. It wasn't until indoor aquaculture facilities began popping up in the eighties and nineties that tilapia took hold at home.

Despite healthy production numbers, local fish account for less than 10 percent of the 200,000 metric tons of tilapia now consumed each year in the United States. In 2001, tilapia landed on the Top 10 list of most popular fish in America and has been climbing ever since. Will it reach number one? Given tuna's head start, that could be tough. But tilapia has already edged out tuna in one race: It's been to space!

Fish in space

On October 29, 1998, a handful of fertilized tilapia eggs blasted into orbit aboard the space shuttle *Discovery*. The eggs were used to test the viability of raising fish in a weightless environment with an eye on providing food for astronauts living on an orbiting station. Although only one tilapia survived long enough to make the return trip, Project AMIGO (Aquaculture MIcroGravitational Orbit) was considered a success. No word on whether the fish tasted best served with a fumé blanc or Tang.

Will tilapia be the first fish served on the moon? Maybe. One small fish for man, one giant leap for extraterrestrial aquaculture. Until then, tilapia will have to settle for being the fish on more plates around the globe than almost any other. Who needs the moon when you're sitting on top of the world?

In the Water
A Mouthful of Motherhood

The hardest thing for a mother tilapia to tell her children is not to talk with their mouths full. Why? To do so would be a bit hypocritical, given that she most likely has a mouthful of kids at the time. Most species of tilapia are "mouth brooders," which means that, after laying and fertilizing a clutch of eggs, mom and sometimes pop incubate them in their mouths until the eggs hatch up to a week later. Even after the fry are free, their parents will continue to provide refuge while the kids find their sea legs.

Pete's Fishes

Thanks to its biblical associations, tilapia is sometimes referred to as "St. Peter's fish." John Dory (*Zeus faber*) also claims to be "St. Peter's fish" and has the disciple's thumbprint on its side (allegedly) to prove it. In which fish should you put your faith? My money is on tilapia (it's less showy).

Li'l Carnivore

In the early stages of life, tilapia display more carnivorous behavior, preferring small crustaceans, fish, and insects, which provide protein for their development. Older tilapia depend more on aquatic plants, algae, and detritus for nourishment.

All of this mouth-to-mouth action takes place only after the water temperature hits 72 degrees F, which in warmer areas means year-round spawning. Males initiate the dance by building a nest in hopes of attracting a mate (or two). Once paired off, he will defend the nest and his mate until the little fry are safely on their own.

Wild tilapia are found throughout the world's tropical and subtropical waters, usually in lakes and rivers, although some varieties thrive in brackish environments. Most tend not to be too flashy in the skin department. Black-and-white or tan-and-white scale patterns produce fairly neutral fashions, although some fish break the mold and wear a smattering of red or blue. A few of the hybrid species were bred to create a more colorful product for the whole fish market.

On the Farm
Pest Controlled

If tilapia weren't such a good source of protein, they'd probably be considered the cockroach of the sea. They'll eat almost anything, don't mind crowded living conditions, are disease-resistant, can tolerate both fresh and salt water, grow rapidly, and multiply like rabbits on crack—all of which makes tilapia a troublesome pest when accidentally (or otherwise) introduced into an ecosystem where they aren't welcome.

These same factors make tilapia ideal for aquaculture, especially in developing countries where intensive (and expensive) farming systems aren't a viable option. It's not quite as simple as—*hey, fish, here's some*

Tilapia Trio

NILE TILAPIA (Oreochromis niloticus), MOZAMBIQUE TILAPIA (O. mossambicus), and BLUE TILAPIA (O. aureus) are the most commonly cultivated species, with the Nile variety by far the most popular of the three. While there are a few obvious external differences (those Jagger-esque lips on the Mozambique, for example), once filleted they're hard to tell apart. Raised in similar conditions, all three species will taste pretty much the same.

Nile

Mozambique

blue

QUICK QUESTION

Can you really grow a fish in a cage? Underwater cage culture is a surprisingly good option for tilapia cultivation. By suspending a large, but lightweight cage in a lake, river, or reservoir, a farmer doesn't have to worry about water circulation, aeration, predation, population control, or how he's going to get the fish out of the water come harvest time. A strong current means there'll be plenty of local cuisine, although supplemental feed is recommended to prevent funky-flavored fish.

Is cage culture cruel? Depends on your point of view. Is it cruel to keep a goldfish in a bowl? Tilapia don't seem to mind the crowded conditions, so in most cases I'd say it was okay.

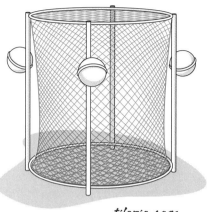

tilapia cage

water, go nuts—but it's close. Even the most primitive ponds can be successful with a little management. Feeding requirements are kept to a minimum thanks to the tilapia's taste for naturally occurring algae and phytoplankton. Keeping the population in check can be as simple as adding a predator fish or segregating the tilapia into more manageable groups through the use of mesh enclosures called "hapas." It's even possible to grow tilapia in existing irrigation systems or rice paddies. The final product probably won't win any international taste tests, but when the main concern is feeding the starving masses, impressing food critics isn't usually an issue.

Homegrown

While it's possible to grow tilapia in the bathtub, a more complex system will produce a superior result in terms of culinary value. Commercial farms around the world grow tilapia in man-made ponds, raceways, tanks, and cages, in water that's circulated, aerated, filtered, and temperature controlled (where necessary).

In the United States, most farmers use indoor reticulating aquaculture systems (RAS), which keep the water a balmy 82-86 degrees F, ideal for tilapia growth and reproduction. Greenhouses are often employed to promote the growth of algae, which contributes to the fish's diet, and helps keep the water clean through the natural uptake of bio-waste such as ammonia.

Of course, tilapia cannot live on algae alone—not if it wants to taste good. To improve the flavor of the fish, farmers often supplement the menu with a protein-and-vitamin-fortified grain-based feed. Depending on the reliance on naturally occurring foodstuffs, it can take anywhere from 1 to 3 pounds of additional feed to produce 1 pound of tilapia.

Fishery

Both California and Florida have modest freshwater tilapia fisheries based on populations that were introduced in the 1960s to help control algae.

Waste Not

At some farms, the odds and ends of tilapia processing are turned into fishmeal to be used in the production of animal feed.

Boys club

One thing you won't find at most tilapia farms is a girl. Males grow faster and more uniformly, and since females tend to hit sexual maturity before they reach market size, they're removed from the equation after brooding.

How do you guarantee an exclusively male population? Turn 'em over. Visual inspection of fry may be the most time-consuming method, but it works. Some farms also treat newborn tilapia with a hormone (methyltes-tosterone), which effectively reverses the sex of 95 percent of the females. Unfortunately, some retailers refuse to buy hormone-treated fish, even if said hormone is long gone by harvest time. Crossbreeding certain tilapia species also produces predominantly male populations, as does breeding an average female with a "supermale." Supermales are equipped with a YY chromosome set, which virtually guarantees off-spring that are 100 percent male.

Once the gender has been established, tilapia fry are reared in a nursery for 5 to 8 weeks, and then transferred to a grow-out pond where they'll swell to market size (about 2 pounds) in 8 to 10 months. Prior to harvest, most fish are transferred to special holding tanks to purge them of any impurities.

Getting the fish out of the water is not always an easy task. Special herding gear and shallow harvest pools are effective in smaller tanks, but at larger ponds seines must be used, often with less than perfect results. Thanks to the tilapia's ability to jump over or burrow under most nets, draining the pond is usually the only way to catch every last fish.

At the Market
Frozen Treat

Tilapia is a fish I buy almost exclusively frozen. It's a convenience thing. I like having a freezer full of fillets that I can call upon whenever the mood strikes. When I first got hooked on tilapia, individually frozen fillets were the only product at most markets. Today, fresh tilapia is readily available. Is the fresh stuff better? Sure. Do I buy it? Rarely. That's not a slam, but an observation of how I cook. It just never occurs to me to buy it.

That shouldn't stop you from buying fresh, at least once, to have a benchmark to judge the frozen product. Most fresh tilapia comes from farms in Central America, which ship the fish to U.S. distributors within a few days of harvest. Whole fish should be clean, with undamaged skin

Hot Water

Fish farmers have found some ingenious ways to heat the local waters to tilapia-friendly temperatures, including: natural geothermal energy, harvesting waste heat given off by manufacturing sites, and even raising fish in the heated effluent ponds of power stations. (Yes, it's perfectly safe. No three-eyed tilapia have made their way to market.)

Gator Bait

In Florida, tilapia are grown in reclaimed phosphate mines as food for farm-raised alligators. I kid you not.

QUICK QUESTION

What is polyculture? Two great tastes that go great together—shrimp and tilapia—can be grown in the same pond since each species occupies its own ecological space. The tilapia act as a biological water treatment system by chowing down on waste and other organic matter that might otherwise require filtering. Harvesting one species at a time can be tricky, which is why some farms keep the fish in cages.

Are They Safe?

Tilapia farms and processing plants are subjected to microbiological testing before being certified safe as required by HACCP (Hazard Analysis and Critical Control Point Program).

and clear, plump eyes. Fillets should be slightly moist and resilient to the touch. If either product smells fishy, turn up your nose and walk the other way.

In terms of flesh color, white to off-white is good; yellow or gray is bad. Don't be surprised to find a series of red stripes along one side of a fillet. The stripes are the result of the skin bleeding through, and, depending on how deep the fillet has been skinned, it will be barely noticeable or cover the entire fillet. For a milder flavor, less red (deep-skinned) is best.

Frozen fillets usually have more noticeable striping, but can be just as tasty as the fresh fish. Unfortunately, not all frozen fillets are created equal. Most of the stone-cold supply comes from China and Southeast Asia, where quality isn't always job one. The trick is to find a superior brand and stick with it. Look for rock-hard fillets with little or no room for air between the fish and the plastic. In general, less packaging is better. If a fillet has multiple wrappers, it's had multiple processors. Ideally, I prefer to buy frozen fish from an outfit that isn't afraid to sell its own product direct to the public. Maybe I'm weird.

tilapia shows its stripes

Alive and swimming

Many ethnic markets (and some fish markets) sell live tilapia out of large heated tanks. Aside from being the freshest fish available, nearly all live tilapia come from U.S. farms, so if you're at all concerned about international aquaculture practices, buying live is your best bet.

Buying a live tilapia (or any live fish) starts with a cursory examination of the tank: Is it relatively clean, not too crowded, and free of floaters? Good. Next, check the fish: Active and attractive are the key ingredients to a top-quality catch. Once you've made your choice, the fishmonger will usually gut and clean the fish for free (although not before weighing it). Additional preparation, such as scaling, skinning, or filleting, may cost extra.

In the Kitchen

Guinea Fish

Tilapia is not a "wow" fish. Serving it to the boss is not going to earn you that promotion you so richly deserve.

BOSS
Johnson, this fish is fantastic! What is it?

YOU
Tilapia, sir. It was only $3 a pound down at the Super Save Mart.

BOSS
Johnson, you cheap bastard!
No raise for you.

Tilapia is, however, mild mannered, easy to prepare, and predictable. While I wouldn't call it comfort food, it comes pretty close. If this seems less than a ringing endorsement, consider: Tilapia is the perfect test fish. Got a new technique to try, a funky flavor combo, or a spicy marinade to modulate? This is your fish. The price is right and the tilapia is willing. Tuna it's not, but tilapia can stand in for most firm, flaky white fillets with reasonably accurate results.

Quality insurance

If the fillets seem mushy or waterlogged after opening, make a note of the brand and don't buy it again. To test for potential off flavors, pat the fillet dry and place it in a microwave safe container, cover it, and nuke it for 15 seconds. If the fish smells muddy or otherwise unappetizing, chances are it's going to taste the same.

Nonthreatening fish

When I'm not playing dress-up, I stick to flavors and cooking methods that accent the fish's mild, nutty flavor, such as baking it in a pouch with some lemon and olive oil, sautéing it with butter and capers, or frying it to achieve a crispy cornmeal crust. Poaching? Sure, in fact, let's try something over-the-top, like a freshly prepared tomato sauce. Too much flavor for ya? Don't be such a wimp. Get it good and bubbly, add the fillets, and in ten minutes dinner is served.

Tilapia is fairly bulletproof when it comes to cooking. Nearly every fillet I've ever seen has been the same size, shape, and thickness. Once you've cooked one, you've cooked them all. When the fillet is firm, white,

QUICK QUESTION

Is rigor mortis an issue when dealing with live fish? Not long after a fish expires, its muscle tissue stiffens, entering a state known as rigor mortis. The trick for fishermen is to get the fish bled and on ice before this happens so the fish can enter rigor slowly and stay there for as long as possible. While in rigor, the flesh is relatively acid happy, which keeps significant bacteria growth at bay (the cold helps, too).

This is not something you'll ever have to worry about unless you catch your own fish or buy it live. Most fish take a few hours to enter rigor, so there's plenty of time to get them cleaned and into a cold environment. Rigor will pass in a few hours, a few days in extreme cases, and then it's cool to cook the fish. Cooking the fish before it stiffens up is possible, but not advisable. The muscles will most likely shrink up, which in a whole specimen results in the fish tearing itself apart. There goes your presentation.

And what of the fishermen who brag about eating fish right out of the stream? Are they nuts? Nope, just hungry. Like I said, it's a presentation issue. The fish will still taste spectacular.

Fashion Statement

Tilapia skin may look nice on the plate, but it doesn't taste very good. Best to remove it before serving. It is, however, strong and fashionable enough that in some countries tilapia skin is used to make belts and purses.

and a little flaky, it's done. Granted, one side of the fillet is thicker than the other, which will no doubt send some chefs into a fillet-trimming frenzy. Relax. I like the contrast of tender and flaky to thin and crispy, but if you're set against any unevenness, keep the thin side away from the center of the pan or simply stick to moist cooking methods such as poaching or pouch cooking.

The whole fish

Grill it, broil it, or roast it—whole tilapia is about as easy as it gets. Start with a whole tilapia (scaled and cleaned, please), season it on the inside with salt and pepper, toss in a few herbs, make three diagonal slits on either side of the fish, stuff each slit with a slice of lime, lemon, or blood orange, season both sides with salt and pepper, lube the whole thing with olive oil, and bring on the heat.

Tilapia isn't especially bony, so your guests shouldn't have too much trouble picking their way through a whole fish. If they give you grief for serving them something with a face, tell them it's bad luck to remove the head before serving. Without his eyes, the fish will get lost on his way to the afterlife and end up haunting the poor soul who blinded him. Yeah, that's nice and creepy. Go for it.

Tilapia Recipes

In keeping with the "guinea fish" theory, I've included a couple of recipes that on the surface may seem a little...odd. In truth, you can use tilapia in just about any of the fish fillet recipes found in this book. Okay, probably not the sushi, but anything else is fair game. Have fun.

NUTRITIONAL INFO

Per 3.5 oz/100 grams (raw)

Tilapia

Calories	85
Calories from fat	9
Total fat	1 g
Saturated fat	0.4 g
Cholesterol	50 mg
Sodium	35 mg
Protein	18 g
Omega-3	0.14 g
Mercury	0.01 ppm

HOW TO STORE: Tilapia

FRESH: Like other freshwater fish, tilapia is well equipped to handle a few extra days in the fridge. Fresh fillets wrapped in plastic and placed in the coldest part of the fridge ought to survive 3 to 4 days, longer if kept on a regularly refreshed bed of ice. That said, if you're going to buy fresh...well, you know what to do. *FROZEN:* Properly frozen fillets will last at least 3 months in the freezer. If they aren't dated, start the clock with a permanent marker before tossing them in the deep freeze. When it comes time to thaw them, plan ahead. All it takes is an evening at rest in the fridge. If time is short, a water bath will speed up the process, while an ice-water bath in the sink along with a trickle of water will dramatically speed up the process. Do not remove tilapia from the package until you're ready to cook.

No-Name Tilapia

Why no name? Because this one I want you to make your own. Over the years, I've made this same recipe with just about every conceivable flavor combination and rarely did it blow up in my face. If you're just not feeling creative and need an easy way out, try Old Bay seasoning or some other simple seafood spice. If you're looking for something to challenge the taste buds of your date, try a tablespoon of pumpkin spices. Seriously.

¼ cup all purpose flour
1 tablespoon seasoning or spice combination of your choice
2 tilapia fillets, 4 to 6 ounces each
Kosher salt and freshly ground black pepper
1 tablespoon unsalted butter
1 tablespoon olive oil

Combine the flour and seasoning in a shallow bowl and stir to combine them. Season the fillets with salt and pepper and then coat each with the flour mixture, shaking off the excess.

Add the butter and oil to a sauté pan set over medium-high heat. As soon as you see some color, add the fillets, and cook until browned, 3 to 4 minutes. Carefully flip the fillets and cook them until firm and opaque throughout, 2 to 4 minutes, depending on thickness.

Serve immediately.

Serves 2

Double Nut Tilapia

Sounds like ice cream, no? This dish does taste a little sweet, which works surprisingly well, considering we're talking about fish. Yes, you can use macadamia nuts, if you like. Hazelnuts? Go for it. Peanuts? Absolutely.

2 tilapia fillets, 4 to 6 ounces each
¼ cup walnuts, chopped
¼ cup almonds, chopped
2 tablespoons dark brown sugar
3 tablespoons unsalted butter
Kosher salt

Combine the chopped nuts in a zip-top bag or between sheets of wax paper and crush, using a mallet, into very small crumbs. Toss the nuts into a shallow bowl along with the brown sugar and mix them well.

Melt 1 tablespoon butter. Season the tilapia fillets lightly with salt and then brush one side with butter. Lay the fillets in the nut mixture, butter side down, coating them thoroughly.

Melt the remaining 2 tablespoons butter in a nonstick sauté pan over medium-high heat. As soon as you see some color, add the fillets, nut side down, and cook until browned, 3 to 4 minutes. Carefully flip the fillets and cook them until firm and opaque throughout, 2 to 4 minutes, depending on thickness.

Serve immediately.

Serves 2

Poached Tilapia
in Red Sauce

Who says fish can't handle a heavy red sauce? Not me, obviously. This is another one of those recipes that is just begging for adaptation. Got a favorite homemade red sauce? Use it. Got a favorite bottled tomato sauce? Use it.

1 large shallot, minced
3 garlic cloves, minced
2 teaspoons fennel seed
2 tablespoons olive oil
1 large can (28 ounces) crushed peeled tomatoes
¼ teaspoon dried oregano
¼ teaspoon dried basil
¼ teaspoon crushed red pepper flakes
Pinch each of kosher salt and freshly ground black pepper
4 tilapia fillets, 4 to 6 ounces each
Fresh basil leaves

Preheat oven to 375° F.

Heat the olive oil, shallot, garlic, and fennel seed in a large saucepan over medium heat. Once the garlic starts to sizzle (but before it browns), add the tomatoes, oregano, basil, red pepper, salt, and pepper. Simmer over medium heat until the sauce thickens slightly, about 10 minutes.

Pour a small amount of the sauce into a baking dish just large enough to hold the fillets in a single layer. Arrange the tilapia fillets in the dish and pour the remaining sauce over them. Bake fillets until firm and opaque throughout, 12 to 15 minutes, depending on thickness.

Transfer the fillets to individual plates and garnish them with basil leaves. Serve immediately.

Serves 4

Cinnamon Crunch Tilapia

Here's the deal: Two of my favorite flavors are cinnamon and nutmeg. Up until now, they have not appeared anywhere in the book (except in the Jerk Seasoning, but that doesn't count). Thus, I present cinnamon-and-nutmeg-flavored tilapia, coated in rolled oats, no less. Trust me, it tastes great. Honest.

1 cup rolled oats
2 teaspoons ground cinnamon
1 teaspoon freshly ground nutmeg
½ teaspoon freshly grated ginger
½ cup all-purpose flour
1 egg, lightly beaten
4 tilapia fillets, 4 to 6 ounces each
Kosher salt and freshly ground black pepper
3 tablespoons vegetable oil

Combine the rolled oats, cinnamon, nutmeg, and ginger in a shallow bowl. Place the flour and eggs in separate, shallow bowls.

Season the tilapia fillets with salt and pepper. Coat each fillet with flour, shaking off the excess. Next, dip the fillets, one at a time, first in the egg, and then in the rolled oats. *NOTE: To keep from gumming up the works, it's best to use one hand for the egg and one hand for the oats.*

Heat the oil in a large sauté pan over medium-high heat. Once hot, add the fillets and cook, 3 to 4 minutes, until golden. Flip the fillets and cook them until firm and opaque throughout, 2 to 4 minutes, depending on thickness.

Serve immediately.

Serves 4

Appendix

The Ones That Almost Got Away

I know what you're thinking. Where's the trout? And sole? And grouper? And the approximately 400 other commercially available species of fish and shellfish not covered by this book? Um...would you believe the dog ate those chapters? No? Okay, if it were up to me, the fun would never stop, but my publisher says the book has to end sometime. Right. I'm not buying it. Thus, attached are a few odds and ends that somehow slipped my mind while researching the mating habits of the Japanese flying squid. Enjoy.

Pretty Fishy

Feel free to judge a fish by its cover: Is it attractive and free of blemishes, bruises, and broken bits and pieces? Buy accordingly.

Which fish tastes "distinctively sweet, but mild, with a firm, yet tender flake"? Could be anything. How about this one: "Rich, full-bodied flavor with a moist, meaty finish"? Yeah, I just made that one up, too, but it sounds like tuna, doesn't it? Or salmon. Or swordfish. See, that's the problem. What does "sweet and mild" mean with regard to fish? How about "rich and oily"? The words certainly mean something, but without taking a bite, how do we know what an oily fish actually tastes like? There should be a standard—an easy-to-understand reference point from which all fish flavors can be derived. If only such a thing existed.

Give me a minute.

Got it.

On the Tongue
Something Fishy

To my palate, there are three basic fish flavors: cod, salmon, and tuna. Cod is lean and mild, with a moist, flaky texture; salmon is moderately rich (oily), with a firm, flaky texture; and tuna is rich, with a firm, meaty texture. Yes, I'm generalizing, and still using too many words. Let's get a second opinion. *Oh, honey…*

"Fishy," my wife says. "Tuna tastes fishy. But in a good way."

I like that. Tuna does have a fairly intense, fishy (in a good way) flavor. Cod, on the other hand, tastes only mildly fishy. Salmon? Right down the middle. So, it's cod, salmon, and tuna—*fishy, fishier,* and *fishiest.*

Of course, each flavor can exist anywhere along the lean and mild to oily and rich spectrum. Chum salmon is mild flavored and not as fatty as coho, which is not as rich and oil-infused as chinook. Albacore tuna is fairly mild, but yellowtail comes across stronger (fully cooked, that is). If cod is the mild, lean base of white and flaky, then toothfish is the oily extreme. Think of it as a triangle with tuna, salmon, and cod at its three points. The center of the triangle is rich and oily, as you move toward the points and beyond, the flavor gets leaner and milder.

Of course, I related cod to toothfish, which seems like a fairly straight line on the mild-to-rich cod-line, but what about mahimahi? Or catfish? Both fall under white and flaky, but mahimahi shares a lot of the same traits as tuna, while catfish seems closer to salmon. No problem!

Every fish has its place in relation to cod, salmon, and tuna. Tilapia is codlike, but milder in flavor. Mahimahi has a bit of cod in it, but ultimately it's more on the side of tuna. Halibut in many ways may be the ideal fish as it has the white flake of cod, the moderate richness of salmon, and a bit of the firmness of tuna (which would be more obvious if this were a pop-up book, but that's not going to happen).

The bottom line: If you've tried cod, salmon, and tuna (which I imagine most of you have), this chart will give you a better idea of how the other fish in this book taste.

There are, of course, a few intangibles. Sockeye salmon has a spicy wildness to its flavor that's hard to describe (other than calling it spicy and wild). Farm-raised catfish also falls a little off the charts thanks to its grain-fed, fishy-fowl flavor. And while there's no "muddy" corner on the triangle, off flavors are out there and occasionally tweak a taste bud or two. For the purposes of this totally unscientific flavor chart, let's pretend they don't exist.

Smell You Later

Does it smell good? If it doesn't, don't buy it.

Eat It Today

You bought it fresh. It's not going to be fresher tomorrow. Why wait?

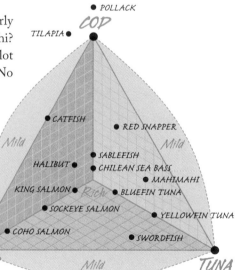

Keep It Cold

On the way home, in the kitchen, right up to cooking— colder is better. At home, cold is 30 to 34°F (-1 to 1°C) in the fridge, or -4°F (-20°C) or less in the deep freeze.

Keep It Dry

Once fish comes out of the water, it stays out the water, until it's time to clean or cook it.

Keep It Alive

If it was alive when you bought it, keep it that way until you cook it.

Crustacean revelations

What about shellfish? Sorry, no brilliant flavor revelations. Lobster tastes like lobster (rich and briny), as do some of the best shrimp. Crab has a similar flavor, but texturally tends to be more flaky than firm. The tastiest squid are definitely on the mild side, while scallops deliver a rich, salty sweetness. In general, clams are mild flavored and a wee bit chewy, but can be plump and juicy. Good mussels are rich and tender. And oysters? Sweet, fruity, salty, fatty, metallic, crisp, smooth, meaty, moist, and firm. I wouldn't know where to begin to draw a picture of that.

On the Road
Vacation Nation

Thanks to the Internet and overnight shipping, it's now possible to get just about anything you want delivered to your door fresh, if not still alive and kicking. But there's fresh and then there's *fresh*. Lobster is livelier in Maine. Halibut is happiest in the Pacific Northwest. *Everything* tastes better in Hawaii.

With that in mind, here's a handy travel map of where to eat what when you're there. These aren't the only places to find each fish, but they're the best. (Go ahead, prove me wrong!)

In the Kitchen
Essential Hardware

If you're going to cook fish there are a few things you absolutely must have in your kitchen. These are those things.

 A sharp knife The only thing you need to turn a fish into food is a sharp knife (been to a sushi bar, lately?). Additionally, the difference between successfully dismantling a king salmon and ruining $50 worth of fish is a good knife. If you don't have one, grab your coat, you're going out. What kind of knife? If I could only have one, it would be a long (at least 8 inches), fairly shallow fish knife, similar to those favored by sushi chefs. A standard 8-inch cook's knife is a fair, more versatile substitute. A flexible fillet knife is also handy for taking apart whole fish.

 A good nonstick pan If you want to cook your fish, a nonstick pan is your best friend, because, let's face it: fish stick. To avoid ruining that crispy, delicious, brown coating, get thee some protection.

 Salt Fish taste more like fish with salt. Use liberally to cook with, sparingly to season after cooking. Kosher salt is king, sea salt is second, table salt is…well, not in my kitchen.

 Extra virgin olive oil For lubrication, for flavor, for life. Just don't fry with it.

 A big spatula, tongs, and a skimmer Technically, that's three things, but each is used for more or less the same purpose: picking stuff up and putting it down. If you've got to grab, flip, or dip, you're going to need these.

 Butter Do I need to explain this one? (Butter + anything else on the planet = good.)

 Parchment paper After a nonstick pan, this is the second most important cooking vessel in your pantry. Fill, fold, crimp, cook, tear, serve, crumble, and throw away.

 Lemon Nothing complements briny seafood like a fresh citrus twang. Lemon delivers the juice, plus it looks great on the plate. (Don't forget about the zest.)

 Freshly ground black pepper If salt is for bringing out the natural flavors of the fish, then pepper is for spicing those flavors up. Does it have to be freshly ground? Yes. Yes, it does. (A one-handed grinder is helpful when seasoning fish.)

 Refrigerator thermometer Ever wonder how cold your fridge really is? This will tell you. Good for finding the "coldest part of the refrigerator" where jerks like me are always telling you to put stuff. An instant-read thermometer is also a must-have for taking the temperature of whole fish and keeping fry oil from going nuclear.

 Capers Are capers really that important? *Yes!* Capers, along with butter and black pepper, will turn any old fish into culinary high art. Capers are the difference between dinner and *"Honey, you're brilliant; let's never eat out again!"* (If you don't want to cook every night for the rest of your life, go easy on the capers.)

And the rest...

For those who must have it all, don't forget: Aluminum foil, plastic wrap, needle-nose pliers (for bones), kitchen shears (for shells and fins), metal skewers (for kebobs and quick-flipping shrimp), soy sauce, peanut oil (for frying), Old Bay seasoning (for tradition), wasabi (for clearing your sinuses), corn meal, flour, *panko* bread crumbs, fresh dill (for salmon), sesame seeds, white wine, beer (for cooking and drinking while cooking), a kick-ass grill, a cast-iron pan, a kick-ass cast-iron grill pan (best of both worlds), sushi rice, nori, a fish-grill basket (for no-stick grilling), fresh lime, a big ol' pot (for boils, boiling, and steaming), a few smaller pots and pans (for any occasion), an oyster knife, a wooden mallet (for cracking), a fish poacher, a fish scaler, and a wok.

Things not to have in your kitchen: one of those rubber "singing" fishes. That's just wrong.

On the Shelf
Suggested Reading

I've got a hundred or so fish and shellfish cookbooks, but there are only a few that I return to again and again. These are the books (along with this splendid tome) that belong in every fish-lover's kitchen.

West Coast Seafood by Jay Harlow is by far my favorite. It's full of great info about a lot of different fishes, and is stocked with plenty of recipes. *Fish & Shellfish* by James Peterson is an excellent seafood recipe and technique resource, but another Peterson book, *Essentials of Cooking*, is best for the novice chef—lots of easy-to-follow photos (of fish and everything else you might want to do in your kitchen). Another very good introduction to cooking fish is Shirley King's *Fish: The Basics*, which tries to cover everything and does a pretty decent job of it.

If you like reading about fish and fishermen (and I assume you do if you bought this book), be sure to check out *The Secret Lives of Lobsters* by Trevor Corson, *Cod* by Mark Kurlansky, *The Hungry Ocean* by Linda Greenlaw, *Their Fathers' Work* by William McCloskey, and *Out on the Deep Blue* edited by Leslie Leyland Fields.

Rewrap It

Get rid of the butcher's paper and rewrap your fish in plastic wrap or aluminum foil (or both) once you get it home. This will keep smells out and in and help the fish stay cool. A quick rinse and pat dry before rewrapping helps, too.

Hot and Fast

When in doubt, cooking less is more, and hotter is better.

Long and Low

If you do cook long, be sure to turn the heat down low.

Enough is Never Enough
More Fish on a First-Name Basis

Can't wait for the sequel? Me neither. Here are a few more fish and shell-fish worth getting to know on a more personal level (by eating them).

Rainbow trout

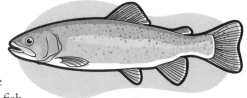

rainbow trout

This is definitely the one that got away. Right up until the typing stopped, there was a trout chapter in this book. And then there wasn't. But this farm-raised beauty is worth picking through the bones to enjoy. Farm-raised or fresh from the creek, rainbow trout (*Oncorhynchus mykiss*) is a tender, flaky fish that's best butterflied and pan-fried (in butter, naturally). Before you poach or grill a whole salmon, try a test run with a rainbow trout. You won't be disappointed.

Grouper

grouper

This is going to sound a little absurd, but one of the most popular grouper varieties is a fish called gag (*Mycteroperca microlepis*). It's taste and texture is similar to that of black grouper (*M. bonaci*), thus gag is usually sold using the less troubling name. Gag and another common variety, red grouper (*Epinephelus morio*), are harvested primarily from Southern and Gulf waters and can be found whole up to 20 pounds at some markets. In terms of taste, grouper is not unlike halibut, although it has the good graces not to dry out if overcooked.

Crawfish

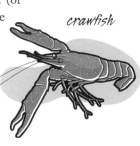

crawfish

Red swamp crawfish (*Procambarus clarkii*) look a lot like little lobsters, and taste, well, a bit like little lobsters. The joy in eating crawfish (or crayfish, or crawdads, or mudbugs) comes not so much from the flavor, but from the experience of shuckin' and suckin' a few dozen freshly boiled daddies right off the kitchen table. For the true craw-fish experience, head to Cajun country (that'd be Louisiana) where most rivers, swamps, and drainage ditches are overrun by the mini-lobstrosities.

Monkfish

A giant, gaping mouth, dozens of pointy teeth, beady little eyes, and a bulbous head sporting a homegrown fishing lure (yes, that's what it's used for), all have helped earn monkfish (*Lophius americanus*) the title of ugliest fish in the sea. Thanks to a texture that's often compared to that of a certain shellfish, it's more pleasantly referred to as the "poor man's lobster" at some markets. Just don't let anybody sell you monkfish "body meat." The tail meat is the only edible part.

monkfish

Dover sole

True Dover sole (*Solea vulgaris*) is a real treat, but most of what is sold in the United States as Dover sole is actually a Pacific variety (*Microstomus pacificus*) that's not nearly as good as the little flatfish found in European waters. And although both are technically flounders, petrale sole (*Eopsetta jordani*) and gray sole (*Glyptocephalus cynoglossus*) manage a reasonable impression of Dover sole, especially when cooked whole.

Dover sole

Sturgeon

If you've ever wanted to eat an armor-plated fish, here's your chance. The Pacific white sturgeon (*Acipenser transmontanus*) has several rows of bony plates running from head to tail. Historically, several species of sturgeon were plentiful in U.S. waters, but overfishing depleted the stock's commercial viability more than a century ago. Today, markets rely primarily on farm-raised product grown in California. The flavor of the fish is mild, but its firm texture is often compared to that of veal. Two things to remember when cooking sturgeon: remove the skin, which otherwise may bring off flavors to the party, and cook longer than you think necessary. Sturgeon can be a bit dense.

sturgeon

Skate

Skate wings have yet to make the transition to sports bar cuisine, but one day…BOOM! Buffalo skate wings. (It could happen.) Until then, we'll have to settle for sautéed or fried skate wing (spicy barbecue sauce optional). Flavor-wise, skate (*Raja* spp.) tastes not unlike a scallop, although texturally it tends to be a little stringy. Dismantling a skate wing (really just a big fin) can be tricky due to a layer of cartilage separating the two layers of flesh. Treat it like another patch of skin and you'll do fine.

skate

abalone

Abalone

Ladies and Gentlemen, allow me to introduce the univalve, the one-shelled wonder that is abalone (*Haliotis rufescens*). Able to eat more than its weight in seaweed in a single day, abalone sports a top shell that's often as beautiful as its meat is tasty. Cultured product has picked up the slack of declining wild stocks in recent years, but top quality fresh abalone is still hard to come by and very expensive (up to $100 a pound).

Pompano

The Atlantic pompano (*Trachinotus carolinus*) is, technically speaking, a cute fish. It's small (never more than 3 pounds), has a sweet face, and sports the most adorable arrow-shaped tail. Pompano is best served whole, which, thanks to its modest size, is almost always how it's sold. Warning: Don't buy "pompano" filets or whole "pompano" larger than 3 pounds—they probably aren't the tastiest fish. Pseudo-pomps don't have the delicate flake or sweet flavor of the Atlantic variety.

pompano

Orange roughy

Sadly, orange roughy (*Hoplostethus atlanticus*) isn't as prevalent as it was back in the 1980s when this fish from down under first popped up on U.S. menus. Originally known as "slimehead," roughy saw its fortunes rise with a name change and an aggressive New Zealand-based marketing push. Slow maturation combined with overfishing ultimately forced local authorities to place restrictions on the fishery, curtailing efforts aimed at world domination. That doesn't mean you should avoid orange roughy at the market. As far as mild, large-flaked, white fillets go, roughy is one of the best.

orange roughy

American eel

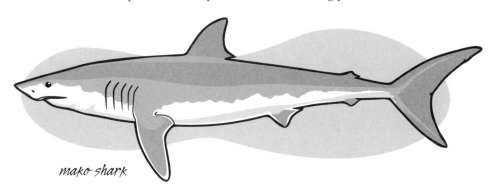

American eel

The American eel (*Anguilla rostrata*) is the opposite of salmon—it spawns in the ocean but matures in freshwater. Most eels are harvested from rivers up and down the Atlantic coast, some at different stages of development. Don't be surprised to find eel still alive at the ethnic markets where it's most commonly available. Eel has a rich, oily flavor that is not for everybody. For a test run, head down to your local sushi concern and order *unagi*. If you dig it, start searching for an eelmonger.

Shark

Cue music. (You know what I mean.) Despite its status as theatrical villain, the average shark is much more likely to be eaten by a human than the other way around. Both mako (*Isurus oxyrinchus*) and thresher (*Alopias vulpinus*) sharks are commonly caught as swordfish bycatch, and when cooked share many of the same characteristics as the popular billfish. Look for ivory to pink steaks with deep red splotches and avoid any that are overly brown or smell strongly of ammonia.

mako shark

Index